P·O·W·E·R &
POWERLESSNESS
in JEWISH HISTORY

P·O·W·E·R &
POWERLESSNESS
in JEWISH HISTORY

DAVID BIALE

SCHOCKEN BOOKS · NEW YORK

Library of Congress Cataloging-in-Publication Data
Biale, David, 1949–   Power and powerlessness in Jewish
history. Includes index. 1. Jews—Diaspora. 2. Jews—
Politics and government. 3. Jews—History—Philosophy. 4.
Power (Social sciences). 5. Israel—International status. 6.
Sovereignty. 7. Jews—United States—Politics and govern-
ment. 8. United States—Ethnic relations. I. Title.
   DS134.B53   1986   909'.04924   86-3850

Design by Thomas Nau
Manufactured in the United States of America
ISBN 0–8052–4015–2 (hardcover)
ISBN 978-0-8052-0841-2 (paperbook)

For Amos Funkenstein
Teacher, colleague, and friend

Contents

Contents

Preface

THIS book originated from a project to publish an anthology of Zionist ideologies since the creation of the state of Israel.[1] In my projected introduction to that volume, I speculated on why these ideologies seemed to be in a state of crisis. My editors at Schocken Books agreed with me that the very weakness of contemporary Zionist ideology seemed to preclude the planned anthology, but they found my introduction suggestive enough to warrant a full investigation of the reasons for this situation. With the war in Lebanon, it became increasingly apparent that the most vital question facing Jews today—one that throws the crisis of Jewish ideology into sharp relief—concerns political power. What began to emerge was an essay on the tensions between Jewish perceptions or ideologies of power and the political realities of Jewish life. Yet, to understand the relationship of the Jews to power today, I found it necessary to examine the historical dimensions of this relationship. What began as an essay on contemporary questions quickly developed into something bolder and quite different: a meditation on all of Jewish history from the point of view of politics and power.

In the normal course of a historian's career, such metahistorical speculations are usually left to one's twilight years, as a kind of summing up of a life's work. My own sense of the state of Jewish historiography has led me, however, to set aside my ongoing historical research to undertake this essay. In a time when Jewish studies, particularly in North America, are enjoying a veritable explosion, it is striking how few his-

torical works on the Jews derive their motivation from the
questions and challenges thrown up by the world in which we
live. Nor do they ask what is the relationship between our
own times and the way we see the past. A certain antiquarian-
ism, reminiscent of nineteenth-century Jewish scholarship,
has seemingly crept into the Jewish academy, and the role of
the historian in the shaping of contemporary consciousness
remains uncertain at best.

My earlier work on Gershom Scholem tried to show how
the research of that great historian of Jewish mysticism was
driven by the cultural and political problems of twentieth-
century German Jews.[2] His personal rebellion against the
world of his fathers found its historiographical analogue in
his "counterhistory" of Judaism. The present book is deeply
influenced by this concept of counterhistory, of an engaged
search for alternatives to conventional interpretations.

My deepest debt for the method, substance, and scope of
this essay I owe to my teacher Amos Funkenstein. A number
of years ago, he set me thinking about the present theme in a
lecture, subsequently published in Hebrew, under the title
"Passivity as the Characteristic of the Diaspora Jews: Myth
and Reality."[3] It was this bold revision of a conventional understanding of Jewish history that became the kernel of my
present treatment of the subject. Professor Funkenstein generously criticized the manuscript and helped me sharpen
many formulations that would have otherwise remained
hopelessly vague. In a more general sense, the work of many
of his students reflects the impact of his concern with Jewish
political ideologies and theories in all periods of history. I
have dedicated this work to Professor Funkenstein since it
belongs integrally to the school of historical interpretation he
has trained and it constitutes, in its own way, a summation of
one aspect of that school.

A number of colleagues and friends have generously read
part or all of this manuscript and have contributed critical
insights. I wish to thank Shlomo Aronson and Steven Aschheim of the Hebrew University, Maurice Kriegel of Haifa Uni-

versity, David Sorkin of Oxford University, David Rapoport of the University of California at Los Angeles, Michael Walzer of the Institute for Advanced Study in Princeton, New Jersey, and Steven Zipperstein of Oxford University. Several of my colleagues and students in the Department of History of the State University of New York at Binghamton also offered timely criticism. I wish to thank those who participated in the 1984 Summer Colloquium and read chapter 4. For more extensive help, I am grateful in particular to John Chaffee, Elizabeth Colwill, and Gerald Kadish. As with any work, but especially an interpretive one such as this, the responsibility for all that follows is entirely my own.

My two successive editors at Schocken Books played a critical role in all stages of the manuscript. Arthur Samuelson helped me formulate what this book was really about and read critically every draft I gave him. Bonny Fetterman was equally supportive and critical in the later stages of writing. I also want to thank Beverly Colman for her many helpful insights and editorial suggestions.

My wife, Rachel Biale, read every draft of the manuscript and contributed her own special combination of intellectual inspiration and emotional succor. Finally, I wish to thank my son, Noam, for reminding me repeatedly that politics and power are not the most important things in life, and my daughter, Tali, for waiting to be born until the day I finished final revisions on the manuscript.

P·O·W·E·R &
POWERLESSNESS
in JEWISH HISTORY

Introduction

The Crisis of Jewish Ideology

O N a June day in 1982, the armed forces of the state of
Israel crossed the Lebanese border, thus beginning the
longest and most divisive war in Israel's history. For many
Jews, including Israel's prime minister, the war demonstrated the power of the Jews to strike back at their enemies,
who, like the Nazis, intended to commit genocide on the Jewish people; the war was an act of delayed revenge for the
Holocaust of the European Jews. For other Jews, it was precisely the contrast between the powerlessness of the Jews of
Europe and the new power of the Jews of Israel that raised
troubling questions about the uses of power: should Jews not
temper power with moral restraint, acting not like all other
nations of the world, but rather as the custodians of a long
ethical tradition born of powerlessness? And, most disturb-
ingly, the Lebanon War suggested to some that the former
victims of persecution and genocide had become perpetrators: Israel's enemies reviled the Jewish state as the reincar-
nation of Nazi Germany.

No nation exercises power in a historical vacuum. The
weight of experience and memory lies heavily on politics,

shaping the way in which each people sees its power and uses it. Jews today cannot think about the power of the state of Israel without at the same moment remembering the utter powerlessness of their European cousins under the murderous regime of the Nazis. Within one generation, Jews have experienced the traumas of powerlessness and the triumphs of power. It is no surprise that many see the last forty years of Jewish history in messianic terms, for if the long history of the exile reached its denouement in the Holocaust, then the state of Israel must surely represent redemption.

The very rapidity with which the Jews have moved from powerlessness to power has produced a crisis of Jewish ideology. The ways in which Jews conceive of politics were developed in Eastern Europe at the turn of the century; the great ideologies of Zionism, Bundism, socialism, and liberalism were all responses to the increasing impotence of the Jews of Europe, an impotence that culminated in the Holocaust. Although some of these ideologies no longer exist and others have changed drastically, they remain the vocabulary of Jewish politics. Today, these forms of discourse appear increasingly irrelevant in the light of the achievement of Jewish sovereignty in Israel and the relative political power of the Jewish Diaspora in the West, especially in the United States. In both Israel and the Diaspora, a new political language is only beginning to emerge, a language for understanding both the possibilities and the limitations of Jewish political power in the modern world.

This new language must come to terms with the nature of power in Jewish history and, in doing so, it must confront the old conception of Jewish history bequeathed by the ideologies of the turn of the century. How did these ideologies see Jewish history? In 1944, when the Holocaust was already common knowledge, David Ben Gurion reflected on Zionism as a revolutionary movement: "All other revolts, both past and future, were uprisings against a system, against a political, social or economic structure. Our revolution is directed not only against a system, but against destiny, against the unique destiny of a unique people."[1] For Ben Gurion, the "unique destiny" of the Jews was the powerlessness that seemed to characterize Jewish history between the ancient revolt of the Jews under the Zealots in 66–70 c.e. and the modern revolt of the Zionists. In its resurrection of the Jewish warrior of old and its victorious march to power against extraordinary odds, the Zionist movement seemed to radically reverse the course of Jewish history and fulfill the dashed hopes of the rebels of Roman times.

The belief that the historical condition of the Diaspora Jews is political powerlessness is often considered the "Zionist" interpretation of Jewish history. Yet, it is a view that is so deeply engrained in the popular Jewish consciousness that even the opponents of political Zionism share it. For instance, Hannah Arendt, one of Ben Gurion's most vociferous critics, wrote: "Jewish history offers the extraordinary spectacle of a people . . . which began its history with a well-defined concept of history and an almost conscious resolution to achieve a well-circumscribed plan on earth and then, without giving up this concept, avoided all political action for two thousand years."[2] Although they disagreed profoundly about political Zionism, Arendt and Ben Gurion retained a similar contempt for the presumed apolitical and passive character of Diaspora Jewish history.

Even more radical opponents of political Zionism than Arendt adopt the same vision of Jewish history, but they do so in order to glorify it. The anti-Zionist writer Michael Selzer sees the passivity of the Jews as a great virtue: "Jewish ethics and purpose derive from the rejection of power, from the actual contempt of power which pervades the Jewish ethos."[3] Judaism for Selzer constitutes a revolution to "radicalize the world through Jewish powerlessness and suffering." In his view, Zionism represents a counterrevolution against the noble essence of Judaism. Thus, from Zionists to anti-Zionists, there is a consensus on the powerlessness and apolitical nature of Diaspora Jewish history.[4]

This book is an argument against this interpretation of

Jewish history. Jewish history cannot be divided into distinct periods of power or powerlessness. During the ancient period of Jewish sovereignty, normally considered to end in 70 C.E., the power of the Jews was severely limited by the great empires of antiquity. Conversely, the period after 70 C.E. was not a period of total political impotence. The key to the Jews' remarkable survival never lay in either one or the other of these two polarities, neither of which exists in pure form in the real world. The Jews possessed an extraordinary ability to maneuver between the extremes of a quest for full sovereignty and a state of political passivity. To adopt either of these two strategies exclusively would have been disastrous and, indeed, nearly was in the case of the revolts of ancient times. Yet, the alternative to revolt was not a retreat into otherworldliness. Jewish history continued to be characterized by a wide spectrum of persistent and ongoing political activism.[5]

Without an appreciation of the political acumen of the Jews in earlier times, their long history can only appear to be a miraculous accomplishment. If we wish to understand Jewish survival from a historical rather than a theological point of view, however, we must look for explanations from the world of power and politics. Without some modicum of political strength and the ability to use it, the Jewish people would certainly have vanished. The history of the Jews is "abnormal" due to their lack of territory for such a long period of time, but their response to this abnormal condition was always in fact political.

Although the problem of power is a continuous thread throughout Jewish history, this book is not a comprehensive political history of the Jews or a history of Jewish political thought. Despite the chronological arrangement of the chapters, there is no pretense here of covering this whole history thoroughly or even of including all relevant material. Instead, my purpose is to advance a particular set of interpretations about the relationship of the Jews to power throughout Jewish history.

I will call power the ability of a people to control its relations to other peoples as well as its own internal political, cultural, religious, economic, and social life. Given the importance military power has come to assume in Jewish life today, particularly in the state of Israel, we must also consider the power of the Jews to defend themselves against physical attack, but not restrict our definition of power to military force alone. There are many means other than physical force that political communities can use to control their relations to other communities and to enforce their will internally.

While power may be found in all spheres of life, I will focus here primarily on political power. Power can only be exercised by a collective, a political body whose members recognize its authority and whose legitimacy is recognized by others. In contrast, individuals who are not organized as a political collectivity may possess influence in society, as a result of, for example, their economic status, but they do not exercise power in a political sense. Similarly, those, such as terrorists, who employ force or violence to achieve their aims do not automatically possess power; on the contrary, violence may well be an expression of powerlessness or of the complete abandonment of the political arena. When I speak of "Jewish power," I have in mind the attempt to exercise strength and authority within a collective framework, informed by conscious political goals.[6]

Power clearly means something different in every age. Today we assume that power means and has always meant state power, yet the concept of the sovereign state and theories of sovereignty are only a few hundred years old. Power in the ancient Mediterranean world, from the Assyrian through the Roman empires, was concentrated in the hands of large empires; in a world of imperialistic powers, sovereignty for most nations in the modern sense was limited. Power for most of the Middle Ages, on the other hand, was fragmented, divided between numerous corporations and guilds; the state was only one of many centers of power. In order to properly evaluate and understand the nature of Jewish power or powerlessness in these different ages, we need to have some notion of what power meant then and we must avoid imposing our concepts on the past. "Sovereignty" versus "exile" may be overly simple and misleading categories with which to judge the rich complexity of Jewish history.

We must be equally careful of trying to comprehend contemporary questions of power using outmoded concepts from the past. The nineteenth century gave us the ideal of the sovereign state as the sole framework for political power. The Zionist movement borrowed this notion to found a Jewish state. As important as state sovereignty still is, its power in the contemporary world is more limited, especially for small states, than nineteenth-century nationalists had hoped. It is therefore necessary to think about Jewish sovereignty in different, perhaps more limited terms, than the founders of Zionism did at the turn of the century. Similarly, we sometimes tend to look back at all of Jewish history through the lens of the Holocaust, as if the history of the Jews in the Diaspora culminates in Auschwitz. The Holocaust may well have something to teach us about our contemporary situation, but other periods of Jewish history suggest different lessons as well.

The historian Yosef Hayim Yerushalmi recently asked whether historians have anything to contribute to the identity of modern Jews.[7] The Jewish tradition, he argues, is strangely unhistorical. The traditional Jew sees his history through the lens of memory, for which all events are cyclical recurrences of ancient archetypes. The exile from Spain conjures up the memory of the exile from Judaea; the pogroms of the Crusades are repetitions of the slaughter of the martyrs by Antiochus Epiphanes. One might say that this very notion of a recurring Jewish destiny remained deeply rooted even in Ben Gurion, the most secular of Zionists: in attempting to revolt against this destiny, Ben Gurion accepted the traditional view of recurrent cycles. The historian, on the other hand, does not see the past as recurring but rather as made up of unique events, each to be understood in its own context. For the historian, the connection between past and present, so intuitive to the traditional Jew, is not at all obvious; historical research could well make the past seem more remote.

If the work of the modern historian only severs us from our history, then indeed he has little to tell us about our contemporary problems. Yet, the historian can play a different role: he can expose our myths about the past. In the words of Walter Benjamin, he can "brush history against the grain" to discover the past that lies buried under products of memory. Historical criticism can liberate us from the burden of a mythical past, while at the same time presenting us with a new past that we may have not considered. Traditional Jewish memory, with its emphasis on recurring persecutions, can only reinforce the traumas of recent Jewish history; history itself, in all its complexity, may provide the needed therapy.

I

Sovereignty and Imperialism in Antiquity

AT the end of his great history of the Jewish revolt against Rome of 66–70 C.E., Josephus Flavius wrote:

> So fell Jerusalem in the second year of Vespasian's reign. . . ,
> captured five times before and now for the second time laid
> utterly waste. . . . From King David, the first Jew to reign over
> it, to the destruction by Titus was 1,179 years. But neither its
> long history, nor its vast wealth, nor its people dispersed
> through the whole world, nor the unparalleled renown of its
> worship sufficed to avert its ruin.[1]

Thus, according to one view of Jewish history, ended the glorious age of Jewish sovereignty, not to be regained until the Zionist movement reestablished the state of Israel in 1948. The destruction of the Second Temple in 70 C.E. is commonly considered to demarcate the fundamental political watershed in Jewish history: the end of political independence and the beginning of the powerlessness of exile. The rabbis, who became the sole leaders of the nation in the wake of the revolt against Rome, instituted radical changes in the nature of Judaism. They not only constructed a religion without Temple sacrifices, but they are said to have abdicated all interest in

10

politics and power in favor of a solely spiritual existence. It was this apolitical Judaism that became the Judaism of the Middle Ages, but the memory of the age of political power was preserved in messianism, the hope for the restoration of the golden age "when the Temple still stood."

This view of the ancient period and the role of the rabbis, so widely accepted in Jewish consciousness, is more romantic than historical. The golden age of Jewish power in antiquity is largely a myth based on exceptions instead of the norm: the political status of the Jews throughout most of antiquity was not full sovereignty but a partial and tenuous independence in an imperial world. For at least two centuries after the destruction of the Temple, the Jews in both the Land of Israel and the Diaspora were not powerless at all but in fact enjoyed forms of self-government similar in many ways to those of the Second Temple period. Rather than an abrupt shift from power to powerlessness, Jewish power in the early rabbinical period, and especially in the century after the Bar Kokhba Revolt (132–35 c.e.), was, if anything, greater than in most of the preceding ages.

The destruction of the Temple dictated a religious revolution for the Jews, but its political meaning was more complex. It brought about a change in leadership from priests to rabbis, but the nature of Jewish power, both internally and in relation to the outside world, remained fundamentally the same. The rabbis built a much more durable political system than had any of the earlier leaders, whether tribal elders, kings, or priests, who were only partially successful in confronting an imperial world and in maintaining some partial semblance of Jewish sovereignty. Yet these earlier attempts, both in their successes and their failures, prepared the ground for the work of the rabbis, which in turn laid the foundations of Jewish life in the Middle Ages.

Under the Shadow of Imperialism

For most of the time from the beginning of the Israelite settlement in the land of Canaan (ca. 1200 b.c.e.) to the fall of the Second Temple, the Jewish people lived in the shadow of great empires, rarely enjoying what would today be called full national sovereignty. The very first reference to the nation of Israel in a non-Hebrew source speaks of Israel's defeat and subjugation. In the stele of Pharaoh Merneptah from the late thirteenth century B.C.E., the name of Israel appears in a list of conquered nations. Israel, the Pharaoh declares in one of the greatest ironies in recorded history, is "laid waste, his seed is not [does not exist]."[2] In the same century when most historians believe the Israelites left Egypt and began to develop into a nation, the ruler of the greatest ancient empire declared them utterly destroyed.

Merneptah's epitaph for the Israelites was premature, for it was precisely the ability of the Jews to survive in a hostile imperial world that constituted their political genius. Lying uneasily in the border region between Egypt to the southwest and the Mesopotamian population centers to the northeast, the land of the Israelites remained throughout the ancient period what it has become again today: a bone of contention between larger states to the north and south, the great powers of ancient times.

The most important political reality of the ancient Middle East was imperialism, and the only possibility for small nations to achieve sovereignty lay in periods of imperial decline. For most of the ancient period, small nations could not aspire to independence and sought instead to maximize their power by striking advantageous alliances with one of the empires. Those like Israel who were in strategic border areas were in positions of some strength because they could always defect to the neighboring empire; but for the same reason they were subject to constant suspicion of treason and brutal suppressions of real or imagined revolts.

The history of the Jews in antiquity demonstrates the persistent importance of imperialism in dictating the fate of small nations.[3] The very settlement in the land in the time of Joshua and the Judges (1300–1100 B.C.E.) came at a moment of Egyptian decline. During the period of the Judges, the fragmented tribes were repeatedly subjugated by neighboring powers and only briefly shook off their oppressors. With the rise of the Philistines, even this limited form of independence seemed threatened. Only under David and Solomon was full national sovereignty established by taking advantage of a temporary decline in imperial power. But David's empire, established around 1000 B.C.E., was very short-lived, as the power of the Syrian Kingdom of Aram grew in the early ninth century, to be followed shortly thereafter by the rise of the Assyrian Empire under Shalmaneser III (858–824 B.C.E.) and Tiglath-pileser III (745–727 B.C.E.). The Assyrians subjected the kingdoms of Israel and Judah to tribute, thus limiting their sovereignty and placing them under the effective control of an outside power. The destruction of the Kingdom of Israel in 722 B.C.E. was not the result of a sudden Assyrian invasion but rather the punishment for a revolt against Assyrian rule, already well established. The Kingdom of Judah, equally subject to tribute, was saved because it chose not to revolt. But, from 722 until it too was destroyed by the Babylonians in 586 B.C.E., Judah's independence was severely circumscribed by imperial domination.

If Jewish autonomy in the First Temple period was under the shadow of Middle Eastern imperialism, the same was even more true of the Second Temple period. In 538 B.C.E., the Persians defeated the Babylonians and created a far-flung, stable empire that included the Second Temple state. Two hundred years after the rebuilding of the Temple (516 B.C.E.), Alexander the Great ousted the Persians from the Mediterranean and established the reign of Hellenism. Finally, the Hellenistic empires in the Middle East were conquered in the second century B.C.E. by the Romans, who continued their rule in one form or another until the Muslim conquest of the seventh century C.E.

The only periods in which the Jews were able to achieve national independence were the very brief interludes between these empires: the reign of King Jeroboam II of Israel (mid-eighth century B.C.E.) during a hiatus in Assyrian power; the reigns of the Judaean kings Hezekiah and Josiah in the seventh century as the Assyrians declined; and the Hasmonean Kingdom (second and first centuries B.C.E.), which was more a consequence of the collapse of the Seleucid Empire than of Maccabean military prowess. Thus, the norm from the time of the Judges to the end of the Second Temple was subjugation to imperial powers, broken by, at best, brief episodes of independence. When the rabbis inherited rule of the nation after 70 C.E., full national sovereignty was more a dream and a wish than a historical reality.

For the most part, the lot of the Jews under these great powers was not different from that of other subject nations. They were allowed a large measure of internal autonomy in exchange for tribute and abandonment of an independent foreign policy. This was as true for the last two centuries of the First Temple period as it was for the Second Temple period. During the First Temple period, Judah and Israel defined themselves as kingdoms, so that they preserved a fiction of independence. In reality, they were only marginally more autonomous than was the priestly Second Temple state of the Persian and Hellenistic eras. In the First Temple period, the right of the Israelites to internal self-government was assumed by the Assyrians and the Babylonians, and was never spelled out in explicit privileges. Under the Persians and Greeks, written privileges were given to the Jews, allowing them to live "according to the laws of their fathers."[4] What had been taken for granted under the less organized earlier empires was now given a formal legal basis. When the Romans succeeded the Greeks, they continued in exactly the same course, for they could not rule their large empire directly, but instead governed through indigenous leaders. The Roman decision to impose direct rule in the first century B.C.E. came not from an intrinsic policy of abolishing local self-government but rather as a result of a breakdown of the Jewish leadership.

In terms of political rights, there was very little difference between the Jews of Palestine and those of the Diaspora, which originated in Babylonian times and spread throughout the Mediterranean under the Greeks and the Romans. Greek law considered the Diaspora Jews a *politeuma*, an ethnic polity with the right to self-government. Roman law defined them as *collegium licitum*, a legal corporation, rather than a *religio licita*, a legal religion, thus laying the basis for their corporate status in the Middle Ages. While the Jews as a collectivity were not citizens in Hellenistic cities such as Alexandria, individual Jews appear to have won citizenship rights. Jews enjoyed a status much higher than that of Egyptian peasants and they saw themselves as virtually equal to the Hellenized citizens. They governed themselves to a remarkable degree, rivaling the autonomy of their brothers and sisters in Palestine. Indeed, the Diaspora Jews were so well organized politically that they were able to undertake widespread military revolts in 115–117 C.E., some of which matched the anti-Roman revolts in Palestine in severity. Thus, while the Temple in Jerusalem made the Jewish community in the Land of Israel more religiously central, the political power of the ancient Diaspora was as great and, in some periods, perhaps even greater.[5]

Revolts and Their Consequences

The Jews were a remarkably contentious people in antiquity and developed a well-deserved reputation for military prowess. Not content to submit to the demands of their imperial masters, they repeatedly revolted in attempts to win full independence. Indeed, the Great Revolt against the Romans (66–70 C.E.) and the Bar Kokhba Revolt (132–35 C.E.) were unique in that they were virtually the only significant revolts against Rome that did not take place on the borders of the empire and that came close to achieving victory. But these uprisings were the last in a long series that goes back to the First Temple period.

The major Jewish revolts of antiquity possess a number of interesting features in common which help illuminate the problematic nature of Jewish power in an imperialistic world. First, there was a persistent conflict between two political parties: those favoring some form of accommodation with the imperial powers and those clamoring for full independence. Second, the relationship between the success or failure of a revolt and subsequent Jewish political survival was often complicated. Failed revolts might ultimately enhance Jewish power by strengthening the partial sovereignty that they had set out to overturn. On the other hand, temporary success might lead paradoxically to less autonomy than before the revolt took place. Finally, the way in which later memory regarded these revolts was frequently at great variance with their actual consequences: some of the most successful revolts were forgotten, while others that had long-term disastrous results were later treated as heroic victories.

In the First Temple period, the debate between "nationalists" and "accommodationists" found concrete expression in the different ways the northern Kingdom of Israel and the southern Kingdom of Judah responded to the crisis of Assyrian domination. Israel revolted against the Assyrians in 722 B.C.E. by refusing to pay tribute, an act which, in antiquity, symbolized a claim of sovereignty. For this refusal, it was destroyed. The Kingdom of Judah, also subject to tribute, did not rebel and therefore survived. In the next 135 years, the debate between the parties of accommodation and rebellion moved to Judah. During the reign of King Hezekiah (late eighth–early seventh centuries), the prophet Isaiah warned against premature revolt against the Assyrians, but Hezekiah eventually did revolt, exploiting a short period of Assyrian weakness.[6]

The most successful policy of survival was undertaken by King Manasseh, who ruled Judah for almost half a century in a period of relative Assyrian strength. Yet, the Book of Kings, edited in a later period, treats this wily accommodationist with the greatest hostility, reviling him as the most sinful of all the Judaean kings.[7] Manasseh had adopted some Assyrian gods into the Temple ritual, a typical form of political obeisance in the ancient world. To the orthodox scribes who edited the Book of Kings, this was a heinous sin, but from a political point of view, Manasseh was quite successful in preserving Judaean autonomy in the last years of the Assyrian Empire. Indeed, precisely because of his shrewd submission when the Assyrians were much stronger, the next king, Josiah, one of the most religiously orthodox rulers in the eyes of the Book of Kings, was able to achieve something like full independence for Judah in the 620s when the Assyrians were in their final decline.

Manasseh's policy fell into disrepute as a result of Josiah's success, with severe consequences as the Babylonians, who had defeated the Assyrians, conquered Judah. The party of independence was not able to adjust once again to life under an imperial power and twice tried to revolt. The party of accommodation, represented by the prophet Jeremiah, failed in its attempt to restrain nationalist passions.[8] In 598 B.C.E., the royal court was deported by the Babylonians, but a Davidic monarch was allowed to remain on the throne. In 586, the Babylonians responded to another attempt at revolt by abolishing Davidic rule and destroying the Temple. Significantly, the Babylonians did not abolish Jewish self-government; they appointed a non-Davidic ruler, Gedaliah, who was subsequently assassinated by Davidic loyalists. Thus, the final destruction of any form of Jewish sovereignty in the Land of Israel came about not because of prior policies of Assyria and Babylonia, but because of the victory of the Jewish party of revolt over the party of accommodation. Indeed, the very ability of the tiny state of Judah to survive as long as it did in the parlous world of the Assyrian Empire was a result of the success of the accommodationists in restraining the forces of rebellion. Jewish historical consciousness, however, represented by the Book of Kings, blamed the destruction of Judah on the "sinfulness" of precisely those, such as Manasseh, who had struggled for a political modus vivendi with ancient imperialism.

Yet, from a historical perspective, the consequences of

the defeated revolts against the imperial powers of First Temple times were not only negative. The restoration of Jewish self-government in Judaea, (the later Roman name for the territory of the Jews) in the late sixth and fifth centuries took place under a new leadership which emerged out of the destruction of the Davidic monarchy and the exile to Babylonia. After the Persian conquest of Babylonia in 538 B.C.E., the Jews in exile there achieved considerable political influence at court and could exploit the new Persian policy of restoring those temple-states that the Babylonians had destroyed. The central figures in the return from exile and the reestablishment of Jewish autonomy in Judaea in the early Second Temple period, Ezra and Nehemiah, were both priests who had become officials in the Persian court.

In Judaea itself, new leaders took power; following the enigmatic career of Zerubbabel, a descendant of King David, no attempt was made to resurrect the Davidic monarchy. In fact, within several generations, the line of David appears to have been lost, perhaps deliberately suppressed by the priests, who dominated the Second Temple state. The political leaders of the Second Temple period accepted the verdict of history: the failure of the Davidic monarchy to preserve the Judaean state demanded that a new leadership take its place. Indeed, this new leadership proved much more adept at accommodation with the imperial world, for the Persian and early Greek periods (ca. 500–200 B.C.E.) were an age of relative peace and prosperity. We have little recorded evidence from this era, but this is a sign less of the retreat of the Jews from politics[9] than of the success of the political leadership in avoiding the disasters of the late First Temple period. The consequences of the defeated revolts of that earlier age were thus new leadership and new stability for a relatively long period of time.

If the long-term result of the destruction of the First Temple was accommodation with the Persian and Greek empires, the consequences of the next major revolt, that of the Hasmoneans, were far less positive. Before considering this revolt, it is worthwhile to mention by way of comparison a much more minor Jewish revolt against the Hellenistic empire of the Ptolemies that took place about 200 B.C.E. The Judaeans, who were under the rule of the Ptolemies in Egypt, revolted by driving the Ptolemaic authorities out of Jerusalem. The Jews took up arms at a time when the army of the Seleucids (the Hellenistic empire in Syria) under Antiochus III was on the offensive against Egypt. The Jews exploited the weakness of the Ptolemies, but, instead of declaring national independence, they proclaimed their allegiance to Antiochus. In recognition of the Jews' assistance in the war, Antiochus renewed their political and religious privileges, granting them the right to "live according to the laws of their fathers." Here, then, is an example of a successful revolt in an imperial context, but successful because it was not a revolt for full independence, taking place instead as part of the struggle between two empires. It is interesting that a moderate uprising such as this never found its way into the memory of Jewish rebellions but remained buried in the *Antiquities* of Josephus.[10]

The Hasmonean Revolt of the 160s B.C.E. presents a totally different picture: a revolt that initially succeeded led to an eventual deterioration in Jewish power. The final consequence of this process of decline was the Great Revolt of 66–70 C.E., during which the Second Temple was destroyed. Although historians continue to debate the causes of the uprising, it is clear that it was preceded by a breakdown in the political leadership that had been so successful at the beginning of the Persian period.[11] The high priesthood became an office to be purchased from the Seleucid king, and it passed into the hands of men who were not from the legitimate family of high priests. The streets of Jerusalem became a battleground between different priestly parties as civil order broke down entirely. It was against this background of anarchy that Antiochus IV's persecution of the Jewish religion took place, whatever its cause. The Hasmonean clan were themselves priests and their revolt, from an internal Jewish point of view, was primarily a struggle for control of the high priest-hood, even if fueled by nationalistic and religious resistance to the Greeks. When Jonathan, Judah Maccabee's brother, became high priest in 154, the Hasmoneans ceased their struggle against the Seleucids and accepted the Hellenistic kingdom as their governors, a sign that they were more inter-ested in high office than in national sovereignty.

In 142 B.C.E., full political sovereignty fell unexpectedly into the laps of the Hasmoneans more as a result of the de-cline of the Seleucid Empire than of shrewd maneuvering by the Jews. But the Hasmoneans squandered the fruits of this victory in internecine strife. The failure of the Hasmoneans to maintain their empire more than eighty years was in large measure due to their inability to establish themselves as le-gitimate and universally recognized leaders. Many Jews, in-cluding the Pharisees (the party that later became the rabbis), rejected the Hasmonean claim to be legitimate high priests. Instead of creating a stable sovereign state for the first time since Josiah nearly five hundred years earlier, their reign was marked by increasing conflict and persecution of their oppo-nents. Their demise came when two Hasmonean descendants, Hyrcanus and Aristobulus, fought over the succession, and one side invited in the Romans in 63 B.C.E..

Although the Romans would have conquered Judaea in any case, the collapse of Hasmonean leadership, a mere cen-tury after Judah Maccabee's revolt against the Greeks, created a serious power vacuum. The Romans preferred to rule through local elites, but they did not find anyone with sufficient authority until they imposed their own agent, the Idumaean convert Herod.[12] Herod's rule combined grandiose building projects with extraordinarily brutal repression. He thoroughly subverted the traditional institutions of Jewish governance, and the high priesthood passed into the hands of families beholden to him who were more interested in private gain than in public worship. Although a Jew (his grandfather was converted by the Hasmoneans as they built their empire),

Herod's loyalty was primarily to Rome. On one level, then, Herod enhanced Jewish power as a result of his favored position in the imperial court, but it was at the expense of a genuinely free political life in Judaea itself. The accomplishments of Herod could not be sustained after his death, and, indeed, the massacres he perpetrated on his own family, not to speak of the rest of the Jewish elite, left him without any serious heirs when he died.

The legacy of Herod's authoritarian rule was chaos. Having completed the dismantling of the traditional institutions of Jewish power begun in the time of Antiochus Epiphanes, Herod left practically no legitimate and recognized leadership behind. The Romans moved into the void and established direct rule of Judaea under procurators. Now the sectarianism that had germinated under the Hasmoneans bore full fruit as anarchy reigned in the countryside and religious strife swept the cities. New messianic movements emerged, of which the band around Jesus of Nazareth was only one. It was this situation of mounting chaos that must be understood as the background to the Great Revolt against the Romans of 66–70 C.E. Although there can be no doubt that the corrupt procurators provoked a rebellious climate, the ability of small extremist groups to capture leadership during the revolt was a result of the breakdown of internal authority.

The priesthood became increasingly corrupt and attracted widespread hostility. The rabbinic sources preserve a variety of sources attesting to the breakdown in the priesthood. Although the rabbis were hostile to the priests to begin with, and their testimony is therefore suspect, some of the stories have a ring of historical truth. For instance, the following denunciation of the high priests sounds as if it might have been an actual popular chant:

> Woe is me because of the House of Elisha, woe is me because of their fist, woe is me because of the House of Ishmael b. Phiabi, who are High Priests and their sons-in-law are trustees and their servants come and beat us with sticks.[13]

Reflecting much later on these events, the rabbis held that the Temple was destroyed as a result of "groundless hatred" (*sinat hinam*). There is probably much truth in their attempt to find an internal cause for this course of events.

As in the revolts against the Assyrians and the Babylonians, the ascendancy of extremists who rejected any form of accommodation with Rome led to catastrophe. According to Josephus Flavius, part of the Jerusalem establishment did favor the war, but this "war party," to which he belonged, had only the limited objective of improving the provincial government. These members of the aristocracy were quickly swept aside by extremists: the Zealots, Biryonim, and other radical messianic groups. For these militants, nothing short of complete victory was acceptable, and the result was the destruction of Jerusalem. The Bar Kokhba Revolt of 132–35, sparked by similar messianic impulses, completed the destruction of the Great Revolt: the Jews of Judaea were exterminated or exiled. Only in Galilee to the north did a Jewish population remain in the Land of Israel.

The success of the Hasmonean Revolt was therefore short-lived, and its long-term consequences were catastrophic. With the Hasmoneans, the Jews sought power beyond the limited autonomy of their temple-state. Their drive for full sovereignty was probably doomed from the outset in light of the Roman conquest of the East. But the failure of the Hasmoneans to provide a stable leadership hastened the slide first to the authoritarian despotism of Herod and then to the chaos of the half-century preceding the final revolt. Ultimately, the victory of the Hasmoneans led to the destruction of the Temple itself.

The Foundations of Rabbinic Power

The destructions of the First and Second temples, although carried out by imperial powers whose policies often provoked revolt, were due in part to the failure of Jewish political leadership. In both cases, the failure of revolts led ultimately to the emergence of more responsible and effective leaders. The Babylonian exile put an end to the Judaean monarchy, which had proven incapable of navigating in the treacherous waters of ancient imperialism, and cleared the way for the priests to take power in the Second Temple period. The priests retained their dominance throughout the Second Temple period, although scribes and other nonpriestly elites also played a role. With the destruction of the Temple, the priests lost their primary religious function, and soon lost political power entirely. With the disestablishment of the priesthood and the eradication of the numerous extreme sects, the way was clear for the Pharisees, or rabbis—who were but one of the Second Temple parties—to seize power and become the sole leaders of the nation. As in the case of the destruction of the First Temple, only the disaster of war could sweep away the old, corrupt leadership and make way for new leaders. The failure of the revolt against the Romans ultimately led to greater stability and greater Jewish power.

What was the nature of rabbinic power? According to one view, the rabbis were passive and apolitical; they were religious leaders concerned with purity and piety, uninterested in political life. During the siege of Jerusalem, the rabbinical leader Yohanan ben Zakkai fled the city and asked for refuge in the town of Yavneh in order to continue studying and teaching the Torah. The Romans, recognizing the rabbis to be "pacifists" and "antinationalists," acceded to the request, and so Judaism was saved even though Jerusalem was destroyed.

As the historian Gedaliah Alon has shown, this conception of the rabbis after 70 C.E. is historically mistaken.[14] The earliest and most reliable sources suggest that Yohanan ben Zakkai supported the war against the Romans until the situation had become hopeless.[15] Far from requesting Yavneh for a spiritual retreat, he was imprisoned there by the Romans in a kind of internment camp for Jewish leaders. He created a legislative court there that only later, under the leadership of Rabban Gamliel, won recognition from the Romans and thus became the center of Jewish self-government. Although the Romans elevated Judaea to the status of a consular province ruled directly by the Senate, they still needed a strong Jewish government to control the internal affairs of the people. With the priesthood thoroughly discredited, the rabbis won this recognition. The historical sources following the Great Revolt portray the rabbis not as a group of otherworldly scholars concerned with purity for its own sake, but as pragmatic political realists determined to preserve their authority and make their interpretation of the law binding. The rabbis came to terms with defeat and constructed new institutions to take the place of the old ones. For example, the Sanhedrin (legislative high court) of Second Temple days was resurrected but was probably a very different institution from its predecessor in terms of its structure and function. Far from being pacifists, these rabbis were nationalists and, as Jacob Neusner has shown, many of the seemingly pacifist sayings attributed to Yohanan ben Zakkai probably date from a much later period.[16]

The proof of this argument can be found in the Bar Kokhba rebellion. Only two generations after the Great Revolt, we find the most important rabbis of the time, including Rabbi Akiva, supporting Bar Kokhba and even calling him the Messiah.[17] It is hard to imagine how the disciples of Yohanan ben Zakkai could have involved themselves in the Bar Kokhba affair if they had forsaken politics. If anything, the Bar Kokhba rebellion proves that the rabbis were susceptible to the same messianic fervor that had provoked the Great Revolt seventy years earlier. A second failed attempt at full independence was necesary to convince the rabbinical authorities that a different course had to be adopted if the Jews were to survive the Roman Empire.

What is most astonishing about the Bar Kokhba rebellion, considering its severity and the damage sustained by both the Jews and the Romans, is how rapidly the Jews were allowed to regain their autonomy.[18] Early in the reign of Antonius Pius (from 138 C.E.), Jewish autonomy was restored under the rabbis, many of whom were disciples of the generation that had supported Bar Kokhba. Where the Great Revolt had led to the transfer of power to a new group (or to a group that had only shared in the leadership), the much more traumatic Bar Kokhba war did not change anything fundamentally. The position of the Patriarch (*nasi*), the rabbi who presided over the Sanhedrin and acted as chief executive of the Jewish community, was reconfirmed. The Sanhedrin, although it moved to the Galilee, continued its work. As with the Great Revolt, failure led paradoxically to greater political stability and internal power.

Following the reign of the Antonines (which ended in 192 C.E.) came the Severans (193–235), under whom Jewish self-government reached a height unknown since the days of Herod. The Patriarch functioned like a monarch, as a passage from the Church father Origen attests:

> And even now, though the Romans are sovereign and the Jews pay them the tax of two drachmas, the Patriarch is so powerful among the Jews, that it seems as if, subject to the Emperor's consent, there is no difference between him and the former kings of the nation, for cases are being tried without official permission, according to Jewish law, and sometimes death sentences are passed, admittedly not completely in public, but not without the Emperor's knowledge.[19]

The Patriarch's court in Sephorris (later Tiberias) became opulent and the Patriarch himself was protected by a bodyguard of German mercenaries. Indeed, the power of the Patriarch was so great that it occasioned the outright opposition of some of the rabbis. The rabbinical government had full powers of taxation and adjudication, including, as Origen reports, even capital punishment (although the latter was not a formal part of its powers). Since the time of Yohanan ben Zakkai, the authority of the court to set the calendar was generally recognized among the Jews of both Palestine and the Diaspora.

With the sanction of the Romans, the rabbis became the

sole Jewish political authority, functioning with all the powers of an autonomous government within the empire. If this power took root following the Great Revolt, it flourished with particular vigor in the period following the Bar Kokhba rebellion until the conversion of Rome to Christianity. Far from putting an end to Jewish power, the failure of the revolts served indirectly to increase it. The Jews had failed to win full independence. But this goal was utopian in the context of the Roman Empire; the more modest possibility of full internal autonomy proved to be very much within reach. And far from developing their authority in total opposition to and seclusion from the Roman Empire, the rabbis were beholden to the Romans for their very position: without Roman sanction and support, rabbinical Judaism would have never been able to consolidate its power and develop the legal and communal system that prevailed throughout the Middle Ages. Some of the Rabbis recognized this reality. Rabbi Judah ben Ilai, in the second century, is quoted as saying: "How beautiful are the deeds of that nation [the Romans]. They set up market-places, build bridges, construct baths." Rabbi Simon bar Yohai, one of the supporters of Bar Kokhba, retorted: "Everything they do for their own good. They set up marketplaces to place their harlots there, baths for their pleasures, bridges to levy tolls."[20] Yet the defeat of Bar Kokhba established the views of Rabbi Judah as politically correct, for the path of revolt could no longer be seen as viable and the path of accommodation had demonstrably produced a golden age of rabbinical power.

Politically and religiously, the destruction of the Temple in 70 c.e. spelled the end of an era: priests were removed from politics and Temple sacrifice became a memory. Yet, in terms of political sovereignty, the subsequent period of rabbinic rule meant no fundamental change in the governance of the Land of Israel, even after the Bar Kokhba rebellion. The Jewish authorities in Palestine continued to enjoy the respect of the Diaspora Jews, even though the Temple no longer stood as the recipient of donations. The internal autonomy wielded by the rabbis exceeded in many respects that of earlier periods. It can well be argued that the centuries of Jewish self-government in both Palestine and Babylonia following the destruction of the Temple were critical in preparing for the Middle Ages: the rabbis developed a Jewish life without a temple and thereby laid the foundation for a decentralized political existence under Christianity and Islam.

The Political Ideologies of Antiquity

There is a persistent tension between the way the Jews of antiquity claimed to perceive their power and the realities of that power as we have described them. The dominant modes of thought in the First Temple period exaggerated Israelite power in order to compensate for a far more perilous reality, while rabbinic political theory, to which I shall turn in the next chapter, often went to the other extreme of underplaying political power in order to avoid a repetition of the failed rebellions.

The two central myths of biblical political theology are the chosenness, or divine election, of the Jewish people and messianism (the urge for full sovereignty modeled on the reign of King David). These two doctrines were related and underwent transformations in the wake of political events. According to the concept of divine election, the Jews are the only people to have received the revelation of a universal God. They must therefore be at the center of world history and, indeed, the later rabbis considered the Land of Israel to be the center of the world. From a political point of view, the doctrine of election was a statement of Jewish power couched in theological terms.

In reality, of course, both the Jews and their land were peripheral to world history in antiquity. Judaea was in the backwaters of the various Mesopotamian empires and of the later Hellenistic and Roman empires. Indeed, pagan critics such as Celsus ridiculed Christianity, and by implication Judaism as well, by pointing to the provinciality of Judaea: "If

God ... woke up out of His long slumber and wanted to deliver the human race from evils, why on earth did He send this spirit ... into one corner [of the Roman empire]?"[21] Judaea lay in the borderland between Egypt and the great population centers to the northeast; its importance was due to the very fact that it was peripheral and not central, located as it was on a trade route in a border area.

Here then is a fundamental contradiction between national myth and historical reality. Had the Jews been closer to the centers of power in antiquity, their chances of survival might have been worse. Certainly, if they had possessed real power on the scale of the ancient empires, they probably would have gone the way of the Assyrians and the Babylonians. But if the Jews had not developed a myth of their centrality, they would likely have vanished like other small nations. The doctrine of divine election proved to be remarkably flexible in meeting the demands of a hostile imperial world. Relative lack of power combined with a myth of power was perhaps one of the keys to Jewish survival in antiquity.

The myth of Jewish origins corresponds to this ambiguous legacy. Was there any other nation in antiquity that proudly admitted to its origin as a motley band of slaves? The early Israelites as we find them in the Genesis stories were wanderers, seminomads perhaps related to the 'apiru, a group of outcasts on the fringes of ancient Middle Eastern society.[22] Moreover, the Bible freely admits that the Hebrews had not resided in their own territory since time immemorial, but, like the ancient Greeks, were a new people, forged as a nation in slavery in Egypt. Yet biblical theology argued that God had chosen this youngest and most disreputable of peoples. The repetition of stories in Genesis of how the younger son is preferred over the elder may well be a piece of nationalistic ideology justifying Hebrew origins: just as the natural law of primogeniture is repeatedly overturned in the choosing of Abel over Cain, Isaac over Ishmael, Jacob over Esau, Joseph over his older brothers, and Ephraim over Manasseh, so God chose the Israelites over all the older nations.

The doctrine of the Chosen People was probably developed to justify the Israelite invasion of the land of Canaan in the time of Joshua and the Judges.[23] Here, too, theory and reality do not correspond. Historians question whether Moses and Joshua led a unified nation and draw instead a picture of a fractious group of tribes with certain religious and ethnic similarities, but lacking anything resembling national unity.[24] The very conquest of the land, portrayed in the Book of Joshua as one swift blow ousting the Canaanites, was in reality a gradual process only completed in the time of David. The theory of chosenness imposed a myth of unity and divine sanction on a fragile political alliance between highly fragmented tribes.

The political theory of early Israelite leadership was a corollary to the doctrine of divine election. The system of judges has been called "charismatic" in the sense that the spirit of God would descend upon a military leader who would then temporarily unite the tribes for purposes of defense.[25] The model for this theory of leadership was probably Moses, although Moses himself is never designated as a judge and his leadership remains without precedent or later imitation.[26] Here, too, divine intervention gave authority to a leader in a time of relative anarchy. Just as the doctrine of divine election promised a powerful future to a shaky coalition of tribes, so the idea of the divine election of the judge papered over a very tenuous system of political leadership.

It was David who transformed this political theory into something entirely new. While Saul appears to have been initially a judge on the old model, David was a mercenary military commander who became king as a result of his ruthless pursuit of power. He was the first noncharismatic ruler of the Israelites. Traditionalists must have perceived the notion of monarchy as a threat to the traditional political theory according to which God, as king, selects His own political leaders. The system of monarchy that David and later Solomon established thoroughly destroyed the traditional tribal structure. Yet, in legitimating his monarchy, David's theolo-

gians adopted the notion of divine election and applied it to
David and to all his heirs. The new theory claimed that God
had chosen not only David, but all of David's descendants as
well. This theology portrayed David and his dynasty as the
adopted sons of God, thus adding a familial touch to the traditional language of election. Psalm 89 is an example of such
Davidic theology:

> I have made a covenant with My chosen one,
> I have sworn unto My servant David:
> I will establish your offspring forever,
> I will confirm your throne for all generations. . . .
> I will appoint him My firstborn,
> Highest of the kings of the earth.[27]

God had become politically superfluous to the continuity of
the political order, for His election of the Davidic monarchy
was passed on biologically. The Davidic theologians did not
reject the old theory of election; they took it over and filled it
with new meaning. This appropriation of a traditional concept to butress a new political system gave the monarchy
great stability, for descendants of David ruled Judah for more
than four hundred years until the Babylonian exile. In the
northern Kingdom of Israel, which seceded after the death of
Solomon, a system of charismatic kingship was reinstituted.
For that reason, the Kingdom of Israel had a far less stable
leadership than did the Kingdom of Judah.

The cooptation of the concept of divine election by the
Davidic theologians became the source of Jewish messianism.
Judaean court theologians in the First Temple period, such as
the prophet Isaiah, hoped for a restoration of the glories of
David's empire, including full political sovereignty. They
tended to see in certain particularly successful kings, such as
Hezekiah and Josiah, political reincarnations of David, the
"anointed" (messiah) of God.[28] Following the destruction of
the Kingdom of Judah, this hope was deferred to a future
descendant of David who might restore the fallen monarchy

and recover national independence. Once the actual line of David was lost in the century following the return from Babylonia, the messianic idea could be infused with a whole new variety of meanings. The prophet Zechariah, who lived during the first period of return from Babylonia (late sixth century B.C.E.), advanced the idea of a priestly Messiah, a notion that resurfaced centuries later in the Dead Sea Scrolls, written by a priestly messianic sect in the late Second Temple period.[29] A host of pretenders to the Davidic line made their appearance at the end of the Second Temple period, ranging from Jesus of Nazareth to the line of the rabbinical patriarchs. In short, it became possible for every group to transform messianism to suit its own claims. From the exclusive political theory of the monarchial establishment, messianism had become equally useful as a theory for rebellions against the established leadership. (Later, we shall see how the rabbis sought to defuse the subversive side of the messianic idea by deferring the hope for full sovereignty and by claiming that the Messiah would surely come from the rabbinical class itself.)

Just as the theory of the divine election of leaders underwent radical changes in the First and Second Temple periods, so the theory of the divine election of Israel as a whole was transformed. If this theory had initially attempted to bestow an ideology of power on a relatively powerless group of tribes, it faced a serious challenge when the imperial nations of Assyria and Babylonia appeared on the scene. Following the destruction of the Kingdom of Israel in 722 B.C.E., a group of Judaean theorists reformulated the covenant between God and Israel. The threat of imminent destruction, brought home by the fate of the north, undoubtedly prompted this development. Evidence that God had chosen the Israelites might be found not only in Israelite success, but in defeat as well. Defeat became a sign of God's power, for He was so exclusively concerned with Israel that He had used the unwitting world powers to punish the Israelites for their transgressions. Defeat was the consequence not of divine desertion of Israel, but, quite on the contrary, of God's love for His people. The prophet Isaiah proclaimed in the wake of the Assyrian invasions:

> O Assyria, rod of My anger,
> In whose hand as a staff is my fury.
> I send him against an ungodly nation.[30]

Since this God used the imperial powers as the "rod of [His] anger," the Israelites could continue to see themselves, even in defeat, as central to world history. Jewish history could continue—indeed, had to continue—even when the state and Temple were in ruins. Thus, the seventh century B.C.E., that hiatus between the destruction of the north and the south, witnessed the development of a thoroughly original political theology that would make possible the continuation of Jewish political life in the Babylonian exile.

The political thought of the seventh century also addressed internal political questions. As is well known, the Prophets attacked social inequality and the breakdown in public morality. This critique cannot be divorced from their reflections on foreign policy, since they assumed that an internally united people would be able to weather the pressures of imperialism. The authors of the Book of Deuteronomy, probably writing at the same time, imposed strict limitations on the power of the king, a position reflected in the critique of the monarchy to be found in the Book of Kings.[31] The social and political criticism of this period were both phrased in religious language, but they amounted to a political response to a very dangerous world.

The new theology of chosenness and the political theory of the Prophets were not doctrines of powerlessness. Prophets such as Isaiah and Jeremiah were neither pacifists nor apolitical moralists. They were part of the Judaean political establishment, and their preaching was the theological expression of their shrewd policy of neutralism and accommodation to the imperial world. Even though their political advice was ignored, their theology was preserved by subsequent generations since it correctly anticipated military defeat and devised a strategy for confronting it. Instead of passivity, the Prophets preached political activism in the wake of the destruction. In one of the most famous passages in Jeremiah, the prophet writes to those in exile: "Build houses, settle down . . . , work for the good of the country to which I have exiled you; pray to the Lord on its behalf, since on its welfare yours depends."[32] Far from advocating a withdrawal from politics, Jeremiah was suggesting the very kind of political activism that several generations later led to the successful return from Babylonia, a return predicated on the political successes of the Jews in the Persian court.

This was the biblical legacy that the rabbis inherited when they sought to construct a viable political theory after the revolts of the first and second centuries C.E. The theory of messianism lay at the heart of both of these revolts, yet it could not be disavowed, for it was too intimately connected with the central theology of divine election. On the other hand, the prophetic model of accommodation offered the possibility of preserving the partial sovereignty of antiquity. The task of creating a new political theory to legitimate and preserve rabbinical power required a delicate balancing act between the messianic urge for full sovereignty and apolitical passivity. In the succeeding centuries, the rabbis of both Palestine and Babylonia confronted this task and laid the foundations of the political theory of the Diaspora which would be carried by the Jews into the Middle Ages. By carrying on a viable political life without a temple, the rabbis laid the groundwork for the continuation of Jewish communities in the Diaspora. The period from the destruction of the Temple to the end of the Patriarchate in the fifth century C.E. marked the transition not from power to powerlessness but from the partial sovereignty of the ancient Israelite state to the autonomous Jewish communities of the Middle Ages.

II

The Political Theory of the Diaspora

IT has often been assumed that, following the destruction of the Temple, the Jews abandoned politics and, in the absence of a political life, developed no political theories. The legal system known as *halakhah* that the rabbis developed in the centuries after 70 C.E. is taken to be devoid of political impulses and fundamentally antithetical to the normal political life of a sovereign nation.[1] The only theorizing about politics was projected into the messianic future: messianic thought, it is generally argued, proves that the Jews were conscious of their political impotence, since they could only long for a restoration of their lost sovereignty in a messianic age.

In fact, however, Jewish thought after 70 C.E. was much more complex. On the one hand, all thinkers recognized the condition of *galut* (exile) as fundamentally abnormal and humiliating. In contrast to the memory (if not the reality) of a golden age of ancient sovereignty and the expectation of a messianic restoration, the *galut* was viewed as a period of abject powerlessness. Yet, most of the very same thinkers recognized the political realities of Jewish life in the Diaspora

34

and developed theories to explain and justify them. The power Jews wielded within their communities and the relationships they established with non-Jewish sources of power all required and promoted the evolution of an authentic political theory of the Diaspora. Jewish reflections on exile therefore operated at once in two dimensions: the theological, to account for the lack of Jewish sovereignty, and the political, to explain the actual power the Jews possessed, both of internal self-government and in the larger societies in which they lived. This duality explains why rabbinic and medieval Jewish literature contains both a theology of powerlessness and a political theory of Jewish power.

It was in the atmosphere of relative power in the century following the Bar Kokhba Revolt that the rabbis developed the political theory that gave conscious expression both to the need for accommodation with the imperial world and to the reality of partial sovereignty or local autonomy. By transforming the ideology of divine election, with its implicit demand for full Jewish sovereignty, into a more realistic theory of Jewish power, the rabbis created the political modus vivendi of the Middle Ages. In the centuries after the completion of the Babylonian Talmud around 500 c.e., the authorities who succeeded the rabbis elaborated and extended rabbinic political thought. Taken together, the writings of the rabbis of the talmudic period and those of their medieval successors constitute a political theory of Diaspora.

Theories of Exile

Following the destruction of the Temple and the defeat of Bar Kokhba, the rabbis took up the old prophetic search for Jewish sins that might have caused these catastrophes.[2] The stories collected in the tractate Gittin of the Babylonian Talmud reflect this search for internal causes. They largely suppressed the memory of the Hasmonean Revolt and clearly voiced their disapproval of the two revolts against the Romans. In the manner of the prophetic response to the Babylonian exile, the rabbis viewed the new exile as a punishment for sins. Extending the biblical doctrine of divine election, they searched for the hand of God in Jewish catastrophes.

At the same time, however, the rabbis introduced an entirely new theology that transformed the theory of divine election and of God's power in history. Far from demonstrating his power, the exile was a symptom of God's own impotence: God Himself had gone into exile with the Jews.[3] This implicit diminution of God's power becomes explicit in a midrash (exposition of a biblical text) that relates how the men of the Great Assembly responded to the destruction of the First Temple and the Babylonian exile by transforming the meaning of the verse "the great, powerful, and awe-inspiring God." Rather than portraying God as powerful in a conventional sense, they claimed that God's power is demonstrated by its absence: "He controls His anger and is long-suffering to evil-doers." The rabbis were nevertheless troubled by this reinterpretation and asked: "Why did these sages alter what Moses had ordained? Rabbi Eleazar replied: 'They knew of the Holy One, blessed be He, that He is truthful, and would say nothing untrue about Him.' "[4] The midrash recognizes the loss of Jewish power by diminishing God's power. Instead of using His power to punish His people, in the way the prophets of late First Temple times argued, God Himself is a victim of the exile. In the sixteenth century, the Kabbalah of Isaac Luria proposed a mystical elaboration of these midrashim in which the very creation of the world involves a self-imposed divine exile: in order to make room for the world, God contracted Himself, leaving a space devoid of His presence.[5] In this new theology, the old idea that God's election of the Jews is proven by Jewish suffering is amended: God Himself suffers with His people.

By subtly subverting the biblical theology of divine election, the rabbis radically transformed the role of God in history. They proclaimed that with the destruction of the Temple, prophecy had ceased.[6] Now in exile with His people, God no longer intervened in history, as He had in the biblical period. This tendency to remove God from the arena of politics was already in motion by the late Second Temple period: the books of Maccabees and the books of Esther and Judith, for example, leave God entirely out of their stories. We shall see shortly how this idea became important in establishing rabbinic hegemony in interpreting the law. This new theology, which existed side by side with the old prophetic doctrine of divine punishment, created a bold opening for human activity. If God's intervention in history had come into doubt, it might now be possible for the Jews to take political action without direct divine dispensation. This duality in rabbinic thought between a prophetic theology of exile and a new theology that might permit human action persisted into the Middle Ages.

Those who consider powerlessness to be the legacy of the Jewish Middle Ages can point to an important group of thinkers who elaborated the prophetic theology according to which the humiliations and political impotence of the *galut* are divine punishment for sin. Under the possible influence of Christianity, medieval thinkers sometimes saw those generations that had particularly suffered, such as the generation of the First Crusades, as atoning for the sins of earlier generations, or Israel in general as atoning also for the sins of the world.[7] For Judah Ha-Levi, the election of Israel was proven by its suffering. Only the Jews give real expression to the religious value of humility since only the Jews are truly powerless. Ha-Levi's elevation of passivity and suffering to a theological principle suggests either Christian influence or an apologetic desire to counter Christian polemics with Christian arguments.[8] In the sixteenth century, Rabbi Judah Loew ben Bezalel (the Maharal of Prague) gave this theology a "scientific" turn: the very powerlessness and lack of sovereignty of the Jews is an unnatural state which can only be maintained by divine intervention. The exile therefore proves that God has continued to choose the Jews and will redeem them from their unnatural condition by returning them to their "natural place" as a sovereign people in the Land of Israel.[9]

Against these theories of exile as an ennobling punishment or as proof of God's continued election of the Jews, another group of thinkers rejected humiliation and advocated militant action when possible, arguing, "When it is within our grasp, kill them." A variety of authorities, such as Eleazar of Worms, Abraham ibn Ezra, Abraham ibn Daud, Abraham bar Hiyya, and Joseph Kimchi, emphasized both the past and present greatness of the Jews and urged that just as the Jews had vigorously defended themselves when they had sovereignty, so they should take action on their own behalf in the Diaspora. Some, like Eleazar, sanctioned the use of arms on the Sabbath. Others, like Abraham ibn Daud in his history of the Jews and Abraham ibn Ezra in his biblical commentary, glorified periods of armed rebellion such as the conquest of the Land of Israel or the Hasmonean Revolt. What all these thinkers had in common was a rejection of subservient behavior: Jews should not accept the role imposed on them by Muslims and Christians. *Galut* had no redeeming merit and should be resisted by whatever means came to hand.[10]

Political Messianism

These two attitudes toward exile naturally produced two very different approaches to messianism, the desire to reestablish the sovereign kingdom of David's time and to rebuild the Temple. In the wake of the messianic rebellion under Bar Kokhba and the threat of Christian messianism, the rabbis were compelled to address the messianic theory they had inherited from Second Temple times. Jewish messianism, as we have seen, was originally part of the official theology or ideology of the Davidic monarchy, but was adopted by radical groups in the late Second Temple period. Messianism lay behind the Great Revolt of 66–70 c.e. and the Bar Kokhba rebellion in the next century. Clearly, no accommodation with Roman power would have been possible without a substantial revision of this revolutionary doctrine.

Since meditations on messianism span many centuries

and include a wide variety of opinions, it is impossible to define *the* rabbinic messianic doctrine.[11] The conventional view of Jewish history argues that the rabbis responded to the manifest dangers of messianism by suppressing its human side altogether and leaving it entirely to divine decision. Jewish messianism from the second-century rabbis through the Middle Ages was synonymous with passivity. There is a great deal of material from the rabbinic period that supports this argument. The rabbis who lived after the Bar Kokhba rebellion bitterly criticized Bar Kokhba by calling him "the son of a lie," a pun on the putative Messiah's real name, Bar Kosiba (*kezivah* means lie or deception).[12] Similarly, the pacifistic and antimessianic sayings attributed to Yohanan ben Zakkai were probably written by post–Bar Kokhba rabbis, eager to establish that an antimessianic position had the sanction of earlier generations.[13] There is also good evidence that some of the rabbinic critiques of the institution of monarchy stem from a similar hostility to messianism.[14] This hostility is best represented in a collection of antimessianic statements in chapter 11 of the talmudic tractate Sanhedrin, which includes the famous curse: "Blasted be the bones of those who calculate the date of the Messiah."[15]

Perhaps one of the most historically significant rabbinic arguments against messianism was the legend of the three "oaths" (*shevu'ot*) sworn between God, Israel, and the nations. The three oaths, which appear in a number of variants, are a *midrash* on Song of Songs 2.7: "Do not make or rouse/ Love until it please."[16] According to the first two oaths, God made Israel swear not to force the coming of the Messiah and not to emigrate en masse to the Land of Israel. In return, the nations of the world swore a third oath not to oppress the Jews "too much." These three oaths have been taken to constitute a kind of political contract of the Diaspora: in exchange for political passivity, the Jews would be tolerated by the nations. Indeed, in our own century, the Satmar rabbi Joel Teitelbaum wrote a treatise, *Va-Yoel Moshe*, attacking

Zionism based on these three oaths; it is one of the most
extreme arguments for total Jewish passivity and against any
human action to end the exile.[17]

Against this hostility to messianism, other rabbinic
sources preserve the legacy of Second Temple apocalypticism, that radical, utopian expectation of an end to this age of
history. Chapter 11 of the tractate Sanhedrin, mentioned
above for its antimessianic statements, also contains a wide
variety of speculations by the rabbis on precisely when the
Messiah would come. Many of these dates fall squarely in the
periods when these rabbis themselves lived, suggesting that
the ban on such speculations was more honored in the
breach. Rabbinic apocalypticism shared with its Second
Temple predecessors the belief in a host of miracles that
would accompany messianic times. Moreover, even the image
of Bar Kokhba was more complicated than the condemnatory
passages might lead us to believe. Side by side with the negative statements are treatments of Bar Kokhba as a hero (*gib-
bor*) of biblical stature.[18]

Between the extremes of passivity and apocalypticism
there was another attitude, that neither suppressed messianic
inclinations nor indulged in wild, utopian hopes. This position, to borrow a phrase from Gershom Scholem, "neutralized" messianism by channeling it into a nonrevolutionary
doctrine related to this world. The theory, which Amos Fun-
kentein has termed "realistic messianism," envisioned the
restoration of Jewish sovereignty as the result of political
action.[19] At the same time, it was profoundly conservative,
avoiding the temptations of another Bar Kokhba Revolt and
emphasizing the basic continuities between rabbinic institutions and messianic times.

The basis for this realistic, political messianism is a saying by the third-century rabbi Samuel that "the only difference between the present and the days of the Messiah is servitude to foreign powers."[20] The idea that only the political fact
of sovereignty distinguishes the messianic age from our times
implies that human action might still be permissible. This

interpretation of Samuel's statement found its clearest expression in Maimonides' *Mishneh Torah* in the twelfth
century:

> Do not think that King Messiah will have to perform signs and
> wonders, bring anything new into being, revive the dead, or do
> similar things. . . . If there arises a king from the House of David
> who meditates on the Torah, occupies himself with the com-
> mandments, as did his ancestor David, observes the precepts
> prescribed in the written and oral law, prevails upon Israel to
> walk in the way of the Torah and to repair its breaches, and
> fights the battles of the Lord, it may be assumed that he is the
> Messiah. If he does these things and succeeds, rebuilds the sanc-
> tuary on its site and gathers the dispersed of Israel, he is beyond
> all doubt the Messiah. . . . Let no one think that in the days of
> the Messiah any of the laws of nature will be set aside or any
> innovation be introduced into creation. The world will follow
> its normal course.[21]

For Maimonides, there would not be a radical break between
this age and the age of the Messiah. Jewish political power
would be restored to a sovereign state but would not be drastically transformed. It is interesting to note that Maimonides'
image of King David is totally unrelated to, and even contradicts, the historical David, whose lawless marriage to Bath-
sheba earned him the rebuke of the prophet Nathan. For Maimonides, David was the epitomy of a constitutional monarch,
obedient to the laws of the Torah. He contrasts this type of
monarchy with the kings from the House of Israel, in which
he includes the Hasmoneans, who were absolute monarchs,
bound by no law.[22]

The emphasis on the subordination of the King Messiah
to the laws of the Torah further points to the continuity Maimonides envisioned between rabbinic power and messianic
times. In his discussion of the laws pertaining to the Sanhedrin (the high court that stood in the Temple), Maimonides
mingled directives to present-day Jewish courts with pre-
scriptions for the messianic high court.[23] He clearly regarded
the judicial power of the Diaspora courts as quite similar to

what it would be when the Sanhedrin is reconstituted in messianic times. In his letter to the Jews of Yemen, which was intended to help suppress a messianic uprising, Maimonides demonstrated that he was thoroughly hostile to apocalyptic messianic movements. His hostility was based not, however, on a belief in political passivity, but rather on its very opposite: the rabbis must be the guardians of the political power that would become the basis for the political program of the King Messiah. Rather than an apocalyptic break between this world and the next, the days of the Messiah would perpetuate rabbinic power in a framework of political sovereignty.

This doctrine of continuity between the rabbis and the Messiah can already be found in talmudic times. In the same passage in Sanhedrin, there are messianic sayings about figures from the courts of the Exilarch (Resh Galuta), the political leader of the Babylonian Jewish community, and the Patriarch, the leader of the Palestinian community. Rav Nahman, the son-in-law of the Exilarch, stated: "If [the Messiah] is among the living, he might be one like myself, as it is said, 'And their nobles shall be of themselves and their governors shall proceed from the midst of them.' (Jeremiah 30:21)." Rav responded that "If he is of the living, it would be our holy Master,"[24] referring to Judah Ha-Nasi, the Patriarch under whom the Mishnah was compiled around 200 C.E. Both the Exilarchs and the Patriarchs traced their ancestry to the House of David, which not only conferred legitimacy on their power, but gave credence to such messianic theories. For these authorities, the coming of the Messiah was guaranteed by the continuity of Jewish government in exile. Instead of sitting disguised as a beggar at the gates of Rome waiting to redeem his powerless people (a theme in some of the rabbinical legends), the Messiah reflected in this theory would emerge out of the institutions of Jewish power in the Diaspora.

By coopting messianism and making it a part of rabbinic political theory, the rabbis neutralized its radical possibilities. The success of this maneuver is evident in the long history of Jewish messianism. None of these many movements emerged out of the rabbinic establishment; they were instead led by outsiders such as Abu Isa, Shlomo Molocho, and Sabbatai Zevi. To be sure, some of these messianic figures briefly captured the imaginations of rabbis as well as the common people. But it was ultimately figures such as Jacob Sasportas and Jacob Emden, to mention two of the leading rabbinical opponents of Sabbatianism, who represented the Jewish political elite. None of the antimessianists opposed the belief in the Messiah as such; what they fought was the usurpation of the rabbinic claim to be the true precursors of the messianic age. As we shall see in the next chapter, this nonmessianic position fostered a repeated urge for Jewish sovereignty in the Diaspora that had no messianic overtones. While the myth of the "three oaths" counseled passively waiting for God's intervention in history, these other rabbinical theories made political activity legitimate both to change this world and to bring the Messiah. By maintaining this political stance but divorcing it from apocalyptic messianism, the rabbinical establishment sought to navigate the political impulses of the Jews into less dangerous waters.

The Legitimation of Rabbinic Rule

By attributing royal characteristics to themselves, the rabbis and other communal leaders cemented their ties to both the monarchs of the past and the monarchy of the future. Even without the messianic dimension, the use of royal attributes conferred an important sense of legitimacy on Diaspora Jewish governments by making the authorities a kind of substitute royalty, kings in exile. The Babylonian Exilarch, as we have seen, claimed descent from King David; he also acted like royalty, with all the pomp of a court and armed guards and bureaucrats at his command. The royal image of the Exilarch was even known to Jews in very distant places. In the eleventh century, a French author wrote of the Exilarch: "Even today, when on account of our sins monarchy and power are lost, we the children of Exile are commanded to appoint unto us a prince of the progeny of David to serve as Exilarch."[25]

These claims occasionally excited challenges by the Babylonian rabbis, who had their own claims to royalty. The tractate Gittin preserves the story of a rabbi named Geniva from the third century:

> R. Huna and R. Hisda were sitting when Geniva happened by. One said to the other, "Let us rise before him, for he is a master of Torah." The other said, "Shall we arise before a man of division?" Meanwhile he came and said to them, "Peace be unto you, Kings, peace be unto you, Kings." They said to him, "How do you know that rabbis are called Kings?" He said to them, "As it is said, 'by me [wisdom], kings rule' (Proverbs 8:15)."[26]

Geniva seems to have considered the rabbis, as the guardians of wisdom, to be substitute kings, a claim that provoked the Exilarch, Mar Uqba, into turning him over to the government for execution. The "crime" of Geniva in the eyes of the Exilarch was nothing short of treason.

The image of the rabbis and other communal leaders as substitute royalty seems to have played a role in later years as well. The poets of the Golden Age of Spanish Jewry (eleventh and twelfth centuries) celebrated the Jewish courtiers with royal language drawn from the Bible and advanced extravagant claims of the royal pedigrees of Samuel Ha-Nagid and other such aristocrats. Drawing its inspiration from Arabic models, this poetry demonstrates a profound desire to imagine the Jewish aristocracy as powerful and glorious. A similar feeling prevailed among the German Jews. One text from Alsace claims that "although we have no king or princes . . . the leaders and heads of the age take the place of the king," while another, by Johanan Luria, refers to the head of the yeshiva (talmudic academy) as a king.[27]

In a similar way, Jewish institutions in the Diaspora might conjure up memories of the age of sovereignty. In an undoubtedly nostalgic passage, Nathan of Hanover, the seventeenth-century chronicler of the Chmielnitski pogroms, wrote of the Council of the Four Lands (see p. 77):

> The pillar of justice was in the Kingdom of Poland as it was in Jerusalem before the destruction of the Temple. . . . The leaders of the Four Lands were like the Sanhedrin. . . . They had the authority to judge all Israel in the Kingdom of Poland . . . and to punish each man as they saw fit.[28]

Just as the rabbis were substitute kings, so the institutions of the Diaspora became surrogates for full political sovereignty. This theory harkened back to the past but also guaranteed the messianic future.

The legitimacy of the political authority of kings and priests in the First and Second Temple periods was based on divine revelation. The rabbinical claims of royalty were attempts to appropriate this old political theory. But in addition to identifying themselves with the ancient kings, the rabbis also constructed an entirely new theory of legitimacy, a theory that sought to replace the claims of monarchy altogether. The Palestinian rabbis developed a "chain of tradition" that stretched back from them to Moses. According to this chain, the process of ordination of rabbis by their teachers had started with Moses. The earliest such chain of tradition appears in the *Pirkei Avot* ("The Sayings of the Fathers"). Here the rabbis trace the lineage of their authority back through the Prophets and elders who inherited the chain of ordination from Joshua and Moses. Astonishingly, this fictitious political history leaves out the kings and priests who, as we have seen, were the political leaders in the First and Second Temple states. Moses is called "our rabbi" (*Moshe rabbenu*), thus turning him into the source of rabbinic legitimacy. This chain of tradition may be compared to the invention by David's theologians of a royal covenant to give legitimacy to his monarchy.

In addition to a chain of authority, the rabbis also claimed that their legislation was not new; it was an "Oral

Law" that Moses had received together with the "Written Law" of the Bible. In a kind of circular argument, they held that possession of this Oral Law was proof of their divine appointment: the chain of tradition and the Oral Law mutually reinforced each other's antiquity and authenticity. These myths of the antiquity of the Oral Law and the rabbis' exclusive claim to knowledge of it became the basis for an irrefutable political theory of rabbinic power.

The lapse of ordination in the fourth or fifth century C.E. and the dispersion of the Jews made such legitimation of power more problematic, but the medieval rabbis put forth similar arguments for their power. Such texts as the *Seder Olam Zuta*, the *Seder Tannaim ve-Amoraim*, the Letter of Sherira Gaon, and the *Sefer ha-Qabbalah* of Ibn Daud were all attempts to establish chains of tradition that would link later authorities to earlier ones who were, in turn, linked to Moses.

Similar theories were applied to other communal leaders. The *nagid* (communal leader) of Spain and North Africa under Islam was a leader without any sacred ancestry, usually rising to his post from a position as a court financier or physician. In his *Sefer ha-Qabbalah*, Ibn Daud relates a story of four emissaries from Babylonia who were captured and eventually came to the West, where they spread the learning of the Babylonian academies. Ibn Daud included this story in his account of the rise of the *negidim* in order to establish the talmudic credibility of the new leaders and to justify the diffusion of power among many Jewish communities.[29]

In the fourteenth century, the process of ordination of rabbis by their teachers was renewed in France and Germany, but with no connection to the earlier talmudic ordination. A myth nevertheless evolved that this ordination was actually based on a genuine chain of tradition: "Every rabbi and expert has been ordained a rabbi by a preceding rabbi all the way back to Moses our Master.... A rod and strap had been given in his hand ... and no householder may in any way question the words of the rabbi."[30] This particular argument was evidently designed to give a weapon to the rabbinical leaders in their struggles with the lay leadership.

The theory of the chain of tradition thus bestowed legitimacy on exclusive rabbinical rule by claiming that the rabbis had inherited their mantle of authority from Moses, not from some new divine dispensation. We have seen that, according to the rabbis, prophecy had ceased with the destruction of the Temple. Having thus banished God from the stage of history, they arrogated to themselves exclusive power to interpret the revealed law. An extraordinary talmudic legend summarizes this theory of rabbinic autonomy. A majority of rabbis take a certain position and are opposed by Rabbi Eliezer, who calls upon a series of divine miracles to prove that God Himself is on his side. The majority rejects this procedure out of hand: "It [the Torah] is not in the heavens" and "We do not pay attention to a heavenly voice [*bat kol*]." The passage ends with God laughing and exclaiming, "My sons have vanquished me."[31] Here, then, is a legend that paradoxically invokes divine authority for the rejection of divine intervention in legal decisions. Once the Written and Oral Law were given, God was no longer necessary for the process of interpretation. This astonishing claim reminds us of the way David's theologians banished God from Israelite politics by making His covenant with David a hereditary one. Small wonder that, in the Middle Ages, Isaac ben Sheshet could write: "If Moses or Samuel were to arise now and make decrees or issue laws in any minor matter [for the country as a whole], they would be regarded as rebels against the State."[32]

The Political Theory of the Jewish Community

The legitimation of rabbinic and lay power was one of the cornerstones of the political theory of the medieval Diaspora. The rabbis and the lay aristocracy formed an alliance of learning and wealth to control the medieval communities. The political power of the Jewish community derived from the non-Jewish governments under which the Jews lived.

Nevertheless, Jewish political theory persistently tried to prove that communal power not only derived from the outside, but also had internal sources of legitimacy.[33] In the fourteenth century, for instance, the Spanish rabbi Isaac ben Sheshet wrote: "There is no doubt that even without the seal of His Royal Majesty ... this community would have had the right to enact ordinances in accordance with the Torah, and to ban and excommunicate and fine the transgressor independently."[34]

What sources did the medieval authorities draw on to give legitimacy to Jewish communal power? The Bible contains no laws that could serve as direct sources for the authority of the Diaspora communities. In part, the very notion of a community was foreign to the Bible, which assumed the existence of a Jewish state. But, surprisingly enough, even the Talmud devotes very little attention to such political theory, contenting itself with laconic statements such as "the townspeople are at liberty to fix weights and measures, prices and wages and to inflict penalties for the infringement of their rules."[35] Nowhere are the "townspeople" defined, nor do we learn what constitutes a town. Yet medieval political theory is based in part on this very passage and much of the discussion revolves around a precise interpretation of what it means.

In addition to this passage, medieval authorities grounded the power of the community in two other principles: the right of expropriation and the notion of the community as a court. According to the Talmud, a court has the right to expropriate property (*hefker bet din hefker*). This principle became the basis for communal taxation.[36] Many authorities argued that the community as a whole could be construed to be a metaphorical court. For instance, Elijah Mizrahi, the leading rabbi of Turkey at the end of the fifteenth and beginning of the sixteenth centuries, wrote: "The community as a whole is like a court in these [communal] matters. They are like judges who assemble in court and are not free to leave although there are differences of opinion between them."[37]

A similar opinion held that the source of the community's authority is an implied contract between all its members. Anyone who disputes the power of the community is like someone who gave his consent and then changed his mind. Interestingly, the medieval Jewish authorities typically preferred this type of contractual language, which was also common in non-Jewish political theory, rather than arguing that communal authority was grounded in the covenant at Sinai. By using the metaphor of the rabbinic court and the language of contract, Jewish political theory in the Middle Ages implicitly distanced itself from its biblical roots, perhaps because the medieval community differed so dramatically from the biblical state.

One of the major sources of dispute in the medieval literature was whether the community decides in a democratic fashion, by majority rule, and who constitutes the community. The minority view, represented by Elijah Mizrahi, favored democracy. The passage quoted above continues:

> pure and impure; innocent and guilty . . . must [all] be counted and must follow the majority decision, as it is written in our holy Torah: "By a majority you are to decide"; and he who opposes the majority is considered a sinner. It makes no difference whether the majority be wealthy or poor, wise men or ordinary people, because the entire community is considered a court in matters concerning its members.[38]

However, many authorities modified the biblical principle of democracy by reinterpreting the meaning of "majority" in favor of the ruling elite. In the tenth century, Hananiah Gaon interpreted the "townspeople" of the passage in Baba Batra to refer to the elders of the city: "The elders have the authority to pass enactments for the members of the city and to coerce them to abide by what they have enacted."[39] In the late thirteenth century, Rabbenu Asher wrote in his *responsa* (legal decisions): "If a community imposes an ordinance in fiscal matters, the 'economic majority' rules. . . . It is illogical that a simple majority composed of those who contribute only a small portion of the taxes should impose a ban on the wealthy."[40] In the sixteenth century, Samuel de Medina of Salonika wrote: "The Torah speaks of 'by a majority you are to decide' only when both parties are equal. . . . But when the two groups are not equal, one man may have the weight of a thousand. . . . Accepting the will of the majority when that majority is composed of ignorant men could lead to a perversion of justice."[41] In all these texts, wealth and learning are taken to be the criteria for who constitutes the "majority."

In the twelfth century, the French rabbi Jacob Tam mounted a different kind of attack on majority rule.[42] He argued that unanimous consent is required for any enactment that involves taxation. He considered the citizens of a town to be like a contractual partnership in which one partner, even if in the majority, does not have the right to coerce another. Rabbenu Tam allowed the majority to impose its will on the minority only in order to enforce laws that had been previously enacted unanimously. But this argument for unanimous consent was not necessarily an attempt to broaden communal democracy. Rabbenu Tam did not actually oppose coercion per se; he objected to coercion by lay leaders. He wanted to restrict coercive power to rabbinical courts. Rabbenu Tam thus rejected the theory of the community as a metaphorical court and limited the judicial power of expropriation to duly constituted rabbinic courts. By undercutting the symbolic interpretation of the community as a court, Rabbenu Tam hoped to restrict political power to the hands of the rabbis. Although his argument for unanimous consent suggests that he favored protection of the poor and weak against the will of the economic majority, Rabbenu Tam in fact was more interested in protecting the hegemony of the rabbis.

Rabbenu Tam's theory of the community must have emerged out of real conflicts between the rabbis and the householders (*ba'alei ha-bayit*) who made up the lay leadership in France and Germany. Although they united to rule the communities, relations between these two groups in the political elite were frequently strained. In the fourteenth century, Rabbi Menachem Meiri observed pragmatically that "[the lay leaders] may legislate without [the rabbi's] permission since they have the power to terminate his appointment."[43] Similar struggles between lay and rabbinical leaders can be found in Poland in the sixteenth and seventeenth centuries, to mention but one other example.[44] But whether power was to lie in the hands of lay leaders or rabbis, it would be kept out of the hands of the poor and ignorant.

It is particularly interesting that this debate uses democratic terminology and the pretense of protecting the weak against the coercion of the strong in order to shore up a manifestly elitist or aristocratic system of communal government. The modern apologetic contention that the medieval Jewish community was democratic is based on a generous amount of mythology, although its underlying theory did use the language of democracy.[45] But the Jewish community was no more egalitarian than were those medieval monarchs who based their legitimacy on the pretense of popular election.[46] Democratic ideals played a definite role in medieval political theory, but they meant something quite different from what they mean today: for instance, there was no notion of universal equal rights. The language of democracy served as the basis for its very opposite: hierarchical forms of government.

A wide variety of opinion can be found in the sources about the areas in which communal authorities might exercise their coercive power. The main controversies surrounded nonlegal issues, the secular needs of the community. For some, such as Rabbi Meir of Rothenberg in the thirteenth century, the power of the community was limited to matters of pressing communal need. But others, such as Rabbi Moses Isserles, who lived in Poland in the sixteenth century, argued that it was only limited by what might violate the laws of the Torah.[47]

If the rabbis imposed some limitations on the power of the community to address communal needs, they invested the

legal system which they themselves controlled with virtually
unlimited power. All authorities agreed that coercion was
legitimate on issues pertaining to the *halakhah* (Jewish law).
In the next chapter we will examine how this power was
actually applied. The theory of the *bet din* (rabbinic court),
like the theory of the power of the community as a whole, was
less rooted in biblical precedents than in ad hoc rabbinic
legislation. In Second Temple times, the Sanhedrin evidently
operated according to certain well-established legal principles, which were enshrined in talmudic law. However, the
destruction of the Temple meant that the Sanhedrin was
abolished, and the legal basis for various procedures, such as
capital punishment, became problematic. Following the sus-
pension of rabbinic ordination in the fourth or fifth century,
the problems of enforcing the law became even greater, since
there was no body competent to impose flagellation or any of
the punishments prescribed in the Bible.

The rabbis nevertheless constructed legal fictions that
allowed them to enforce the law. The principle of judicial
expropriation cited earlier allowed extraordinary power to
the courts beyond that stated in the law. For example, a rabbinic court might annul a marriage it disapproved of by ret-
roactively expropriating the symbolic money with which the
groom "purchased" the bride. Another principle was *hora'at
sha'ah*, which might be translated as "exigency jurisdiction."[48] The classic statement of this principle is in the Babylonian Talmud:

> It once happened that a man rode on horseback on the Sabbath
> in the days of the Greeks and he was brought before Bet Din and
> stoned; not because he deserved the penalty [according to law]
> but because the exigencies of the hour [*hora'at sha'ah*] de-
> manded it. Another incident occurred with a man who had in-
> tercourse with his wife under a fig tree and he was brought
> before Bet Din and flogged; not because he deserved such a
> penalty, but because the exigencies of the hour demanded it.[49]

In some of these cases, no actual law was violated, and the
rabbis imposed punishments simply for behavior of which

they did not approve.[50] These floggings, called "floggings for rebelliousness" (*malkot mardut*), were extralegal in the sense that the normal restrictions on procedures for conviction and severity of sentence were suspended. Since a court flogging to punish rebellious behavior or to meet the "exigencies of the hour" might exceed the stipulated thirty-nine lashes, it might actually commit capital punishment by such a sentence. In fact, although talmudic law made capital punishment almost impossible to carry out, even when the courts were still legally empowered to do so, some medieval authorities advocated the death penalty under these new legal categories.[51] By creating the category of emergency legislation, the medieval rabbis boldly expanded both the boundaries of talmudic law and the means of enforcing it. While the lapse of ordination and the demise of the Sanhedrin theoretically limited the power of the medieval authorities, these legal devices made possible a much more comprehensive and coercive legal system than one based solely on the ancient institutions.

The rabbis enforced the exclusive power of their courts by forbidding Jews recourse to gentile courts. While the right of judicial autonomy derived from gentile privileges, the rabbis nevertheless made it a principle of their legal theory. One talmudic passage states this principle, which was honored for most of the Middle Ages, as follows: "It has been taught: Rabbi Tarfon used to say: In any place where you find heathen law courts, even though their law is the same as the Israelite law, you must not resort to them."[52]

The theories of the legitimacy of rabbinic rule and of the powers of the community and the rabbinic courts gave genuine political authority to the leadership of the Jewish communities of the Diaspora. Although this power derived from extra-Jewish sources, the persistent attempt to give it an internal theoretical basis testifies to the positive consciousness the Jews had of their political status. Had they seen themselves as thoroughly powerless, it is hard to imagine them developing such a coherent political theory.

"The Law of the Kingdom Is the Law"

Although medieval Jewish theorists sought to ground Jewish self-government in an internal political philosophy, they also recognized that the power of the Diaspora communities actually derived from the host governments. They developed a contractual theory of the exile to explain what obligations Jews owed to the non-Jewish government and what powers were left to the Jewish community. The legal basis for the relationship between the Jewish community and the state lay in the doctrine of *dina de-malkhuta dina* ("the law of the kingdom is the law").[53] The principle was first enunciated by the third-century Babylonian rabbi Samuel, who was close to the Persian court and wished to ground the status of the Jewish self-government in law. Significantly, Samuel was the same authority who stated that only subjugation to non-Jewish rule distinguished his age from the days of the Messiah (see above, p. 40): Samuel's approach to both contemporary and eschatological questions seems to have been thoroughly political and pragmatic.

In the four places Samuel's principle appears in the Talmud, it affirms the authority of the gentile ruler to enforce certain laws pertaining strictly to financial matters (*mamona*), such as the collection of customs and taxes and the promulgation of land ordinances.[54] In all other areas, the Jewish community presumably retained full jurisdiction. This strict limitation on the powers of gentile rulers had its basis in the actual privileges the Jews enjoyed, and it persisted throughout the Middle Ages.

Samuel stated his principle without any reference to biblical precedent, and subsequent authorities were compelled to search for the sources of its legitimacy. According to some, non-Jews are commanded by the laws given to Noah to preserve society, and Jews who live in non-Jewish societies must obey their laws. Rabbi Hanina articulated this position in the

Talmud, adding a rationale that foreshadows the political theory of Thomas Hobbes: "Just like the bigger fish of the sea swallows its fellow, so with human beings, if it were not for fear of the kingdom, every bigger one would swallow his fellow. And that is why we learned: 'Rabbi Hanina the deputy priest says: Pray for the well-being of the kingdom for were it not for fear of it, one would swallow his fellow alive.' "[55] For others, the right of the king to enact laws is contractual and the Jews, like all other residents of the land, implicitly accept this contract. The Spanish Jews in Solomon ibn Verga's *Shevet Yehudah* say to the king: "You are our king and we are your people, and if we do not do your will, then you will exile us to another land."[56] For others still, the king's ownership of the land gives him legislative rights that the Jews must accept if they wish to reside in his kingdom. Solomon ben Adret wrote: "Precisely in the case of gentile kings did they say 'the law of the kingdom is the law' . . . because the king can say to them: 'If you will not obey my commands, I will exile you' for the land belongs to him."[57]

For most authorities, the scope of *dina de-malkhuta dina* with respect to the king's financial powers was construed to be quite broad, as long as royal ordinances did not directly infringe on Jewish law and did not discriminate specifically against the Jews. Yet, in some instances, even discrimination against the Jews as a group was considered legally valid as long as it fell equally on all Jews.[58] On the other hand, the rabbis also imposed important restrictions on the principle that theoretically limited royal prerogatives. They distinguished between the legitimate "law of the kingdom," typically defined as ancient law, and the newer, more arbitrary "law of the king."[59] In denying recognition to new legislation, the rabbis adopted the general medieval prejudice in favor of old custom law. They also distinguished between legitimate taxes and *gezelah de-malkhuta* ("robbery by the kingdom").[60] The king did not have the right to interfere in the orderly administration of internal Jewish law but only in matters between Jews and non-Jews. For example, the king was not thought to have the right to appoint officers within the Jewish community if the community opposed the nominees.

These distinctions were all very important, for they gave a legal basis to the right of resistance to the king, a right also enshrined in general medieval law. Even where the Jews did not possess the actual power to resist unjust decrees, their theory gave them an internal sense of what was legitimate for the king to demand of them and what was illegitimate. The right of resistance, even if only theoretical, meant that the Jews saw themselves as free people in a contractual relationship with the state rather than as impotent subjects of an arbitrary monarch.

The assumption behind *dina de-malkhuta dina* was that, in exchange for recognition of the rights of the monarch, the Jews would receive internal autonomy. The political theory of the "law of the kingdom" was therefore inextricably linked with the theory of Jewish self-government outlined above. The principle claimed that Jewish law was sovereign and that the contract with the state implied that each side gave up a part of its sovereignty: the Jews gave the king certain rights of taxation and the king gave the Jews the right to govern themselves in all other matters. Later on, in the nineteenth century, those desiring to disband Jewish communal self-government often argued on the basis of *dina de-malkhuta dina* that Jewish law itself recognized non-Jewish authority. But this argument ignored the fundamental meaning of the principle: by recognizing the authority of the state in a few limited areas, the Jews would receive full autonomy in return. And if the state exceeded its authority, the Jews, in terms of their own political theory, would have the right to resist and to disobey the state in whatever way they could. Far from a principle admitting the political subservience of the Jews, *dina de-malkhuta dina* was a pithy summation of the whole political theory of Diaspora: that the Jewish communities preserved the sovereignty of the ancient Jewish state in exile.

The persistence of this tradition of political thought demonstrates that the long Diaspora was not a political vacuum, for it decisively linked the sovereignty of antiquity with the secular politics of modernity. In their theories of political messianism, communal power, and contract with the gentile rulers, the rabbis articulated an accommodation with the larger world in which the Jews might retain some elements of political life. The Jewish institutions of the Diaspora, conceived as substitutes for monarchy and statehood, might form the real basis for renewed sovereignty. The conservative impulse of medieval Jewish leaders was not a product of passivity toward politics or of an acceptance of suffering but, on the contrary, an expression of the political power they wielded and wished to continue to wield even after the arrival of the King Messiah. The political thought of the Middle Ages represents an attempt to reconcile the limitations on Jewish politics imposed by the condition of exile with the relative power Jews actually enjoyed in their Diaspora communities.

III

Corporate Power in the Middle Ages

THE biblical Book of Esther foreshadows all of the ingredients of Jewish power in exile. Here are the Jewish aristocrats, close to the center of power in the Persian court, whose political acumen saves their people from destruction. But the Jewish people in Esther are not merely passive victims, miraculously rescued by the court Jews. Instead, they take up arms at the end of the book and slay their opponents. Even if it does not represent an actual historical event, the Book of Esther furnished the Jews of the Greco-Roman Diaspora and, later, the Jews of the Middle Ages with a powerful myth of political action in exile.[1]

The Book of Esther portrays in the form of a historical romance the political theory of the Diaspora that we traced in the last chapter. The implication of this theory is that the Jews had a sense of their own power, even as they were acutely conscious of their condition of exile. This dual self-image corresponds closely to the ambiguous reality of the Jews' status in the Middle Ages, both in their relationship to the societies in which they lived and in their internal power. Jewish political theory was not produced in a vacuum, but

58

rather emerged out of a complex political situation in which the partial sovereignty of antiquity continued throughout the Middle Ages in the form of communal autonomy. Rather than a pariah people on the outermost margins of society, the Jews of the Middle Ages, in both the Christian and Muslim worlds, inhabited an uneasy region close to the centers of power, at times enjoying considerable influence and security and at others experiencing terror and persecution. Throughout the Middle Ages, the Jews played political roles, even under the constraints of their inferior and alien status.

How to define the Jewish Middle Ages is a thorny question. The very term "Middle Ages" is really only Christian, since Christianity believes in an age between the two appearances of the Messiah. For Jews and Muslims, the term is misplaced. I shall define the Jewish Middle Ages as that period after the Jews had ceased to have a political center in the Land of Israel but still enjoyed political autonomy and a protected or privileged status in the lands of their dispersion. Many of these characteristics apply as well to the Greco-Roman Diaspora, so the beginning of the Middle Ages remains fuzzy. This definition also excludes other features of the Jewish Middle Ages and may well appear to be arbitrary and even circular: it assumes what still remains to be proven, namely, that the Jews possessed genuine political autonomy in the Diaspora. But since periodization is a creation of historians rather than history, we will have to make do with such a tentative and problematic definition. Given such characteristics, the length of the Jewish Middle Ages varied markedly from one community to another: it ended in Spain with the rise of a unified state and the expulsion of the Jews in 1492; in Western and Central Europe with the rise of the absolutist state in the sixteenth and seventeenth centuries (already foreshadowed in the expulsions from England and France in the thirteenth and the fourteenth centuries); in Eastern Europe with the breakup of the medieval Polish state in the eighteenth century; and in the Middle East with the decline of the Ottoman Empire under the im-

pact of European imperialism in the eighteenth and nineteenth centuries.

The Political Status of the Medieval Jews

To understand Jewish political life in the Middle Ages,
we need a precise definition of the difference between "privileges" and "rights." Since the American and French revolutions, rights have been held to be universal and equal, but in
the Middle Ages there was no such concept of human rights.
Instead, groups or even individuals were beneficiaries of distinct privileges, which might raise them above other groups
but also could be arbitrarily withdrawn. From a modern
point of view, the status of the Jews in this system looks very
much like second-class citizenship. But, as Bernard Lewis has
written about the Jews under Islam:

> Second-class citizenship, though second-class, is a kind of citi-
> zenship. It involves some rights, though not all, and is surely
> better than no rights at all. It is certainly preferable to the kind
> of situation that prevails in many states at the present time,
> where the minorities, and for that matter even the majority,
> enjoy no real civil or human rights in spite of all the resplendent
> principles enshrined in the constitutions, but utterly without
> effect.[2]

Religious mentalities dominated both the Christian and
Muslim Middle Ages, and theology strongly influenced the
political status of the Jews, as members of a different religion.
Yet, it was the very ambiguity with which Christian and
Muslim theology viewed Judaism that created Jewish vulnerabilities and opened opportunities for Jewish power.[3]
Both Christianity and Islam dictated that Jews be maintained in a second-class position divorced from political
power. Since Christianity claimed to have superseded Judaism, the Jews had to be kept in a degraded condition. As a
"fossil people," a relic of God's chosenness which had now
passed to the "Israel of the spirit," the Jews could not possess
any political or spiritual power. Powerlessness was proof of

their theological rejection. For Islam, as for Christianity, failure to accept the prophet's message had turned the Jews into historical anachronisms who deserved both symbolic and actual degradation. Islam required that Jews be deprived of both the instruments and symbols of worldly power. They were not allowed into government service and were humiliated in symbolic ways, such as being forbidden to ride horses. The main practical impact of the law of the *dhimma* (the Islamic law governing non-Muslim subjects of Muslim states) was financial, for the *dhimmis* were required to pay a special poll, or head, tax.

Yet the theologies of Christianity and Islam dictated that the Jews be protected. Christianity viewed the Jews as living proof of the veracity of the Old Testament prophecies of the Messiah, and their conversion to Christianity was regarded as a necessary prerequisite for the Second Coming. The Jews had to be preserved for these purposes and therefore were entitled, from a theological standpoint, to protection. Islam treated Judaism and Christianity as "religions of the Book." As such, both minorities received protection and were theoretically not forced to convert. Although the poll tax constituted a considerable burden, the law of the *dhimma* otherwise interfered very little in the daily lives of Jews and other subject non-Muslims. The tension between toleration and degradation in Islam and Christianity produced a reality less monolithically hostile for Jews than theological images would suggest. The Jews often exploited their protected status to become a vital part of the societies in which they lived, possessing considerable political and economic power beyond what their theoretical status allowed them. In medieval Christian Europe, the existence of an independent secular law next to Church law made it possible for the Jews to evade the strictures of theological inferiority. The Jews were successful in exploiting the fragmentation of power in Christian Europe by playing off secular against religious authorities. In Islam, where church and state were unified, fewer such legal and political possibilities existed, although persistent failures to enforce the law of the *dhimma* opened avenues to power that would have otherwise remained closed.

If toleration had a theological rationale, it was also motivated by practical concerns. Throughout the Middle Ages, the Jews proved to be remarkably adept at forming strategic alliances with both secular and religious powers. As an urban, merchant class, they were particularly important in the development of new cities, a role that they played in eleventh-century France and Germany in alliance with the monarchs and in sixteenth-century Poland in alliance with the nobility. As a group outside of the existing social hierarchy, they could serve the needs of new and rising forces in society. The ability to find allies among new elites can be traced from late antiquity and throughout the Middle Ages. In Babylonia, as early as the first and second centuries c.e., the Jews allied themselves with the new political power of the Arsacid Parthians. They found allies in the Muslims of ninth- and tenth-century Iraq, the French and German kings from the Carolingian period to the eleventh century, the Christian forces of the Spanish *reconquista*, and, finally, the Polish nobility of the fifteenth and sixteenth centuries. In the Rhineland in the tenth and eleventh centuries and Poland in the fifteenth and sixteenth centuries, the Jews were invited in by the rulers. In the Rhineland, they received privileges as individuals or as families, but these privileges gradually developed into corporate privileges as the European Middle Ages became increasingly feudal. These privileges led to a variety of rights, including the right to internal self-government and the right of royal protection.

The history of the Jews in the Middle Ages is the history of such alliances with the ruling powers. The belief in an alliance between rulers and the Jews persisted as a myth long after it had ceased to mean what it did in the Middle Ages (see chapter 4).

The legal status of the Jews in places such as Spain, France, Germany, and Poland was considerably better than that of enserfed peasants and in many cases approached that of the nobility and the burgher class.[4] In medieval Christian Europe, the Jews were considered to be free people. One medieval writer, Martin Didaci d'Aux, observed of Christian Spain:

A Saracen or a Jew cannot oblige himself by contract or loan to become anybody's slave. . . . Not even the king can sell them except in retribution for a crime. Neither do they really deserve to be called captives or serfs in the sense that they may be sold, because according to law they have the liberty of moving about.[5]

The Sachsenspiegel, the German law code of the thirteenth century, similarly regarded the Jews as free. Freedom of movement, which was necessary for those engaged in commerce, distinguished the Jews from those bound to the land and made the status of the Jews closer to that of knights, who had the legal right to live wherever they wished.

The Jews also saw themselves as free. According to Meir of Rothenburg, who wrote in the second half of the thirteenth century, when Jewish status was already in decline:

Jews are not subjugated to their overlords as the Gentiles are, in the sense that they have to pay taxes to a particular overlord even when they do not live in his domain. The status of the Jew in this land is that of a free landowner who lost his land but did not lose his personal liberty.[6]

Since the Jews were typically urban dwellers, they fought for the same rights as those enjoyed by burghers. They took full part in the life of their city, sometimes occupying municipal offices and contributing to the town's armed defense. In many medieval towns in Germany, France, Spain, and Italy, they were able to obtain full and equal citizenship.[7] A fifteenth-century Italian jurist formulated the municipal status of the Jews in general terms: "Jews are considered to be of the same people and of the [political] body of the same city, although they may not be considered members of the same spiritual body."[8] As equal citizens, the Jews had the same rights as all other citizens to acquire property and sell it, live where they wished, and, in some cases, even hold municipal office. While some special restrictions and special taxations might still apply to them, the Jews of the High Middle Ages were not the ghettoized, disenfranchised minority of later times.

But even if Jews did possess certain privileges in medieval society, is privilege the same as power? The very essence of a privilege is that it depends on someone who grants it. If power means the ability to act autonomously, the Jews surely could not be called powerful. They did not wield power in the modern sense of sovereign state power, but in the Middle Ages such a notion of power hardly existed. In an era of political fragmentation and insecurity, virtually no group in society might be considered autonomously powerful. Medieval society was hierarchical and was built on complex relationships of loyalties and privileges. Even kings were not fully autonomous in their power over their territories, for they had to contend with princes and bishops who might have conflicting loyalties to other authorities. Monarchs, nobles, and clergy competed with each other, and their spheres of influence often overlapped in bewildering patterns. States as such were exceptionally weak, even in periods of relative stability such as the Carolingian era. Consequently, political sovereignty, in the sense of political power located exclusively in the hands of a central state, did not exist in the Middle Ages. It was only in the thirteenth and fourteenth centuries at the earliest that monarchs began to consolidate their power and lay the basis for later absolutism. Not until several centuries later was there anything one could speak of as a modern state.

In such a heterogeneous and uncertain world, power meant not autonomy or sovereignty but the protection of a powerful master. Medieval law saw the free person as "a protected individual. . . . Originally anyone who was not unprotected or rightless was called free. . . . The very idea of freedom necessarily presupposed a master who protects and safeguards."[9] Power in the Middle Ages involved not only the power possessed by a group in its own right but also what allies it could call upon to protect it. For the Jews, to win privileges and protection was a sign of power. If they were dependent on the good graces of secular and religious rulers for their very existence, this was very much the norm in the Middle Ages. For instance, in 1103, following the Crusader pogroms of 1096, the Jews were granted royal protection through the Land Peace (*Landfrieden*) of the German king. This Land Peace included a variety of groups in need of protection, such as priests, monks, widows, orphans, virgins, and merchants. Some of these clearly required special royal protection, since they either had no other protectors or could not directly protect themselves. But the Jews, like the merchants, did not entirely lack means of self-defense. The inclusion of the Jews in the Land Peace testifies to the failure of earlier promises of protection, but it also accorded to them the protection of the king. Such royal protection was particularly necessary for those who traveled between towns and needed better protection than a local lord could provide.

The very fact that the Jews could call upon or solicit royal protection attests to their relative power in the medieval hierarchy. In Aragon in 1392, the king regarded those who persecuted the Jews as rebels against the state. He wrote to his brother, who had witnessed riots in Valencia and had not intervened, that he should have "put to the sword or hanged 300 or 400 men during these riots against the Jews."[10] In sixteenth-century Poland, kings obliged city councils and burghers to defend Jews when they needed help and threatened the death penalty against attackers or those who accused the Jews of "profanation of the wafer," that is, desecrating sacred objects from the mass.

Despite the real disabilities that governments often imposed on them, the Jews could generally count on protection from secular and religious authorities. The most significant massacres and persecutions of the medieval period were the work of rebels or antiestablishment mass movements, frequently of a religious nature. The Almohads of the twelfth century were Muslim schismatics; the Crusaders of 1096 represented forces that established authorities viewed with considerable suspicion (in fact, the Second Crusade of 1146, which was under much tighter papal and royal control, indulged in fewer anti-Jewish excesses than the First); the Black Plague incited popular uprisings and caused the breakdown of government control; and, finally, the Ukrainian massacres of the mid-seventeenth century, under the Cossack hetman Bogdan Chmielnitski, were the consequence of a rebellion against the Polish authorities, whom the Jewish chroniclers of the time portray as frequently trying to help save the Jews. Thus, the Jews, who were often close to the centers of power, had much more to fear from popular uprisings than they did from established authority.

In light of the generally protected status the Jews enjoyed in the medieval political order, terms that might seem to imply humiliation and discrimination take on a different meaning. A key example is the definition of the Jews as "serfs of the royal chamber" (*servi camerae*).[11] The term would seem to contradict their free status in medieval privileges and law codes. The notion of the Jews as enslaved has a long theological background, going back to the Church fathers of late antiquity, but this formulation had little effect on actual law. The term *servi camerae* begins to appear in reference to the Jews as early as Louis the Pious of France (ninth century), but it seems to have found its clearest expression in the privilege that Frederick II of the Holy Roman Empire gave to the Jews in 1236, in which he calls them *servi camerae nostrae* ("the serfs of our chamber"). Although the concept of serfs of the chamber came to have a humiliating meaning and could subject the Jews to threats of financial extortion from the king, its main significance was that the Jews paid taxes directly to the royal coffers. They were therefore protected against taxation by local lords, which was a considerable privilege. The status of the Jews deteriorated when these local lords succeeded in subjecting them to taxation. Thus, *servitus camerae* was by no means equivalent to peasant serfdom and it did confer upon the Jews the benefits of royal protection. Even in the period when the Jews were formally serfs of the king, they continued to act and to be treated as free people, and, especially in the medieval German cities, to enjoy most of the rights of burghers.

Similarly, the distinctive Jewish garb or markings in many medieval societies, although they could be humiliating, could often mean something quite different as well. In the cacophony of corporations, guilds, ethnic groups, and religious orders that made up medieval society, the Jews were but one distinctive group among many, rather than the only foreign element in a homogeneous body politic. Each of the many classes and corporations distinguished itself publicly by its dress. At least some of the Jewish dress of the Middle Ages, such as the Jewish hat, originated out of choice rather than compulsion. By the later Middle Ages, Jews were required to wear certain identifying marks as signs of humiliation, but the principle of outwardly symbolizing group differences was generally accepted in the medieval world and was not peculiarly anti-Jewish in origin. Medieval society thought that Jewish costumes had not changed since ancient times and were a sign of the antiquity of the Jews. One saint even went so far as to claim that he beheld Jesus clad *more Judaico vestitus* ("dressed according to the Jewish fashion"), thus indicating that such clothing was not necessarily a sign of degradation.[12]

The yellow patch, which marked the first stage in the Jews' journey to extermination during World War II, originated in the Islamic world. It was not originally intended as an instrument for segregating and humiliating the Jews—as it was in Nazi-occupied Europe—but to proclaim publicly that its wearers enjoyed official protection. A fourteenth-century Egyptian text compares it to the protective power of an amulet: "It is to be fastened upon their heads to preserve them just as amulets are fastened. . . . [The] yellow badge is required so their red blood will not be spilled; that they are safe as long as it is firmly attached."[13]

There were, of course, significant exceptions to the protection the Jews generally enjoyed from their powerful allies, most notably the expulsions from England, France, and Spain from the end of the thirteenth to the fifteenth centuries. These expulsions represent the beginning of the end of the medieval system of privileges and protection. The Spanish case is particularly instructive. The Jews were expelled from Spain in 1492, at precisely the time that Spain underwent an enormous political transformation. Under Ferdinand and Isabella, Aragon and Castile were united and Granada was reconquered from the Muslims. The *reconquista*, some four centuries long, was completed and the monarchs set out to create what was perhaps the first absolutist Christian state. As opposed to the rest of Christian Europe, church and state were powerfully united.

In this religious and nationalist atmosphere, the Jews—and especially the *conversos* (those Jews who had converted either voluntarily or by force to Christianity)—were perceived as a threat to the new unity. The Inquisition directed much of its attention toward these converts, whom it accused of secretly spreading Jewish beliefs among Christians. (Jews were immune from direct persecution by the Inquisition, whose jurisdiction included only Christian heretics.) The distinction between "new" and "old" Christians introduced at this time violated Church law, which regarded anyone who accepted baptism as a full-fledged Christian. This doctrine of the "purity of the blood" with all its racial overtones violated the Catholic principle of reluctant toleration of the Jews and pointed ahead to anti-Semitism of a more modern sort. The persecution of the *conversos* and the expulsion of the Jews was therefore less a product of the Middle Ages than it was an ominous foreshadowing of a new world in the making. We shall return to this point in the discussion on absolutism (see chapter 4), the period during which the state became far less hospitable to the Jews. But up to the end of the thirteenth century in Western Europe and much later in Eastern Europe, the system of privileges and protection guaranteed the Jews a generally favorable alliance with the ruling forces.

The complicated mix of secular and religious law in Christian Europe made it possible for the Jews to acquire a political status much more favorable than one might assume by reading theological tracts or by looking at Jewish history solely through the prism of medieval massacres. At the same time, however, the uncertain position of the Jews could lead to such massacres or to catastrophic expulsions. In the Muslim world, where the law of the *dhimma* afforded much more explicit and unchallenged protection and where the hatred of Jews endemic to Christianity did not exist, massacres and expulsions were less common. On the other hand, because Islamic law prescribed a degraded status for the Jewish community, the kind of quasi equality occasionally achieved by the Jews of Christian Europe was unknown in the Middle East. We may generalize that individual Jews achieved greater political power under Islam, while the Jewish community as a whole enjoyed, if sporadically, a better status under Christianity. Under Christianity, the political history of the Jews was subject to greater extremes than under Islam, but in both societies the Jews found ways of engaging in political life even where theology formally dictated that they remain powerless and apolitical.

Jewish Political Activity in the Middle Ages

The Jews persistently sought to exploit their political status to further their collective self-interest. Jewish political activity in the Middle Ages took two forms: external and internal. The first refers to the relations between Jews and their host societies and the second to the internal politics of the autonomous Jewish communities.

Throughout the Middle Ages, the Jews enjoyed considerable influence in high governing circles in many of the lands in which they lived. The Exilarch in Babylonia had access to the Babylonian court and was, in fact, appointed by the Arsacid and Sassanian governments.[14] In the Islamic world, although Muslim law forbade consulting non-Muslim doctors, many rulers had Jewish court physicians, a position of considerable political influence. The first Ra'is al-Yahud ("Head of the Jews") in Egypt was a court physician, as were a number of his successors, including Moses Maimonides.[15] Although Jews were formally barred from government service, their financial and commercial expertise made them indispensable to areas of government connected with finance. In the Ottoman Empire, they controlled the collection of customs, the mint, and the farming of taxes. An example of a politically influential Jew in Turkey of the sixteenth century was Joseph Nasi, who used his position to foster Jewish settlement in Tiberias. In Muslim and Christian Spain, Jewish communal leaders such as Hisdai ibn Shaprut, Samuel Ha-Nagid, and Isaac Abravanel were also important government officials. In fact, it is striking how Jews continued to hold important positions in Spain up to the time of the expulsion. The phenomenon of Jews in politics is particularly remarkable under Islam, which so strictly excluded *dhimmis* from political power, and is a striking example of how law and reality do not always correspond.

Such extraordinary political power seems to have been more common in the Islamic world and in Christian Spain than in northern Europe. But if the Jews of England, France, Germany, and Poland were not to be found to the same degree in the circles of gentile power before the emergence of the court Jews in the seventeenth century, neither were they entirely divorced from political life in those lands. For instance, Jews must have held governmental positions in medieval towns in Germany, since Frederick II prohibited the practice in the privilege that he gave to Vienna in 1237.[16]

The penetration of Jews into the centers of power often involved them in political machinations with little connection to the Jewish community per se. According to Abraham ibn Daud's *Sefer ha-Qabbalah*, the Jews took sides in the struggle for succession of the Berber king of Granada in 1026–27.[17] Those supporting the losing side were forced to flee to Seville. The involvement of Jews in royal politics probably prompted the recurring fantastic tales concerning gentile rulers such as the Sassanian Yazdagird I (early fifth century) and the Polish Kasimir I (early fourteenth century), who reputedly had Jewish wives or mistresses in the manner of Queen Esther.[18]

Many of the Jews who were influential in medieval politics were at the same time the most important leaders of their communities. This dual power characterized the Resh Galuta in Babylonia, the Ra'is al-Yahud in Egypt, and the *negidim* of Spain. It was not, however, a medieval invention, for it had ancient precedents in Ezra and Nehemiah, who were at once leaders of the Jewish community and officials in the Persian court in the fifth century B.C.E. and used their influence to establish the Second Temple state. While one can point to similar cases of Jewish access to the inner corridors of power in early modern and modern times—such as the court Jews in absolutist Germany, Gerson Bleichroder in Bismarck's Prussia, or Henry Kissinger in America—there are none in which the figure in question was first and foremost a Jewish leader. Thus, one of the dominant characteristics of Jewish political activity in the Middle Ages was the congruence between communal leadership and service in non-Jewish governments.

In addition to their interest in court politics, these Jews participated in political life in defense of Jewish interests. Many communities had an official *shtadlan* or intercessor who acted as the recognized Jewish ambassador to the gentile government. The power of the *shtadlan* lay in the Jews' position in the hierarchy of power. In Poland, for example, he was paid a substantial salary and was expected to be able to speak fluent Polish and represent the Jews in law courts and before the king.

The Council of the Four Lands, which was the supracommunal governing body of the Polish Jews, maintained a virtual "Jewish lobby" at the Polish parliament. In the eyes of enemies of the Jews, the power of this lobby was such that, according to a statement from 1669, "in practice Jews do not let any law materialize which is unfavorable to them."[19] Although this is certainly an exaggeration of the Jews' actual power, it indicates the vigorousness of Jewish political activity.

Jewish power in the Middle Ages did not lie solely in political activity or in economic status but sometimes in physical strength as well. The prevalent image of the medieval Jew is that of a martyr dying without resistance for his faith. This is an erroneous view of medieval martyrdom. The Jews were not merely passive objects, at times protected by powerful rulers and at others slaughtered by the mob. In widely scattered times and places, they took up arms in self-defense and to pursue political objectives. The earliest examples are the Jewish military uprisings throughout the Roman Diaspora in 115–17 C.E. These revolts were no less severe than the two great revolts in Palestine of 66–70 and 132–35 and, in Egypt, succeeded for a time in overwhelming substantial Roman forces. Another example from late antiquity is the revolt of Mar Zutra, the Babylonian Exilarch who created an autonomous Jewish state for some seven years until he was defeated by the Persians in 520 C.E. The account that has been preserved of this revolt, whose historicity may be doubted, suggests that the Babylonian Jews organized an effective military force.[20] In the eighth century, a messianic figure named Abu Isa led an armed rebellion in Iraq; he was defeated and killed in battle.[21]

In Western and Central Europe, the *Waffenrecht*, or arms law, allowed Jews to carry weapons; even when the law was revoked in the thirteenth century, violation carried no penalties as it did for the peasants. The right of the Jews to bear arms strengthens the conclusion that their status was in general higher than that of the peasants. They were allowed to issue duel challenges and the arms they carried were not merely defensive. A *responsum* of Meir of Rothenburg from the thirteenth century concerns a Jew who hires another Jew to teach him how to use a sword and then changes his mind. Meir rules that the erstwhile student must pay his tutor, since learning swordplay is a necessary skill which may often save a person's life.[22] In an illustrated manuscript of the Sachsen-spiegel, a Jew is shown armed on horseback.

There are several rabbinic texts, such as the *Or Zarua* of Isaac ben Moses of Vienna and the *responsa* of Meir of Rothen-burg, as well as a communal regulation from thirteenth-century Spain, that discuss whether Jews should be allowed to carry arms on the Sabbath, implying that they carried them the rest of the week.[23] Eleazar of Worms, describing the siege of Worms in 1201, says: "It happened once that great armies besieged Worms; then we allowed all Jews to carry arms on the Sabbath."[24]

Intriguing additional evidence of Jews carrying arms can be found in illuminated medieval *Haggadot* (Passover ritual books) from a wide variety of European countries. The wicked son (*rasha*), who rejects the importance of the Passover holi-day, is typically portrayed as a man armed with a sword or a pike and often dressed in armor. Clearly, the attitude toward Jews bearing arms reflected in these pictures was not a posi-tive one. The Prague Haggadah of 1526 bears a caption over a picture of the armed *rasha* that reads: "woe to the wicked son and woe to his neighbor." Yet, this evidence confirms that Jews did indeed carry arms, even if those who did so were regarded as somewhat brutal and uneducated; the armed Jew might be religiously indifferent, but he was still a Jew. One even wonders whether the Prague Haggadah may in fact be-tray a certain hidden admiration for the armed Jew who could intimidate his enemies.

During the First Crusade, the Jews "armed themselves in the inner court of the bishop [of Mainz] and they all advanced toward the gate to fight against the errant ones [i.e., the Cru-saders] and the burghers." Similar incidents occurred else-where, in which as many as five hundred Jews took up arms.[25] During the Second Crusade of 1146, the Jews bought the right to the fortress of Walkenburg and "the remaining Jews who were in the lands of the king gathered together and defended their lives."[26] The right of the Jews to the local fortress proves that they were not helpless victims protected by the rulers, but were expected to participate in their own defense. Unlike monks who did not carry arms or women who could not, the Jews were frequently an armed minority in the Rhineland. It is, however, a sign of the deterioration of the Jewish position in France and Germany that they began to lose their right to bear arms throughout the thirteenth century. By the fourteenth, the not uncommon portrayal of armed Jews in earlier manuscripts had disappeared.

To be sure, in most cases during the Crusades, if their protectors failed them, the Jews were not sufficiently powerful to overcome the Crusaders. Instead, they frequently turned their weapons on themselves and committed suicide. Hitherto, *kiddush ha-shem*, or allowing oneself to be killed rather than transgress God's law, had been an act of passive resistance. By turning their weapons on themselves, in the manner Josephus describes of the defenders of Masada at the end of the Great Revolt, the Jews turned martyrdom from a passive to an active deed. Despite the prohibition on suicide, this new definition of *kiddush ha-shem* struck deep roots in the popular consciousness, and the practice recurred in later persecutions.[27]

In Poland, similar kinds of evidence can be found in a later period, the sixteenth to the eighteenth centuries. In the eastern provinces, such as the Ukrainian borderland, synagogues were fortified and in some places it was required "that every householder shall have as many guns as the number of men and that he shall keep cartridges and three pounds of gunpowder for each gun."[28] During the Chmielnitski uprising, the Jews frequently joined with the Poles in defending their towns against the Ukrainians. As during the earlier Crusader pogroms, the chronicles of the 1648 massacres make clear that Jewish martyrdom was not always the result of physical passivity.[29]

There is also evidence that Jewish communities resorted to force to defend themselves against common criminals. In the Islamic world, Jews were not allowed to carry arms, so the kind of armed activity we find in Europe was not possible.

However, despite the subservience that Jews had to display toward Muslims, neither were they entirely passive. In thirteenth-century Baghdad, for example, the son of the vizier killed a Jew and his wife and made off with their money. The text relates that "the neighbors caught up with him and seized him. They brought him to the Bab al-Nubi [one of the city gates] where he was executed by being cut in half."[30] Surely these Jews must have had a great deal of self-confidence to deal this way with the son of the vizier. Polish Jews seem to have followed a similar policy of "blood vengeance" in the seventeenth century. If a man was murdered on the road, his relatives were obligated to bring the murderer to court. If they were not able to do this themselves, the community would assist in catching the criminal "in order that it should become known that Jewish blood is not free for all."[31] In the eighteenth century, the Polish memoirist Ber of Bolechow related an incident in which a Jewish householder kills one robber and wounds two more with firearms that he has in his possession.[32] In eighteenth-century Germany, the carrying of arms by Jews is reflected in Gotthold Ephraim Lessing's play *The Jews*.

In addition to using arms in self-defense, Jews also participated in various places in the armies of their country. One document suggests that they paid for the privileges they received from the Carolingian kings in France with active service in the king's army as well as with money:

> Our forefathers, the people of Israel, came into the land of the king, who promised to protect our persons, our wealth, and our property. And we and our forefathers have survived as a result of this promise for many years since the time of the death of King Charles [Charlemagne] who conquered many lands, as did those who came after him, with the help of the people of Israel who were with them with their bodies and their wealth, since they themselves entered into the fray of warfare and risked death for the salvation of the kings and princes who were with them.[33]

Jews in the Middle East also took up arms to assist the Muslim armies that overran areas of the Byzantine Empire. In the medieval cities of Europe, Jews were expected to participate in civic defense together with the non-Jewish burghers. Finally, as late as 1794, Jews formed a Jewish regiment to assist the Poles in an uprising against the Russians in Warsaw. These were most likely unassimilated Jews, since the process of assimilation had scarcely begun in Poland.

In antiquity, the Jews of Palestine were known for their skill in the production of arms. There is some evidence that this skill was not entirely lost in the Middle Ages. For instance, the Spanish Jews who came to Turkey after they were expelled in 1492 were reported to have brought with them modern military technology. One traveler who visited Turkey in 1551 wrote: "[The Jews], not long since banished and driven from Spain and Portugal . . . , have taught the Turk several inventions, artifices, and machines of war, such as how to make artillery, arquebuses, gunpowder, cannonballs, and other weapons."[34]

Perhaps the best-known Jewish military figure of the Middle Ages was the poet and communal leader, Samuel Ha-Nagid, who led the armies of Granada in the early eleventh century. He left an array of military poems describing his exploits in battle. Reflecting a clear understanding of the use of force in politics, this Jewish Machiavelli wrote: "Take risks when you aim for power and defeat the foe with the sword."[35] As perhaps the only Jewish general of medieval times, Samuel was obviously exceptional, but his grasp of the relationship between force and politics was shared by most Jews of the Middle Ages.

The fact that Jews were permitted to carry arms during part of the Middle Ages and that they used them in their own defense should be kept in proper perspective. Even if they were not passive, they were still extremely vulnerable when bereft of powerful allies. In both the Crusades and the Ukrainian uprisings, support by the governing authorities was less than totally reliable; when support was withdrawn, Jewish self-defense was rarely effective. The Jews did not possess sufficient force to rely on themselves alone; they had to base their power on political intercession and alliances as well. Moreover, the Jewish value to gentile rulers did not lie in their military prowess. Despite these qualifications, however, the prevailing picture of the Jews as militarily impotent is just as unhistorical as the notion that they were politically impotent. The great Jewish military prowess of antiquity—demonstrated in the Great Revolt, the rebellions in the Diaspora in 115–17 c.e., and the Bar Kokhba Revolt—did not disappear with the loss of Jewish sovereignty.

Jewish Self-Government

The political activity of the Jews was closely bound up with attempts to preserve and extend communal autonomy, the most important of the medieval Jewish privileges. There was frequently a direct correlation between the power of the Jews in the political hierarchy and the degree of internal autonomy they possessed. For instance, in 1476 the Spanish monarchs Ferdinand and Isabella revoked the right of the Jewish community councils (*aljamas*) to exercise criminal jurisdiction.[36] This severe restriction, which was more a consequence of the new, absolutist theory of the Spanish state than of direct anti-Semitism, set the stage for the expulsion of the Jews sixteen years later. As the Spanish state redefined itself to exclude foreign elements, it almost inevitably had to limit the internal power of the Jewish community. Similarly, the degree of Jewish influence in Poland coincided with the pinnacle of Jewish self-government in the sixteenth and early seventeenth centuries. As the position of the Jews deteriorated in the eighteenth century, the state attempted to take over direct rule of the Jewish communities; it abolished the Council of the Four Lands in 1764.

It was entirely consistent for medieval political theory to grant discrete corporations, and especially separate ethnic groups, rights of internal self-government. Germans, Ruthenians, and Armenians in medieval Polish cities also enjoyed such rights. In fact, the Jews were initially treated as Germans, since they had migrated from Germany to Poland. These minorities were not full-fledged citizens of the Polish cities and were therefore not represented in the city governments, but they had their own parallel institutions. Jewish self-government, because it had a firm status in medieval political theory, was generally not the object of anti-Jewish polemics. The accusation that the Jews formed a "state within the state" really only became important in the eighteenth-century Enlightenment.[37] Yet, as Salo Baron has pointed out, Jewish communal autonomy in Western Europe was often far greater than that enjoyed by the medieval cities in which they lived, perhaps as a result of the Jews' special status as *servi camerae*. The almost total autonomy that the Jewish leadership possessed in setting and collecting taxes was one characteristic of Jewish privileges that went far beyond that of any other group. Moreover, the supracommunal synods and councils that Jewish leaders convened in France and Poland were unique. As Baron writes, "Can one envisage such national or regional convocations of villeins assembled to vote new taxes or new methods for their effective collection almost on the level of regular diets?"[38]

The jurisdiction and powers of the Jewish communities of the Middle Ages naturally varied widely depending on place and circumstance. But there are certain common features to communal power throughout the Middle Ages and throughout the Diaspora. We have already seen how the political theory of the medieval Jewish community granted enormous power to the communal authorities. Historical reality corresponded closely to theory, for the communities typically controlled wide areas of daily life. They regulated the religious behavior of their members by enforcing Jewish law. They enacted regulations (*takkanot*) to supplement the law and fit it to particular circumstances. The communities also controlled social welfare, education, and other civic needs, as the political theory of the community dictated. Their legal jurisdiction frequently extended far beyond religion and philanthropy to full control over civil and criminal law in cases involving only Jews. In Babylonia during the talmudic period, Jewish courts had jurisdiction over murder, theft, torts, commercial transactions, and "personal" law (marriage, divorce, and inheritance). In this way, the Jewish authorities had virtually all the powers of an autonomous state with the exception of control of foreign affairs.[39] The power of the Babylonian community was certainly no less than that of the priestly state of the Second Temple period.

No later Jewish community had quite as much power as did the Babylonian, but many possessed most of the same elements. Yitzhak Baer records the crimes punished by the *aljama* of Burgos in the thirteenth century:

> [The] record lists a graduated scale of fines for various degrees of assault and vilification. Similar penalties are incurred for the desecration of the Sabbath or holidays by drawing another's blood by a blow, by forcing him to testify in a non-Jewish court, or by bearing arms, sitting on the wall of a house with one's feet dangling or leading an animal to water by a chain.[40]

The Spanish Jewish communities also controlled the economic life of the Jewish market, setting prices and excluding imports of certain items in order to protect local producers.

In Poland, too, the Jewish courts had wide jurisdiction over civil matters between Jews and, in some regions, criminal matters as well. Conflicts between Jews and non-Jews were settled in "courts of the Jews" which were staffed by judges appointed by local rulers, often in consultation with the Jewish authorities. These latter courts were supposed to use Jewish law, but usually applied Polish law as well. In addition to their juridical powers, the communities typically acted as full-fledged urban governments which administered the Jewish quarter. The Cracow ordinances of 1595 cover religious and commercial matters and even prescribe how refuse is to be disposed of.[41]

The Jews enjoyed power over their own lives in many

cases because the gentile governments charged the Jewish authorities with the collection of taxes from the Jewish population. From the point of view of the Polish government, the justification for allowing the growth of the extensive system of councils and supracouncils among the Polish Jews was to assure proper collection of taxes. The abolition of the Council of the Four Lands in 1764 was connected to the desire of the Polish government to collect Jewish taxes directly. Jewish power therefore derived from the fact that the communities were regarded as arms of the gentile governments, whether for purposes of taxation or internal control.

How did the Jewish communities enforce their will? They could make use of the non-Jewish authorities. For instance, the crown officers might be induced to fine a Jew in Aragon for "wearing his hat on the Sabbath without a string."[42] Or, more importantly, Jews accused of informing on other Jews could be handed over to the Spanish authorities for execution. But the communities also had considerable powers of enforcement of their own by the use of a ban, or *herem*. Such bans often forbade business dealings with the guilty party, which could easily ruin those whose livelihoods depended on business relationships with other Jews. The communities also possessed the right of *herem ha-yishuv*, meaning that they could withdraw someone's residency privileges. To lose one's right of residency was a terrible fate in the Middle Ages, when settlement was a privilege rather than an automatic right and was often severely restricted.

In addition to the *herem*, the Jewish community could enforce its will by fines or by corporal punishment. Although biblical and rabbinic law limited the number of strokes that a criminal might receive in a flogging, courts could impose virtually unlimited "floggings for rebelliousness" (see above, p. 53).[43] Communities might use corporal punishment to control matters that we today would consider private. In the minute book of the Council of Lithuania, a threat is made against those who marry in secret without the presence of ten witnesses:

[They shall be] excommunicated and ostracized in this world and the world to come. . . . The court shall punish them severely by hanging them from a post and administering forty lashes without any possibility for ransom. They shall be punished and tortured with all manner of sufferings and excommunications as a means of prevention against the promiscuity of the generation.[44]

There is also scattered evidence that the Jews may have occasionally administered capital punishment directly. There are some theoretical discussions of the death penalty in the Talmud, although it appears that the Jewish government probably did not actually carry it out. The one case of murder that we have in the fourth century was tried by the Exilarch, and the punishment was blinding (a punishment not to be found in either biblical or rabbinic law!).[45] In Spain, the communities imposed the death penalty on informers, but the execution was carried out by the government. This privilege went back to the Muslim period in Spain, even though Islamic law did not theoretically countenance such power for the Jewish community. Maimonides suggests that the Jewish authorities did not hesitate to use this authority: "It is an everyday occurrence in the cities of the West [i.e., Spain] to execute the informers who by their informing are known to have caused loss of Jewish property, and to hand such informers over to the non-Jews for execution, beating, or imprisonment for their crime."[46] Rabbi Asher ben Yehiel, who moved from Germany to Toledo, expressed astonishment that the Jews of Spain tried capital cases without a legally constituted Sanhedrin.[47] In the sixteenth century, Rabbi Shalom Shakhna (d. 1558), who was chief rabbi of Lesser Poland, received the right to impose capital punishment as part of his authority on his appointment in 1541.

The Jewish authorities were also capable of using torture to extract confessions, even though confessions are not, strictly speaking, admissible as evidence in a Jewish court. Yitzhak Baer believes that the Jews adopted the inquisitorial procedures of Roman and canon law from their Christian contemporaries in the thirteenth century.[48] In Central Europe in the eighteenth century, a Jew suspected of rape was dragged to the local rabbi and beaten until he confessed.[49]

The Jewish communities at the peak of their power controlled much of daily life. The community councils and courts represented the executive, legislative, and judicial branches of government. In many cases, the structure of the Jewish government was modeled after the governing institutions of the non-Jewish majority. The Jewish Council of Thirty in fourteenth-century Barcelona apparently imitated the city's Council of One Hundred. The community councils attempted to concentrate as much power in their hands as possible. In 1327, the Barcelona council gained control of all official appointments within the community and forbade the influential from petitioning the king directly for such favors. The stronger the community, the more it attempted to block access to non-Jewish courts, already forbidden by the Talmud, and thus to make any kind of independent life impossible outside its jurisdiction.

Leadership in most communities was in the hands of the wealthy and the learned, a fact that Jewish political theory attempted to legitimize. In most cases, there was very little participation by the lower classes in political life. H. H. Ben-Sasson estimates that the right of election to the regional councils in Poland "belonged to some 5% of all householders and that at times it fell as low as 1%."[50] Occasionally, the sources reveal revolts in the lower classes, such as the attempt by a group in Saragossa in 1264 to challenge the taxation system that favored the wealthy or the move to democratize the Barcelona Council of Thirty in 1386. There were similar cases of tension and conflict between the classes in fifteenth- and sixteenth-century Poland.[51] In general, however, power remained in the hands of rabbis and householders, and it is to them that one must turn in studying the internal political life of the Jews.

There is a tendency to see the Jewish leadership as monolithic and therefore to ignore the very active political struggles within the communities. In virtually every period, however, it is possible to write a history of Jewish politics based on conflicts over leadership and power. The tensions between the Exilarch and the Academy heads in Babylonia during talmudic times, although sometimes portrayed as struggles between secular and religious figures, were really power conflicts between two institutions that were both simultaneously secular and religious. In Germany in the fifteenth century, a rabbi named Seligmann of Bing tried to convene a synod to legislate against the proliferation of divorces and hasty remarriages evidently typical of the time. He ran into vociferous opposition from other rabbis, not on the grounds of the substantive issue but rather over legislative power: who had the right to convene synods and which communities would control them?[52] In sixteenth-century Poland, a power struggle developed between the householders who controlled communal institutions and local rabbis. Here, wealth and learning, which were often united in other places, came into conflict.[53]

It is also possible that conflicts which appear to have been purely intellectual had a significant political dimension. For instance, during the eighteenth century, a violent dispute raged between groups of rabbis led by Jacob Emden and Jonathan Eibeschutz over whether or not Eibeschutz was a secret Sabbatian (follower of Sabbatai Zevi). Each side banned the books of the other, and the conflict quickly became a struggle over who had the power to decide on the orthodoxy of books.[54] These are, of course, only a handful of examples among many, but they suggest that a rich political life—one in which conflicts developed over control of power—was always present in the Jewish community.

The Urge toward Statehood

Medieval Jewish thought considered the Jewish communities and their leaders to be surrogates for the ancient sovereign Jewish state and guarantors of the future messianic state. Rabbis and other leaders assumed royal titles. In some cases, rabbinical authorities undertook actions to instigate the coming of the Messiah. A striking example of such rabbinic messianism was the attempt by Jacob Berav in Safed in the late 1530s to reinstitute the ancient ordination of rabbis and reconstitute the Sanhedrin. Berav clearly conceived of these steps as preludes to the establishment of a messianic state in the Holy Land. After ordaining some of his disciples, including Joseph Karo, the author of the definitive law code, the *Shulhan Arukh*, Berav was blocked by the Jerusalem rabbis, who feared the loss of their authority to the Safed community.[55]

As noted in chapter 2, such attempts to create a messianic state in the Land of Israel were generally not undertaken by the rabbis, but instead by rebels such as the sixteenth-century Marrano Shlomo Molocho or the seventeenth-century messianic pretender Sabbatai Zevi. Among establishment figures there emerged a different kind of urge toward statehood, namely, the urge to set up a Jewish state somewhere in the Diaspora, without any direct connection to the messianic desire for a future renewal of sovereignty in the Land of Israel. This nonmessianic desire for statehood has received very little attention, but it is eloquent evidence of the political consciousness of the Jews quite apart from messianic expectations. Many of these stories may be legendary, but what is important is that the impulse existed, even if the Jews did not actually create such independent states in the Diaspora. For this purpose, legends can be as revealing as facts.

In the talmudic period, there were at least two reported attempts to form Jewish states in Babylonia. The first seems to have been a Jewish principality in Nehardea in the first century c.e. under two Jews named Anileus and Asineus.[56] The second, mentioned earlier, was the result of a short-lived revolt by the Exilarch Mar Zutra II at the beginning of the sixth century, which ended with the crucifixion of Mar Zutra by the Persians. Since the only source we have for this Jewish state is the later collection of legends *Seder Olam Zuta*, the whole story may be fantastic. More likely to have been historical are the stories about the conversion of the Caucasian kingdom of the Khazars to Judaism, which probably took place in the eighth century.[57] Jews in Spain, such as Hisdai ibn Shaprut and Judah Ha-Levi, the author of *The Kuzari*, were fascinated by the idea of the Jewish kingdom of the Khazars but attributed no messianic significance to it: the fact that Jews might exercise sovereign power somewhere apparently had no implications for the eventual coming of the Messiah.

Reports also circulated in the twelfth and thirteenth centuries about an eighth-century Jewish principality in Narbonne under the Carolingians in which Jews not only enjoyed vast communal privileges but also owned the land. The first *nasi* (patriarch) of this quasi state was ostensibly a Babylonian descendant of David named Makhir, who was sent to the Frankish kingdom where he received the territory of Narbonne and married a local noblewoman (a Latin source has him marrying King Pepin the Short's sister Alda). Although the most recent scholarship throws serious doubt on the historicity of this Jewish principality, belief in the legend symbolized the desire of the Jews for the continuation of the Patriarchate, with its royal lineage, in the lands of the Diaspora.[58]

The persistent legends of a Jewish kingdom beyond the imaginary river Sambatyon are also indicative of the desire for Diaspora statehood. During the seventeenth century, the kingdom beyond the Sambatyon played a role in the fantasies of the disciples of Sabbatai Zevi. The Sabbatian propagandist Nathan of Gaza believed that the Messiah would go to this mythical kingdom and return with his bride to conquer the Holy Land without violence.[59] Similar fascination with exotic Jewish kingdoms excited interest in David Ha-Reuveni, who appeared in Italy in the sixteenth century claiming to represent an Oriental Jewish monarchy. Both Jews and non-Jews, including the Pope, were prepared to believe Ha-Reuveni, presumably because they regarded the existence of such a kingdom as entirely probable.

The Sabbatian movement is of considerable interest in terms of the Jewish desire for a monarchy. The followers of Sabbatai Zevi gave their messianic hero royal titles even before he had established a kingdom. It is possible that this urge for a Jewish king, perhaps influenced by European absolutism, explains the widespread attraction to Sabbatai Zevi even more than the mystical ideas that formed the ideology of the movement.[60]

The desire for statehood, whether in the full messianic sense in the Land of Israel or in the Diaspora without messianic overtones, demonstrates the persistent vitality of Jewish politics, just as do the internal politics of the Jewish community and the political activity of the Jews in their societies. We must be careful, however, not to distort the meaning of Jewish power in the Middle Ages. Just as the myth of medieval powerlessness has warped our view of Jewish history, so might an attempt to correct that myth create its opposite: a countermyth of Jewish power. The very real power Jews possessed must always be understood together with the disabilities under which they suffered and the persecutions they faced. When their alliances failed to protect them, they were perhaps more vulnerable to murderous attack than any other group in medieval society. But in an age when security was uncertain and fragile, when the reign of law was much more tenuous than it is today, Jewish vulnerabilities were not just the result of religious hatred, but part and parcel of the insecurities endemic to medieval society as a whole. Yet, the Jewish response to insecurity was not, as the nineteenth-century historian Heinrich Graetz claimed, to "la[y] aside [their] weapons of war . . . [and] free [themselves] from the bonds of self-interest."[61] On the contrary, the Jewish Middle Ages represent a period of intense political activity, in which defense of Jewish self-interest, even to the point of taking up arms, was very much the norm. Without this enduring political life, such a dispersed and outnumbered people could scarcely have survived.

IV
Absolutism and Enlightenment

THE High Middle Ages, up to the late twelfth or thirteenth century, in Central and Western Europe were a time of relative power for the Jews, but in subsequent centuries their status and influence deteriorated. Between the end of the thirteenth and the end of the fifteenth centuries, the Jews were expelled from England, France, Spain, and, more sporadically, various principalities in Germany. Much of the freedom that Jews had enjoyed in those countries in which they remained, such as Italy and Germany, was curtailed by new civil disabilities. In Poland and the Middle East, this decline set in later than in Western and Central Europe. The turning point for the Polish Jews came with the Ukrainian massacres of 1648. In the next hundred and fifty years, the Kingdom of Poland gradually collapsed until it was partitioned by Russia, Austria, and Prussia, a development with devastating consequences for the Jews. In the Middle East, the Ottoman Empire was a favorable place for Jews in the sixteenth and seventeenth centuries, but became an increasingly hostile environment in the eighteenth and nineteenth centuries.

Why did the relatively favorable atmosphere of the Middle Ages—at least favorable in terms of the relations between the Jews and the centers of power in their societies—change for the worse? Religious developments in Western Europe certainly played an important role. In the twelfth century, Christian thinkers argued that the Jews were followers of a new religion (*nova lex*), the Talmud, and therefore no longer qualified for the toleration accorded the Chosen People of the Bible by Church dogma. New monastic orders such as the Franciscans and Dominicans took up this argument in the thirteenth century and instigated a new form of anti-Jewish hostility, leading to the burning of the Talmud in 1240. Later on, in the sixteenth century, the tensions caused by the Reformation upset the uneasy equilibrium in Church theology between toleration and persecution of the Jews, and the papacy promulgated new anti-Jewish decrees. The Protestants, for their part, were fascinated with the Jews as a result of their interest in the Bible, but, for unclear reasons, many of the Protestant sects, especially Lutheranism, developed a virulent anti-Semitism that foreshadowed the exterminatory language of the Nazis.[1]

Deterioration in the power of secular authorities also contributed to the decline in Jewish status in a number of places. The Black Death in the fourteenth century traumatized society and undermined much of the social basis for tolerance of the Jews. With the breakdown in governmental authority at the time of the plague, vicious rumors that Jews were poisoning wells swept through the population. The decline of the Kingdom of Poland in the seventeenth and eighteenth centuries and the impact of European imperialism on the Middle East in the nineteenth century contributed to the deterioration of the Jews' position in those areas.

More important than political decline in changing the Jewish status was the slow growth of the absolutist state. In the Middle Ages, Jews profited from the division of power between the Church, the kings, and the nobility. But if the fragmentation of power served Jewish interests in the Middle

Ages, the concentration of power in the hands of absolutist monarchs in later years ultimately subverted the Jewish position by destroying their old communal autonomy.

Along with these external factors, a variety of internal developments weakened the authority of the medieval Jewish communities. The expulsion from Spain in 1492 destroyed the largest and most prosperous Jewish community. Many Jews were forced to convert to Christianity, and those who later returned to Judaism after living as New Christians often felt less allegiance to the community. These Marranos were frequently the source of controversies and rebellions. In the seventeenth century, the messianic movement of Sabbatai Zevi split Jewish communities down the middle and created an opposition force to the conservative rabbinic leadership.[2] In eighteenth-century Poland, as the Jewish population grew, many Jews left the old noble cities and took up residence in small villages. The formally constituted communities continued to have legal and fiscal jurisdiction over these outlying villages, but communal controls undoubtedly weakened.[3] Out of the increasing power vacuum in the traditional leadership of Eastern Europe came a number of new movements in search of power within the Jewish community: Hasidism, the yeshiva movement (*mitnagdim*) that opposed the Hasidim, the Musar movement of Israel Salanter in the nineteenth century, and, finally, the Haskalah (Jewish Enlightenment).

Absolutism and the Jews

Absolutism is the political system in which all power is concentrated in the hands of a monarch and his bureaucracy. The so-called Age of Absolutism is usually considered to be the period from the middle of the seventeenth century to the early nineteenth, but the seeds of the absolutist state can be found as early as the thirteenth century in England, France, and Germany.[4] Though halting, these early efforts at centralization of power foreshadowed the development of the absolute nation-state. In the last chapter, we saw how the expul-

sion of the Jews from Spain was but a symptom of the attempt to create a unified nation-state; this was equally true
for England and France. Without denying the many social
and religious causes for these expulsions, the political framework in which they took place was closer to absolutist nationalism than to the medieval state. This new nationalism regarded the Jews as a foreign body, to be either thoroughly
absorbed or expelled.

Just as the beginning of the absolutist age is unclear, so is
it difficult to speak of an age of absolutism occurring at the
same time in all places and meaning the same thing. Russian
absolutism began with Peter the Great in the first part of the
eighteenth century but culminated only in the reign of Czar
Nicholas I (1825–55). In the Middle East, the Ottoman Empire might be considered a kind of absolutist regime, starting
as early as the fifteenth century, but its characteristics were
thoroughly different from the absolutist states of either Western or Eastern Europe.

The absolutist state evolved into its first developed form
on the European continent in the seventeenth and eighteenth
centuries in France and Germany, particularly in Prussia.[5]
The devastating Thirty Years War eroded much of the basis
for local power, which was in the hands of the landholding
nobility and the cities. Into this vacuum moved the princes
and kings, who now sought to develop monarchical power not
as "the first among equals" in relation to the estates or of
corporations, but as absolute and exclusive. They created a
new, professional bureaucracy and standing armies, neither
of which had real precedents in the Middle Ages. With these
innovations, monarchs sought to establish institutions independent of the nobility that provided means of ruling all of
society in their sole interests.

No pure absolutist state can be found in the age of absolutism. The nearest one was probably the police state of Napoleon Bonaparte; true absolutism found perfection only in a
totalitarian state such as Stalinist Russia in the twentieth
century. All of the earlier absolutist states still had to contend

with the power retained by the nobility and other groups. In Prussia, for instance, the new bureaucracy was really an arm of the landholding aristocracy rather than an independent agent of the king. But the logic of absolutism, if not the actual practice, was to dismantle the medieval corporations as independent centers of power and concentrate all political authority in the hands of the sovereign.

The medieval status of the Jews necessarily became a casualty of this assault on the corporations, not because the absolutist regimes were particularly hostile to the Jews—some were more than others—but because they were hostile to any power concentrations outside of their immediate grasp.[6] It is this fact, more than any other, that explains their ambivalent relationship to the Jews. In order to establish tighter and more direct control over settlement in their states, absolutist monarchs took over control of residency rights from the Jewish communities which had enjoyed these rights for most of the Middle Ages. Residential restrictions became common in Italy and Germany, where there had been none at all in the Middle Ages: the ghetto was invented in sixteenth-century Italy and quickly spread to Germany. In Central Europe monarchs made strenuous efforts to prevent "foreign" Jews from entering their territories, and they issued elaborate regulations defining the status of "protected" or "privileged" Jews. The protected Jews included only the most wealthy members of the community and their employees and servants. The poorer classes, which undoubtedly included the majority of the Jewish population, often lived in these states without a secure legal status and were subject to arbitrary expulsion. This hostility to any but the privileged Jews led to a number of mass expulsions, the worst being that from Vienna in 1670.

The East European Jews were also subjected to unprecedented residential restrictions when the Russian state seized most of the old Kingdom of Poland at the end of the eighteenth century. The czarist government created a Pale of Settlement and, during the nineteenth century, also sporadically expelled the Jews from border areas and villages. These kinds of residential restrictions were not the rule in Poland before it was partitioned, but were rather the infamous legacy of Russian autocracy. In the late nineteenth and early twentieth centuries, the czarist government instigated pogroms against the Jews as part of a desperate attempt to shore up the autocratic state at a time when revolutionaries were trying to bring it down. If Jews in Eastern Europe previously fell victim to rebels against the state, as was the case in 1648, the rise of Russian absolutism made them increasingly victims of the state itself.

The state interfered in the internal life of the Jewish community to a degree never seen in the Middle Ages, with the possible exception of the Byzantine Empire of late antiquity. Even privileged Jews were restricted in their business activities and places of residence. The state dictated who could marry and how many marriages might take place. Rumors or actual legislation to set a minimum age of marriage, which was unheard of earlier, caused a stampede among many Jews in the eighteenth and nineteenth centuries to marry off their children as young as eight and nine.[7] Never before had the state or any other non-Jewish body legislated private matters such as marriage, which had always been the exclusive province of the autonomous Jewish community.

All these measures had a common logic: to decrease the corporate powers of the Jews and to place them directly under the authority of the state. Yet, the primary motivation of the state was not hatred of the Jews, although certainly many monarchs and their ministers harbored no great love for the Chosen People. Rather, interests of state dictated these policies, many of which were applied equally to other groups. In this sense, absolutist policy toward the Jews differed fundamentally from anti-Jewish enactments in the Middle Ages, which frequently had more specific religious motivations.

An example of the motivations behind absolutist policy is Czar Nicholas I of Russia, whose reign is still remembered as one of the most bitter in modern Jewish history. Under Nicholas, the Jews were conscripted into the Russian army for the first time, many of them at age twelve or even younger. These "cantonists" were subjected to inhuman pressures in order to make them convert. The missionary impulse behind Jewish conscription surely stemmed from religious motives, but the decision to draft the Jews in the first place was part of Nicholas' nationalistic policy in general and had little to do with anti-Jewish sentiments. It was under Nicholas that Russia became a true absolutist state, in ideology if not in practice, and the ideology of a unified autocratic state demanded the same obligations of all subjects, whatever their ethnic group. The policy of Russification was not directed just against the Jews, but against other nationalities as well, although the particular brutality with which czarist Jewish policy was enforced was undoubtedly a product of traditional anti-Semitism.[8]

Yet, the logic of absolutism pointed equally to toleration of the Jews as well as to increased disabilities. The new concept of a nation-state with sovereign power residing solely in the monarch laid the basis for equality of rights. The famous essay by Christian Wilhelm von Dohm, an enlightened German bureaucrat, "Concerning the Amelioration of the Civil Status of the Jews," published in 1781, suggested granting the Jewish corporation the same rights enjoyed by other religious communities.[9] The charter granted by Frederick II of Prussia in 1750 also treated the Jews less as a foreign community and more as individual subjects of the state. Even the Russification policy of Nicholas I, for all its missionary and coercive overtones, flowed from a desire to "modernize" the Jews and integrate them as individuals into the state. Indeed, many of the absolutist policies which appeared abhorrent to the Jews were intended for what the state perceived to be to their benefit.

Although the American and French revolutions were the first to treat Jews as full and equal citizens, it is not surprising that many of the early steps toward emancipation came from absolutist rulers such as Joseph II, who issued an Edict

of Tolerance for the Austrian Jews in 1782, or Napoleon Bonaparte, who emancipated the Jews of Italy and Westphalia.
The absolutist government of Prussia emancipated the Prussian Jews in 1812. In addition, the first serious reforms of the
Jewish status in Russia were undertaken by a czar, Alexander
II (1855–81), who succeeded Nicholas I. Despite the influence
of the European Enlightenment and the French Revolution
on these acts, they were equally a product of the logic of
absolutism, a logic that might at one time dictate repression
of the Jews and, at another, their emancipation. The same
logic applied to the behavior of these states toward their
populations as a whole: police-state repression on the one
hand, and gradual steps toward a modern, tolerant society on
the other.

   Loss of internal Jewish power was the price that absolutist regimes exacted for opening up their societies and econo-
mies to greater Jewish participation. Edicts abolishing Jewish communal autonomy typically accompanied edicts of toleration or emancipation. For instance, two years after Joseph
II issued his Edict of Tolerance, a step close to full emancipation, a further edict abolished rabbinic courts. These types of
regimes wanted to create a direct relationship between the
individual and the state. The judicial autonomy of the rabbis
stood in the way of this new concept of citizenship. The absolutist regimes also opposed the farming out of taxation and
sought to collect taxes directly. In the Middle Ages, the Jewish community had derived much of its power from its official
function as tax collector for the king. One sign of the deterioration of medieval privileges was the abolition of this power.
As we have seen, the Polish government dissolved the Council
of the Four Lands in 1764, in order to collect Jewish taxes
itself. In 1844, the Russian government abolished the *kahal*
(the governing body of the Russian Jewish communities) and
substituted its own Jewish agents for tax collection.

   The abolition of the *kahal* was part of Czar Nicholas' absolutist program to "modernize" and "Russify" the Jews:
even though Nicholas' reign was far more detrimental to the

Jews than was Joseph II's in Austria, this link between a desire to integrate the Jews and an attack on communal autonomy characterized all absolutist regimes. In practice, Nicholas' ukase did very little to change Jewish self-government since the same leaders often assumed the new positions, but it did create a perception among many Jews that their traditional autonomy had significantly declined. Although Jewish courts continued to issue rulings, one Lithuanian rabbi wrote in 1846: "The honor of our life has been removed by the orders of His Imperial Majesty and his ministers that we may no longer judge cases between Jews in Jewish courts . . . as has been the custom in our country until now."[10]

The Grand Sanhedrin which Napoleon convened in 1807 was to serve the same purpose of linking full citizenship for the Jews with the abolition of Jewish communal authority. Napoleon demanded, in a list of questions that he posed first to an Assembly of Notables and then to the Sanhedrin itself, that the Jews give up all their medieval judicial and legislative powers in exchange for citizenship and equal rights. But the very act of convening a Sanhedrin, with all its archaic overtones from the time of the Temple, suggests that Napoleon had a grandiose, exaggerated view of Jewish power. He assumed that a convocation of rabbis and other Jewish notables might actually have the authority to rewrite Jewish law and thus voluntarily renounce the social contract of the Middle Ages. Napoleon paradoxically called upon the Jews to exercise more power than they actually had in the Middle Ages in order to abdicate that power. In the end, rather than abolishing Jewish communal institutions altogether, Napoleon established a network of *consistoires*, councils that would rule the Jewish communities under the strict supervision of the government, similar to the control he established over the Catholic Church.[11]

In addition to the actual abolition or taking over of communal institutions, absolutist regimes tried to exploit the existing leadership to enforce new policies repugnant to the Jews. The Russian Jewish communities were required to

meet the conscription quotas of the czarist government and
the communal leaders employed kidnappers (known in Yiddish as *khappers*) to snatch children for the purpose. The col-
laboration of these leaders with the notorious policies of the
government seriously undermined their authority. Such actions tragically foreshadowed the behavior of a few leaders of
the Judenräte (Jewish councils; see below, p. 142) during the
Holocaust.[12]

These policies created severe communal tensions. In 1853,
the leadership of Grodno appears to have cooperated with the
government in its decree against traveling without a passport.
A contemporary source describes how a rabbi, Eliyahu Shik,
rallied community members against the leadership:

> [He] called on everyone to revolt against the heads of the com-
> munity and to tear the *kahal* building to shreds. . . . With an axe
> in his hands he ran in front of the crowd that had gathered, each
> man armed with an axe; before they were stopped, they had
> broken the iron bolts on the door of the *kahal* building and freed
> the three prisoners incarcerated there.[13]

Before ending this discussion of the ambivalent relationship of absolutism to the Jews, it is necessary to mention the
very different situation in the Middle East and, particularly,
the Ottoman Empire. With the rise of Spanish absolutism at
the end of the fifteenth century and the expulsion of the Jews
from the Iberian Peninsula, the Ottoman Empire became a
haven for Jewish refugees, in much the same manner as the
Kingdom of Poland received Jews from Germany in roughly
the same period. Individual Jews often rose to positions of
considerable power throughout the Ottoman Empire, even
though Islamic law banned them from government service. In
the eighteenth century, Christians replaced Jews in many of
these positions, largely because the Christians now had better
international contacts. In the early nineteenth century, Sul-
tan Mahmud II (1808–39) sought to create a modern bureaucracy and army. In so doing, he abolished the Corps of Janis-
saries, a semiautonomous military unit with which Jewish

merchants and purveyors had important relations. The destruction of this important military force spelled the end of Jewish economic power and political influence in the Ottoman Empire. This negative consequence of the creation of a modern army was the opposite of what happened in Central Europe, where the development of modern standing armies opened up new opportunities for Jewish businessmen.

The extension of the *millet* system to include the Jews in 1835 was another case in which developments in the Ottoman Empire differed from those in absolutist Europe. Under this system, religious minorities were organized throughout the empire as one community with a central governing official. The chief rabbi, called the *hakhambashi,* wielded considerable power and the authority of the conservative rabbinate therefore increased at a time when Jewish corporate autonomy was weakening in Europe.

Despite these differences between Europe and the Ottoman Empire, the position of the Jews deteriorated in both cases. As the Ottoman Empire ran into financial problems, the European powers increasingly interfered in Ottoman affairs. The imperialist nations tried to provide protection for Christians and, to a lesser extent, Jews. In reaction, Muslim society applied the discriminatory laws of Islam to minorities much more strictly than had been the case previously. The European influence also had a direct negative impact on the Jews, for it exported Christian anti-Semitism to a culture that had never harbored such violent hatred of the Jews. In 1840, a Capuchin friar and his Muslim servant disappeared, and a number of Jews confessed under torture to their murders. The French consul appears to have had a hand in inciting the accusers. Although another imperial power, Britain, intervened to protect the Jews, the affair would probably never have taken place had it not been for European imperialism, since there is no precedent for such accusations against Jews in medieval Islam.[14] The Damascus Blood Libel, as this incident came to be called, became a symbol for the deterioration of the Jewish situation in the Middle East.

New Leaders and the Struggle for Communal Power

In addition to undermining the Jewish communal structure of the Middle Ages, conditions in the absolutist states fostered the development of new Jewish elites. In Germany and Austria, following the devastation of the Thirty Years War, princes sought new sources of finance. Lacking the indigenous bourgeoisie which was developing in France and England, they turned to a small group of wealthy Jews as purveyors of supplies to the new armies and as financiers. These "court Jews" were exempt from the residency and travel restrictions that pertained to the rest of the Jewish community, and they often adopted the culture of the aristocracy. The privileges these Jews enjoyed made them in a sense the first "emancipated" Jews. The wealth of the court Jews was based less on old-style moneylending and more on commerce; they were products of the new mercantilist era rather than vestiges of the Middle Ages.[15]

The court Jews also differed significantly from medieval Jewish courtiers such as Samuel Ha-Nagid and Isaac Abravanel. While these earlier political figures were also leaders of the Jewish community, the court Jews were first and foremost partisans of the absolutist princes. The rulers would often make them the "elders" of the Jewish communities, but this was externally imposed communal power, not acquired in the traditional way. Although the court Jews frequently used their influence to intercede on behalf of their communities, the external source of their authority and their separation from the life of the community often brought them into conflict with the rest of the Jews.

The ostensible power of the court Jews has led some observers, such as Hannah Arendt, to argue that the absolutist period was when the Jews enjoyed their greatest power during the Diaspora. For Arendt, the demise of the absolutist state and the emergence of a state dependent on the "mob" spelled the end to Jewish power.[16] Interestingly enough, anti-Semites also used the image of the court Jew to argue that all Jews are wealthy and powerful. The Rothschilds, who were not court Jews in the precise sense of the term, became for nineteenth- and twentieth-century anti-Semites the symbol of this Jewish power. The Nazis exploited the image in a vicious anti-Semitic film, *Jud Suess*, based on the life of the spectacular seventeenth-century court Jew Suess Oppenheimer.[17] In reality, however, the power of the court Jews was quite precarious. They were all too dependent on individual patron princes whose death could mean the loss of their own position or even their lives, as the story of Suess Oppenheimer, who was hanged after his patron died, demonstrates.

The court Jew, for all his wealth, represented a hollow form of power, based as it was on the vagaries of individual whim and politics rather than on a recognized place in the social structure. It was a transitory kind of power and it vanished as soon as the state found other sources of finance and supply. The court Jews were extraordinary exceptions, products of an age in which individuals might achieve great wealth and power only to be swept away by the swift torrent of rising capitalism. What is important about the court Jews from the perspective of Jewish politics, however, is that they represent a new form of leadership, quite different from that of the Middle Ages, a leadership pointing ahead toward the period of emancipation in which traditional structures of authority would be replaced by new sources of power.

In Eastern Europe, the crisis of the Kingdom of Poland in the eighteenth century created the conditions for the emergence of a new Jewish leadership there too. In the early part of the century, itinerant wonder-workers and preachers wandered the countryside and found a ready audience as poverty and political conditions weakened the traditional Jewish community. In the middle of the century, Hasidism developed out of this milieu of mystics and magicians, offering a kind of countercommunity around its own charismatic leaders.[18] The hasidic masters (*zaddikim*) often attracted disciples from a wide geographical area, thus tending to divorce the disciples at least partially from the authority of the *mara de-atra*, the official communal rabbi.

Hasidism emphasized prayer as opposed to the traditional value of study, but its ideology would not have been so provocative if it had not also constructed a social system to put its ideas into practice. As such, it constituted a challenge to the political hegemony of the old leadership. The creation of hasidic communities clustered around the *zaddikim* instigated a countermovement called *mitnagdim* (literally: opponents), who tried to preserve traditional authority against the challenge of Hasidism.[19] Despite their conservatism, however, the *mitnagdim*, too, sought innovations, especially in the area of yeshiva study. In response to the perceived anti-intellectualism of the Hasidim, the *mitnagdim*, disciples of Elijah, the Gaon of Vilna, attempted to revitalize talmudic study by establishing the great Lithuanian yeshivas, including the famous one at Volozhin. In the nineteenth century, a further attempt at renewal in the nonhasidic Orthodox world took place under the leadership of Israel Salanter, who created the pietistic Musar movement.[20]

All these movements within the traditional world of the East European Jews reflected the decline of the old leadership, a decline that accelerated as Russian autocracy replaced the Kingdom of Poland. They represented efforts to produce new leaders, not merely for religious reasons, but to fill a political vacuum in the Jewish communities. The vicious struggle between the Hasidim and the *mitnagdim*—including their mutual denunciations to the czarist government—was essentially a political battle, despite the religious arguments that each side used. By the nineteenth century, the Hasidim had successfully entrenched themselves in large areas of the Ukraine, Poland, and Hungary where they wielded power in a manner frequently more autocratic than their opponents had earlier. Some of the *zaddikim*, such as the Ruzhin dynasty, lived in opulent palaces and imitated the absolutist monarchs in their courts.

The warfare between the Hasidim and their opponents

foreshadowed the even more violent conflict between the traditional authorities and the new movement of Jewish enlightenment, the Haskalah. Once again, mutual denunciations to governmental authorities, writs of excommunication, forceable breakups of marriages, and even physical violence characterized this struggle. Despite the ideological arguments for which the Haskalah is primarily known, it was first and foremost a political bid by a group of intellectuals in Germany, Austria, and Russia to become the leadership of the Jewish community. While the elite of the Jewish community throughout the Middle Ages always included intellectuals, to use the modern term, the *maskilim*, or adherents of the Haskalah, represented something new. Like the intelligentsia of nineteenth-century Russia, these intellectuals formed their own social group in opposition to the establishment community. They produced their own newspapers and periodicals and met in their own clubs and societies. Even their use of Hebrew was a symptom of their revolt, since it was a demonstrably different language from the medieval Hebrew used by rabbis and merchants. In order to demonstrate their distinct difference from normative Jewish culture, they virtually created a new, flowery form of Hebrew modeled in a self-conscious and mostly unsuccessful way after the biblical language. The *maskilim* became an opposition intelligentsia largely because of the persecution and resistence they encountered in the traditional Jewish world, but they claimed to represent the "true" Judaism against the obscurantism of the rabbis. They presented themselves as an authentic leadership to the Jewish community rather than as the splinter sect they actually were.[21]

In Germany, the Haskalah began during the eighteenth-century Enlightenment. By the middle of the nineteenth century, the Reform Jews, who were the spiritual descendants of the eighteenth-century *maskilim*, won the following of the majority of German Jews and achieved control of the official institutions in many Jewish communities. The Orthodox, finding themselves a minority, petitioned the government to allow them to secede from the official community, a reversal from the Middle Ages when it was they who would expel rebels. By claiming the right to secede from the community, the Orthodox, led by Samson Raphael Hirsch, ironically took refuge in the "modern" principle of freedom of religion against the "enlightened" Reformers. Other Orthodox Jews, such as Rabbi Moses Sofer, unwilling to become a minority sect within Judaism, retreated to the East when the battle against Reform in Germany appeared to be lost.

In Eastern Europe, the *maskilim* remained in the minority for most of the nineteenth century. Even if they failed to make significant inroads in the Jewish community, however, they found allies in the absolutist bureaucracy. The governments of Nicholas I and Alexander II were the midwives for the birth of the Haskalah, just as, in Germany earlier, absolutism had created the court Jews. By establishing government schools for the Jews, at which Russian and secular subjects were taught, in the reign of Nicholas and by opening up Russian gymnasia and universities to Jews during the reign of Alexander, the regime created a Russified intelligentsia. These intellectuals saw themselves as allies of the government in the mission of "modernizing" the Jews.

What is striking about the Haskalah is that it emerged only in absolutist states and not in democratic countries such as England or France. Only in those lands where emancipation was delayed or incomplete, where the Jews were caught between the promise of individual freedom and the reality of continued group disabilities, did a specifically Jewish movement of enlightenment emerge. As the rabbis and communal leaders either lost their formal authority or were perceived to be losing it, the stage was set for an Enlightenment alternative to the traditional leadership, first in Germany, then in Austria-Hungary, and, finally, in the Pale of Settlement of nineteenth-century Russia. And, as a result of the historical congruence between absolutism and the Haskalah, the political ideology of this movement became the Jewish equivalent of the theory of the absolutist state.

The Political Ideology of the Haskalah

Historians have typically described the Haskalah in terms of its proposals for educational, social, and religious reform.[22] It sought to open up Jewish education to the Western sciences and to teach the Jews the languages of the countries in which they lived as well as to revitalize the Hebrew language. It proposed the "productivization" of the Jews, by which it meant moving Jews from the "useless" occupations of commerce and moneylending to trades and agriculture. Finally, the Haskalah prepared the way for movements of religious reform, even though its adherents were not always religious reformers themselves. All of these goals and tendencies stood at the heart of the Haskalah program for "modernizing" the Jews.

Yet, the function of the Haskalah in modern Jewish history and the deep structure of its ideology were fundamentally political. The *maskilim* understood that a new social compact was in the making between the Jews and their societies. While the *maskilim* were never more than a tiny group of intellectuals within the Jewish world, it was their ideology, and that of their successors, that decisively shaped the way many, if not most, Jews by the end of the nineteenth century came to understand the politics of "modernization." In their veneration of the state, their critique of the traditional Jewish community, and their new interpretation of Jewish history, the *maskilim* elaborated a political ideology that influenced all subsequent Jewish ideologies.

The *maskilim* glorified the modern state, an ideology that took its cue from the absolutist political theory that emphasized state sovereignty over the power of particular corporations. They took the medieval doctrine of *dina de-malkhuta dina* ("the law of the kingdom is the law") and turned it into a historical rationale for the Jews' loyalty to the states in which they lived.[23] In the Middle Ages, the principle served as the basis for the Jews' understanding of their contract with the gentile state. It gave a legal basis for ceding certain powers to the state and for expecting certain communal powers in return. The principle was limited solely to the state's right to tax the Jews and even then sanctioned only taxes levied equally. It was never understood to mean that the Jews had some higher allegiance to the state as such. On the contrary, it signified the pragmatic division of sovereignty between the state and the Jewish community.

For the *maskilim*, however, the state was to be invested with full sovereignty and the Jewish community rendered politically impotent. This radical reinterpretation of a hitherto narrowly defined, pragmatic principle can be seen in the answer that the Assembly of Notables gave to Napoleon in 1806: "In the eyes of every Israelite, without exception, submission to the prince is the first of duties. It is a principle generally acknowledged among them, that, in everything related to civil or political interests, *the law of the state is the supreme law.*"[24] No longer limited to fiscal matters, the law of the state was to be considered supreme in *all* areas of life, save religious ritual. Here was the basis for rejection of Jewish law in favor of absolute loyalty to the secular state. Ironically, Jewish law itself provided the means of its own dissolution!

If the French Jews at the time of Napoleon were willing to abdicate all civil and political legislation to the state, nineteenth-century German reformers went even further by using the principle that "the law of the kingdom is the law" to renounce even religious laws. The reformers held that if the Sabbath and marital laws interfered with the integration of the Jews into German society, the state had the right to overrule them. By the 1840s, the principle that had defined the limits of state law throughout the Middle Ages came to mean the very opposite: that Jewish law had no authority in any area if the law of the state contradicted it.

The revolutionary new understanding of *dina de-malkhuta dina* reflected an attitude toward the state utterly different from that of the Middle Ages. Although Jews had always recognized the importance of a practical alliance with

political authority, they never regarded the state with anything akin to modern patriotism. The new attitude began to
emerge several centuries before the Haskalah, probably
under the impact of absolutism. It is ironic that these first
statements of allegiance to the state came not during the
Middle Ages, when the Jews owed their very existence to governmental protection, but in the period when the state turned
dangerously hostile to the Jews. As the Jews were expelled by
the monarchs of France, Spain, and Portugal, they clung to
the illusion that their medieval alliance with the government
continued to exist. After the expulsion from Spain, Solomon
ibn Verga, the author of *Shevet Yehudah*, did not blame the
kings and princes for Jewish suffering. He portrayed the
Spanish rulers as the friends of the Jews, and the fact that the
Jews were permitted to take their property with them as a
sign of continuing favor.[25]

Similar expressions of loyalty to the state can be found in
a variety of other texts from before the Haskalah. David Gans,
the seventeenth-century historiographer, wrote of his native
Bohemia: "For the honor of this land, the land of Bohemia in
which I live, may the favor of God be upon its inhabitants."[26]
In seventeenth-century Italy, Simone Luzzato articulated a
new theory of the relationship of the Jews to the state: the
modern state needs the Jews for purely economic reasons
based on the theory of mercantilism; because of the nature of
their guild, the Jews are uniquely capable of fulfilling important roles in the economy of Europe. For Luzzato, the Jews
are the "leaven of absolutism," the agent that can expand the
power of the absolutist states.[27] In Germany in the eighteenth
century, Jacob Emden absolved the contemporary nations of
Europe from responsibility for the destruction of the Temple.
Emden argued that the nations of Europe were not the descendants of ancient Rome, the claims of the Holy Roman
Empire notwithstanding; he therefore cleared the way for a
much closer relationship between the Jews and the nations in
which they lived.[28] While prayers for the welfare of the kingdom were common throughout the Middle Ages and, indeed,

had a firm talmudic basis, these new anticipations of modern patriotism are quite different in tone from medieval political pragmatism. The *maskilim* could draw from this new identification with the state, which had been developing among Jews for several centuries.

The veneration for the state can also be traced to the seventeenth-century philosopher Baruch Spinoza, who in this context may be considered a proto-*maskil*. In his *Theologico-Political Treatise*, he argued against the meddling of religion in politics.[29] Religion must be subordinated to the state. In his appeal for tolerance of ideas and the freedom of philosophy from the tyranny of religion, Spinoza idealized the secular state. The power he invested in the state was in part a reaction against the power assumed by the Church and the synagogue in the Middle Ages; it also fits into the political theory of absolutism, which found expression in other seventeenth-century writers such as Thomas Hobbes.

As a result of his hostility to religion, the Jewish community of Amsterdam excommunicated Spinoza. A victim of persecution as well as a forerunner of the Enlightenment, Spinoza served as a model for many of the *maskilim*, who themselves suffered at the hands of the traditional Jewish community. For such outcasts and rebels, the state seemed a promising refuge from the arbitrary coercion of religious authority. To the *maskilim*, the absolutist state was close to a messianic redeemer from the servitude of the Middle Ages. Naphtali Herz Wessely, an eighteenth-century *maskil*, hailed Joseph II's Edict of Tolerance in messianic language, calling the Austrian emperor "God's anointed" after Isaiah's prophecy about Cyrus the Great.[30] In the nineteenth century, the Russian Haskalah poet Judah Leib Gordon used similar language to describe Alexander II and concluded his patriotic poem "Awake My People" (1863) with the lines:

> To the treasury of the state bring your strength,
> Take your share of its possessions, its bounty.
> Be a man abroad and a Jew in your tent,
> A brother to your countrymen and a servant to your king.[31]

The *maskilim* viewed the state as a "benevolent father," an agent that could bring about the regeneration of the Jews. Since they considered the state—and, indeed, only the state—to have the ability to redeem the Jews, they addressed petitions to the bureaucracy for enactments favoring enlightenment and civil rights. These petitions were fundamentally different in character from the attempts by medieval Jewish politicians to intercede with the government; the *maskilim* saw the state not as a potential agent of protection, but as a messianic redeemer, an ally in the battle for enlightenment.

It was not only radical reformers and *maskilim* who were enthusiasts for the modern state. Similar attitudes can be found among the Orthodox, and, in fact, it remains true today that Orthodox Jews in general display great patriotic allegiance to the states in which they live, with the ironic exception of the anti-Zionist Neturei Karta group in modern Israel. Although the Orthodox rejected the new interpretation of *dina de-malkhuta dina*, they made their peace with the law of the state wherever possible.

In the eighteenth century, an Orthodox rabbi named David ben Nathan of Lissa wrote a sermon attacking Wessely, who had connected Joseph II's Edict of Tolerance with his own program for enlightenment. Ben Nathan argued that the edict was not designed to undermine traditional Judaism, as was Wessely's program. The emperor's intentions were pure, while Wessely's were antithetical to all the principles of Judaism. For this Orthodox thinker, the state was really on the side of the traditional faithful, despite the attempts by the heretical *maskilim* to distort its goals.[32]

In the nineteenth century, the founder of German neo-Orthodoxy, Samson Raphael Hirsch, developed a complete theory of the identification of the Jews with the state. Hirsch wanted the Jews to become full citizens of the non-Jewish state, and he argued that the obligations of citizenship need not contradict Orthodox practice. Unlike the Reformers, he believed that the Messiah would ultimately restore the Jews to national sovereignty, but he also held that the national

dimension of Judaism could be realized before the coming of
the Messiah in the modern states of Europe. Judaism required a political framework—but not necessarily a political
framework of its own. He therefore attempted to preserve the
political dimension of Orthodox Judaism by divorcing it from
its medieval political context and wedding it to the modern
state.[33]

Ironically, the Orthodox, like their opponents, learned to
make use of modern political processes to fight for their positions. Many nineteenth-century Orthodox German Jews
feared that full emancipation or equal citizenship would undermine both the Jewish community and the Jewish religion.
They consequently voted in large numbers for the more conservative German parties, who were less sympathetic to Jewish emancipation than were the liberals. For these Orthodox
Jews, such an "unholy alliance" with anti-Jewish forces was
preferable to the dubious benefits of emancipation and
assimilation.

Not all the *maskilim* accepted the state as it was. As the
struggle for emancipation dragged on in the states of Central
and Eastern Europe, many of the followers of the Haskalah
realized that only reform of the state itself could lead to full
political and social integration for the Jews. The Hegelian
philosopher Samuel Hirsch proposed a strange vision of a
"Christian state" as the answer to the problem of emancipation.[34] According to Hirsch, Christianity had become
contaminated with the idea that the state must be subordinated to the Church. True Christianity was really much closer
to the ethical ideas of Judaism, for which the state constituted the highest ideal. Once Christianity returned to its
"Jewish" origins, he suggested, it would be ready to emancipate the Jews. Here, then, is a peculiar utopian vision of the
state. Even though Hirsch did not mean the existing state, the
state remains the pinnacle of society. By arguing that adher-
ence to the state was the essence of Judaism, Hirsch turned
Hegel, for whom the state was the true expression of freedom,
into a crypto-Jew! Hirsch's notion that only a revolutionary

transformation of the state would make possible Jewish emancipation resembles the argument of another Jewish disciple of Hegel—Karl Marx.

Perhaps the only dissent to this celebration of the state—whether existing or utopian—can be found in the writings of the iconoclastic German Jewish philosopher Solomon Ludwig Steinheim.[35] Steinheim saw the state in general as a pagan institution whose essence is tyranny and repression. He argued that Judaism's political ideal is theocracy, by which he meant something like Kropotkin's anarchism: a society without formal political institutions which would be governed by "natural" associations on a small scale (families, tribes, and so forth). But such an anarchistic theory remained a total anomaly in nineteenth-century Jewish thought and, as an exception to the rule, it only highlights the centrality of the state in all the other writers.

The Haskalah and Jewish Self-Government

Hand in hand with their veneration of the state, the *maskilim*, like other European Enlightenment writers, attacked the political institutions of the Middle Ages. As their conflict with the rabbinical establishment grew sharper, they increasingly saw rabbinical authority as symbolic of the degradation of the Middle Ages. An implicit alliance was struck between the *maskilim* and the absolutist regimes since each, for their own reasons, could not countenance a continuation of Jewish judicial autonomy.

Spinoza linked his celebration of the secular state with an attack on the involvement of religious authorities in politics. Later *maskilim* followed the same course. Moses Mendelssohn, the founder of the German Haskalah, argued against any religion having the power to discipline its members by excommunication or other means; only the secular authority should possess the right of coercion, and then not in matters pertaining to opinion and conscience. Mendelssohn developed this argument in the form of a political theory of the separation of church and state. Significantly, he portrayed Judaism—as opposed to Christianity—as a religion without coercion. Judaism, a revealed legislation, did not seek to impose dogmatic beliefs on its adherents or to coerce them in their observance. The laws were meant as pedagogical tools, a notion that Mendelssohn took from Maimonides but devoid of the coercive power that Maimonides certainly advocated.[36]

Mendelssohn evidently considered the practice of excommunication and the judicial authority of rabbis in the Middle Ages to have been an aberration, a distortion of the true essence of Judaism. In claiming that "true Judaism" was fundamentally different from the way it was actually practiced in medieval times, Mendelssohn paved the way for the claims of Reform Judaism in the next century. But where the opponents of the Jews (and not a few of their defenders as well) saw Jews as backward and medieval, Mendelssohn claimed that authentic Judaism was more modern than Christianity. Only Judaism, he argued, anticipated the ideal modern society in which religion and state would be separated.

Mendelssohn's rejection of rabbinical judicial authority opened a Pandora's box of questions. Saul Ascher, although a disciple of Mendelssohn's and one of the founders of Reform Judaism in Germany, pointed out that Mendelssohn's ambiguous definition of the halakhah (Jewish law) as "revealed legislation" could not stand up under scrutiny and that the logical conclusion from Mendelssohn's own premises was a total rejection of Jewish law.[37] Mendelssohn, said Ascher, could not reject the coercive power of the rabbis without undermining the whole legal structure that they represented and that in fact gave them the authority to coerce. Law without power is meaningless; therefore, the rejection of rabbinic power would necessarily lead to the rejection of the law. Here was the kernel of Reform Judaism, a movement born of the historical circumstances that stripped the rabbis of their authority.[38]

Willingness to relinquish communal power and hostility

to the rabbis became the hallmarks of much of subsequent Haskalah ideology. This explains the enthusiasm of the Russian *maskilim* for the government's various schemes to educate and appoint officially sanctioned rabbis.[39] As peculiar as it may seem in the light of Czar Nicholas I's policies toward the Jews, the *maskilim* believed that if the rabbis were government officials, they would help to pave the way for enlightenment. Presumably, these rabbis would have nothing in common with traditional rabbis, except for their titles: they would instead be enlightened communal leaders who would replace the old leadership under the aegis of the government.

The attack on the rabbis went hand in hand with an attack on the medieval political system that had denied the Jews equal rights. David Friedlaender, another of Mendelssohn's disciples, saw the lack of civil emancipation and the power of the rabbis as simultaneous roadblocks to enlightenment. The only solution was a political revolution in both the gentile and Jewish worlds,

> to throw off the heavy yoke under which the king and the judges of this country [Prussia], who are not of our people, have harnessed us; to throw off, furthermore, that other yoke which we have taken upon us with the rule of our own rabbis and communal leaders. Only if we are free, neither afraid of the ruling party nor intimidated in our enlightenment by the threat of excommunication and the refusal of burial rites, will it be possible to raise Israel's prestige, our Torah and the teachings of Moses from the dust.[40]

A thorough reinterpretation of the whole social contract between the Jews and gentile society lay behind this manifesto. Throughout the Middle Ages, the Jews had accepted a dependent, though not necessarily inferior, status in exchange for communal autonomy. By the eighteenth century, whatever advantages such a position might have had had long disappeared and it was now an anachronism in the modern absolutist state. From the point of view of a *maskil* like

Friedlaender, the Jews gained nothing by giving up the rights of citizenship in exchange for communal power. The political theory of the Haskalah, articulated here by Friedlaender, called for a renunciation of both sides of this bargain and the fashioning of a new social compact: Jews as individuals would be admitted to society and would, at the same time, be liberated from the bonds of their own coreligionists.

This new political theory thus envisioned a transfer of power from the community or corporation to the individual: the very power that had been invested in the communal structure was now to be returned to the individual Jew so he could reinvest it in the secular state. Whereas the Jews had possessed a certain status, they would now possess the power of individual citizens. Or, in the words of Count Stanislas de Clermont-Tonnerre in the debate on the emancipation of the Jews in the French National Assembly in 1789: "The Jews should be denied everything as a nation, but granted everything as individuals."[41]

Haskalah and History

Moses Mendelssohn created a fictitious picture of historical Judaism in suggesting that, if the rabbis had wielded political power in the Middle Ages, they did so in opposition to the true apolitical essence of Judaism. While Jewish thinkers in the Middle Ages defined exile to mean national impotence, they never considered Judaism to be apolitical, nor did they shrink from using the actual power they did possess. The Haskalah reading of Jewish history produced a new myth: that of Jewish powerlessness in the Middle Ages. This myth was a consequence of the political struggles in which the *maskilim* engaged. The Jews faced a new accusation as they fought for emancipation: the charge that they were a "state within the state." In the Middle Ages, they did indeed constitute such a political entity, but not because they were unique. Only in the modern period, when the state laid claim to political sovereignty, did Jewish political autonomy become a problem. The effort of the *maskilim* to claim that the Jews were neither a nation nor political was part of their effort to persuade the world that Jews would accept the conditions of citizenship.

The beginnings of this new interpretation of Jewish political history, like the new veneration of the state, can be found earlier, in the works of Jewish writers from the Renaissance. Starting with Solomon Ibn Verga, a number of authors wrote the first histories of the Jews that departed from theological explanations of the exile and attempted to see the Jewish condition in political terms. In his *Shevet Yehudah*, Ibn Verga criticizes the Jews for fanning Christian hatred by competing too ostentatiously with the Christians, a sign of Jewish political incompetence. Then he goes on to argue that the Jews find themselves in exile because they relied on God to defend them and "they did not therefore learn the art of war since they did not need it . . . and when they sinned, God hid His face from them. . . . They were not familiar with the instruments of war and God was not with them, so they were left utterly naked, falling like sheep without a shepherd."[42] Here is the opposite of a theology of exile: by relying upon God, the Jews failed to attend to the affairs of this world and therefore were incapable of defending themselves. For Ibn Verga, the Jews—not God or the Gentiles—carried the primary responsibility for their political catastrophes. With this argument, Ibn Verga may have been first to accuse the Jews of deliberately choosing a stance of powerlessness in the Middle Ages.

Perhaps the most radical new interpretation of Jewish history was that of Spinoza. His *Theologico-Political Treatise* is constructed around a devastating critique of the Bible as a source of philosophical truth. Spinoza read the Bible not as a book of timeless truths but as a historical source relevant only to the period of the ancient Hebrews. He attacked all the beliefs of the Jews in their own chosenness, revelation, prophecy, and miracles. From a historical point of view, the chosenness of the Jews lay not in a special relationship to God nor in some philosophical understanding, but in the political talents necessary to build a state. This state was a theocracy (Spinoza had in mind the period before the creation of the monarchy by Samuel). Although Spinoza certainly did not consider theocracy a model for his own time and although he demonstrated how its intrinsic flaws led to its eventual demise, he still admired the ability of the Hebrews to construct a long-lasting state. Moreover, the identity of state and religion in this ancient theocracy was much healthier than the medieval situation in which religion competed with the state for authority. Despite Spinoza's hostility toward the Jewish religion, he clearly considered the biblical Hebrew state to be an extraordinary achievement. The essence of Judaism is political, he suggested; therefore, after they lost their state, the Jews had no further basis for existence. The Judaism of the Middle Ages—including the power of the rabbis—was a thorough distortion of biblical Judaism and a travesty of history. But since the essence of the Jews is their political talent—which could only find expression in the sovereign state—Spinoza believed that they might once again justify their existence by founding a new Jewish state.[43]

Spinoza's interpretation of Jewish history was thoroughly political, but due to his narrow identification of politics with the state, he could not find anything of value in Diaspora Jewish history. Lack of a state meant utter powerlessness and therefore, given the essence of Judaism, historical redundancy. Perhaps David Ben Gurion was right in his contention that, had Spinoza lived in the twentieth century, he would have been a Zionist. But in the absence of a renewed Jewish state, the only alternative Spinoza saw for anyone who did not wish to remain a historical fossil was to join those peoples that did possess a state.

Many of the later *maskilim* agreed with Spinoza about the powerlessness of the Diaspora Jews, but they presented it as a sign of virtue. Some went much further than Spinoza by rejecting any political understanding of Judaism. Immanuel Wolf, one of the founders of the Wissenschaft des Judentums

(Science of Judaism), the nineteenth-century movement to study Jewish history scientifically, argued that the essence of Judaism is not political but spiritual, namely, the idea of monotheism. Wolf suggested that the very spirituality of the Jews demonstrated their high level of culture, which made them prime candidates for integration into modern German society. The persecutions of the Middle Ages had suppressed their spiritual culture, but it was in the process of renewal as a result of enlightenment.[44]

Isaac Marcus Jost, who in the nineteenth century wrote the first general history of the Jews, opened his work with the question: "Can there be a history of slaves?" He concluded that there could not, unless one construed their history as other than political and social. Since, according to Jost, the "true fatherland" of the Jews was God and religion, a history of the Diaspora was possible, but a history whose subject was, once again, pure spirituality.[45] Similarly, Abraham Geiger, the leading proponent of Reform Judaism in Germany, argued that Judaism survived precisely because it did not require a political framework. Geiger also claimed forcefully that the Pharisees or rabbis of Second Temple times were apolitical antinationalists, i.e., good models for nineteenth-century Reform Jews.[46] It was from arguments such as these, rooted in nineteenth-century needs, that the myth of the apolitical rabbis originated.

Heinrich Graetz, perhaps the greatest of the nineteenth-century Jewish historians, modified the antipolitical interpretation of the earlier Wissenschaft des Judentums. He proposed, in effect, a synthesis between Spinoza and his later critics: the essence of Judaism was both political and religious. Each period of Jewish history realized a different dimension of its essence. The First Temple period was the age of politics, the Second Temple period the age of religion, and the Middle Ages the age of speculation in which Judaism reached its highest expression: self-conscious reflection on itself. As history progressed, Judaism gradually shed its political dimensions and became essentially spiritual. In the introduction to volume 5 of his *History of the Jews,* he wrote: "History still has not produced another case of a nation which has laid aside its weapons of war to devote itself entirely to the peaceful pursuits of study and poetry, which has freed itself from self-interest and let its thoughts soar to fathom its own nature."[47]

Graetz may have celebrated the spirituality of the Middle Ages, but he did not accept it as the end of Jewish history; in his vision of a messianic Jewish state that would combine both the political and spiritual dimensions of Jewish history, he may have anticipated later religious Zionism. Despite his reluctance to give up the national component of Judaism, Graetz in the main accepted the fundamental assumption that Judaism had lost touch with political power when it lost its state: the Jews became a spiritual people in medieval times, giving up political "self-interest" in favor of intellectual and religious achievements.

For the Haskalah writers, the primary symptom of the lack of Jewish politics in the Middle Ages was physical persecution. Just as the European Enlightenment viewed the medieval period as an unrelieved "dark age," so the *maskilim* saw for the Jews only a dark landscape of massacres and persecutions, broken by occasional rays of spiritual light. This view of medieval Jewish history as a time of *Leiden und Lernen* ("suffering and learning") Salo Baron termed the "lachrymose" theory of Jewish history, a theory that found achievements in this period only on the intellectual plane and considered the political and social realms a disaster.[48]

The concept of historical powerlessness evolved by modern Jewish thinkers was a logical consequence of their ideology of emancipation because it corresponded neatly to the exigencies of the absolutist regimes under which they lived. In order to win allies in the non-Jewish world and create a constituency for their leadership among the Jews, the *maskilim* developed an ideology that rejected and even denied the forms of medieval Jewish power. The power that the rabbis exercised, they claimed, was based on an illegitimate interpretation of the "essence" of Judaism and was not part of the intrinsic nature of the religion. They proposed a new social compact between the Jews and their societies in which the old leadership would be stripped of its authority and Jews as individuals would gain access to the state, at whose door they clamored for admission.

V

Between Haskalah and Holocaust

IN the short period between the end of the nineteenth century and World War II, a new Jewish political life emerged. For a brief moment in Jewish history, between the Haskalah and the Holocaust, a host of political parties and movements competed for the support of the millions of European Jews, especially in Eastern Europe. In the smallest Jewish communities, political parties, youth movements, newspapers, and clubs flourished. Zionists, Bundists, liberals, assimiliationists, religious revivalists, and socialist revolutionaries of all stripes and colors vied with each other for followers. This quest for power was rooted in an increasing sense of the impotence and impoverishment of the European Jews. No one could afford to remain indifferent. Whether a solution to the problems of the Jews lay in Jewish nationalism or in a cosmopolitan revolution was far from an academic question. If Jewish nationalism was the answer, should such a solution take place in Palestine, Europe, or elsewhere? If revolution was the goal, what model of revolution should be followed and how might it include the Jews?[1]

Between the years 1917–19, the four major Jewish ideologies of this period,—Zionism, socialism, liberalism, and territorialism—seemed coincidentally to achieve the first stages of success. In November 1917, the Zionist movement won its long-sought charter when Great Britain, in the process of conquering Palestine, issued the Balfour Declaration. Earlier that same year, the Russian Revolution had overthrown the yoke of czarism, under which the largest mass of Jews still lived. For many, revolution held the only promise for a solution to the continuing inequality and persecution of the Jews in Russia. As a result, all of the parties that supported the February Revolution, from the Cadets to the Bolsheviks, had a disproportionately large number of Jewish members. For those committed to a socialist solution to what was called the Jewish question, the seizure of power by the Bolsheviks in November 1917 seemed to herald a messianic era. On the other hand, the creation of the Weimar Republic in Germany at the end of World War I seemed to signify the triumph of liberalism, for only in Weimar did the long struggle for the social as well as political emancipation of the Jews in Germany achieve fulfillment. And, finally, the Versailles peace conference established the principle of the national rights of minorities in the new states of Eastern Europe, a development with potentially far-reaching consequences for the large Jewish populations, especially in the reconstituted Polish Republic. This seemed to be the realization of the program of the socialist Bundists and other "territorialists," who fought for Jewish political and cultural autonomy in multiethnic Eastern Europe.

Within the next few decades, however, three of these four ideologies suffered their death blows in Europe: socialism as a result of Stalin's purges, liberalism in Weimar Germany with the rise of the Nazis, and territorialism with the emergence of fascist regimes in Eastern Europe—and, finally all three with the Holocaust. All the "European" solutions of the Jewish question became victims of the Nazis since, after the Holocaust, there were no longer significant numbers of Jews in Europe whose "question" needed to be solved. With the demise of these "European" solutions, only "extra-European" ones remained for world Jewry: Zionism and American pluralism, two alternatives that rose on the agenda during this fateful period.

The New Jewish Nation

The new political movements were the result of fundamental changes in Jewish life in the second half of the nineteenth century, particularly in Eastern Europe. A tremendous population explosion took place primarily in that region, and to a lesser degree in Central Europe. For reasons that are still unclear, European Jews multiplied at a rate faster than their non-Jewish neighbors, increasing from 2.75 million in 1825 to over 8.5 million in 1900. Together with this population explosion came an enormous movement of Jews into cities. The Jews had been an urban people since late antiquity. In Eastern Europe, they were always a large proportion of the population of private, noble towns. In the nineteenth century, as the European countries began to urbanize in the modern sense, Jews moved into large cities at a far higher rate than non-Jews. The population of Berlin increased twelve times in the course of the nineteenth century, but the Jewish population of Berlin increased twenty-seven times. In the Russian Empire, the process of dispersing into tiny villages, which had occurred in the eighteenth century, was substantially reversed in the nineteenth. The small towns or *shtetlach* could no longer support the population, and tens of thousands of Jews migrated to the cities or the new territories.[2] Jews rose from 25 percent of the population of Warsaw in 1860 to 33 percent only a decade later. In city after city in western Russia, they became either a near or a clear majority.

With the population explosion and urbanization came rapid impoverishment, as the traditional Jewish occupations of small-scale commerce and independent artisanry became either unprofitable or impossible. Within the brief period of one or two generations, many Jews by the end of the nineteenth century had become industrial workers, although typically in small shops owned by other Jews who were often almost impoverished themselves. At the same time, partly as a result of pressures and incentives from the Russian Government, a small group of Jews turned to farming. The "productivization" of the Jews, which the *maskilim* had advocated, began to take place in Russia, although not necessarily along the ideological lines envisioned by the intellectuals.

As a result of these changes, the Jews were no longer a tiny minority scattered in a sea of Gentiles: in areas of the Ukraine, Poland, and White Russia, they began to feel like a nation. Of course, the Jews had always seen themselves as a nation in exile as well as a religion, but they had not been a nation in any concrete sense since late antiquity. Not only did they lack territory and a common language, but, with the exception of Spain before the expulsion and Poland before 1648, they were a tiny population in both absolute and relative terms. Some of the great communities of the Rhineland during the time of the Crusades, for instance, numbered only several dozen families. By the end of the nineteenth century, the Pale of Settlement had become the home of an enormous Jewish population with a social and economic structure increasingly resembling that of a modern nation. While some of the earlier *maskilim* may have been able to abandon the idea that the Jewish people constituted a nation, the new politics had no choice but to accept it, since the Jews had become a nation in reality and not only in memory. All of the Jewish political movements of the end of the nineteenth century, including "antinationalists" such as the socialist revolutionaries, had to grapple with the fact that Jews were a nation as a result of demographic and social realities.

Jewish culture in the second half of the nineteenth century reflected the emergence of a modern Jewish nation. Yiddish became a literary as well as a spoken language. Not only did the Yiddish renaissance include great authors such as Mendele Mocher Sforim, Y. L. Peretz, and Sholom Aleichem, but it also prompted the creation of a "lowbrow" popular literature, perhaps as important a sign of a national culture as "high literature." Hebrew remained the preferred language of the literati, but the explosion of Yiddish culture signified a popular movement. The journals and newspapers created by the *maskilim* were no longer read only by intellectuals; they became the fare of the masses of Jews. In the midst of a still religiously traditional society, an extraordinarily vital secular culture began to grow.[3]

Not only the Jews now regarded themselves in national terms: the anti-Semites of the late nineteenth century began to view the "Jewish problem" in much the same way—as a national or racial concern rather than a religious conflict. As European nationalists began to define themselves around racial or ethnic categories, they saw the Jews as a foreign virus in the body politic. The wave of anti-Semitism that swept both Western and Eastern Europe in the 1880s and 1890s was organized for the first time in political parties and was a product of this new nationalist hostility to the Jews.[4]

The rise of a new form of anti-Jewish feeling was a symptom of the growing crisis regarding Jewish emancipation in Europe. In Russia, the liberal reforms of Czar Alexander II failed to lead to civil emancipation of the Jews. When Alexander was assassinated in 1881, the new czar, Alexander III, took the throne to the echoes of the first anti-Jewish pogroms in over a century. Alexander III's government enacted a series of measures sharply curtailing Jewish participation in Russian society. The government of his successor, Nicholas II (1894–1917), presided over an even more bloody series of pogroms in the first years of the twentieth century. Instead of moving toward emancipation, Czarist Russia seemed to be heading in a more and more reactionary direction.

In Germany, the emancipation of the Jews of Prussia in 1812 and those in some of the other German states occupied by Napoleon marked a false dawn, for in the wake of the Congress of Vienna, (1814–15), emancipation was either withdrawn or drastically limited. It was not until 1871, when Bismarck created a unified Germany, that the Jews were finally emancipated, but even then certain restrictions remained. The great depression of the 1870s created fertile soil for the growth of the new racial and political anti-Semitism that erupted in the 1880s. Instead of emancipation producing acceptance of the Jews, it seemed to exacerbate old tensions and create new forms of hatred.

Even in France, which had emancipated the Jews during the French Revolution, the new disease of anti-Semitism struck. It infected the political system in the 1880s and 1890s, first in the Panama Canal scandal and then in the Dreyfus Affair. If the land of equality, liberty, and fraternity could succumb to anti-Semitism, then emancipation elsewhere seemed a dubious prospect.

The new anti-Semitism, together with the mushrooming number of impoverished Jews, provided the impetus for the greatest migration of Jewish history: from Russia and Eastern Europe to Western Europe and, most significantly, from Europe as a whole to other continents.[5] It now became increasingly apparent that the long European age of Jewish history was coming to an end. The task for Jewish politics was no longer to remake society so that it would tolerate all religions, as it had been for the Haskalah. It was now necessary either to remake society or remake the world so that it could swallow and digest all national groups. For that reason, the solutions proposed were more radical than they had been in the past, and the movements more revolutionary. If European society could not be transformed, the problems of the Jews would have to be solved outside of Europe. Through emmigration, more and more Jews were voting for this solution with their feet.

New Political Tactics

Jews began to perceive themselves as a national body dispersed over many countries as opposed to a discrete corporation in each country, and they began to act more internationally than they ever had in the past. In earlier periods, they had always had a sense of national identity across political borders. This consciousness certainly played an important role in seventeenth-century Sabbatianism, which found adherents throughout the Jewish world. Yet this sense of Jewish solidarity largely disappeared with the movements of emancipation and enlightenment, as Jews increasingly identified with the nations in which they lived: the concepts of "German Jews," "French Jews," and "Russian Jews" were modern inventions. With the rise of anti-Semitism, the old sense of identification with Jews elsewhere reasserted itself. What was new in the nineteenth century was that, probably for the first time since antiquity, Jews acted to defend the rights of Jews in other countries.

The first international political action based on national solidarity was in response to the Damascus Blood Libel of 1840 (see p. 97). Perhaps as a result of the involvement of the European powers in the affair, the Damascus Blood Libel attracted Jewish attention throughout Europe, and Jewish notables intervened to free the Damascus Jews. During the following decade, a number of Western Jews, including the English philanthropist Moses Montefiore, tried to intercede on behalf of the Jews in Russia, thus establishing a tradition that continues to this day. In 1858, a celebrated case in which an Italian Jewish boy named Edgardo Mortara was secretly baptized and abducted by the Catholic Church attracted a similar political response. As a result of these episodes, the first international Jewish organization, the Alliance Israélite Universelle, was formed in France in 1860 for the purpose of Jewish self-defense and self-improvement around the world. The Alliance played a particularly important role in creating awareness of the Oriental Jewish communities and in promoting settlement in the Land of Israel long before the Zionist movement.[6]

In individual countries as well, Jews organized politically to defend their interests. In America, England, France, and Germany where integration was at least possible, Jewish political parties as such did not emerge, but self-defense organizations were created. The Centralverein was founded in Germany in 1893 in the wake of the new political anti-Semitism. Representing the liberal mainstream of German Jewry, the Centralverein undertook an active political struggle to defend the Jews against the outbreak. Far from passively accepting their fate in fin-de-siècle Germany, Jews quickly grasped the necessity of operating within the German political system to assert their interests.[7] In America, the American Jewish Committee and the American Jewish Congress were created in 1906 and 1916 respectively, at first to protect the rights of foreign Jews, but later to defend the interests of American Jews as well.[8]

It was in the Russian Empire, starting largely in the 1890s, that the Jews achieved the most impressive level of political and economic activism. The Jewish socialist labor movement called the Bund borrowed tactics of mass political mobilization from other European movements, and in the first decade of the twentieth century it instigated more strikes than any other labor union in Europe. Between 1903 and the 1905 revolution, the Bund and other political groups organized Jewish self-defense groups that actively opposed the Black Hundreds and the Cossacks. The strength of the Bund is revealed in this excerpt from a memorandum written by a czarist official in 1903:

> The Jewish political organization, the Bund, acts with enormous energy, is rapidly strengthening its ranks and having created . . . a fighting detachment has become almost omnipotent. Proclamations . . . are distributed in thousands of copies; workers' strikes . . . are organized. . . . Strikes, street demonstrations in which red flags are hoisted, demonstrations in theaters, resistance to authorities occur primarily in . . . Vilna, Grodno, Kovno, Belostok, Brest, Smorgon Krynki, and others.[9]

This obviously hyperbolic view of Jewish power contrasts strikingly with the passivity frequently associated with the East European Jews, but even if exaggerated, the mere existence of an image of Jewish power was significant in a time of persecution. If the image of passivity is unconvincing for the Middle Ages, it is equally false for the period of pogroms at the beginning of the twentieth century. This tradition of resistance continued later, in the 1930s, when Polish Jews again faced anti-Semitic attacks which Bundists, Zionists, and others met with a variety of tactics including armed self-defense.[10]

The emergence of Jewish political parties in many states of Eastern Europe was characteristic of the new politics. Following World War I, the Jews entered the political life of the new states and demanded their rights as a national minority. In Czechoslovakia, they created their own party, which won 104,539 votes in the election of 1929 and waged a vigorous fight against anti-Semitism. Jewish politics also developed in Rumania, Lithuania, and Latvia.[11] The greatest political activity was in interwar Poland, where a host of Jewish parties competed for power within the Jewish community and also ran their own slates for the Polish parliament.[12] The parties represented various types of Zionists, from bourgeois to socialist; the Bund; and religious groups, including the religious Zionist (Mizrachi) and the ultra-Orthodox Agudat Israel. In a shrewd bid to enhance the power of ethnic minorities in Poland, the Zionists organized alliances with other national minorities to win parliamentary elections. In the face of increasing anti-Semitism, Jewish political activity reached a high-water mark.

The emergence of religious political parties was perhaps the most unusual element of the Jewish political renaissance in interwar Poland. Some religious Jews had become active in the Zionist movement as early as the 1880s. Soon, a non-Zionist religious party was organized as well. In 1914, Orthodox Jews formed the Agudat Israel in reaction to the increasing success of Zionism. In Poland, the Agudah became an Orthodox political party devoted to defending the interests of traditional Judaism within the Jewish communities and in Polish national politics. In pursuit of its own interests, it did not always join with the other Jewish parties in presenting a united front in Polish politics. The very existence of the Agudat Israel symbolized dramatically the shift in power within the Jewish world. No longer did the religious constitute an "establishment" leadership; they were now but one faction among many, and not necessarily the most powerful. To the degree that the Orthodox understood this shift in power and organized to combat it, they implicitly accepted the premise of modern politics. Claiming to represent a "traditional" way of life, the religious parties in fact acted in a thoroughly modern fashion.[13]

New Leaders

The emergence of Orthodox political parties was a symptom of the fear of the traditional leadership, already in decline as a result of absolutist policies, confronted with new forces in the Jewish community. Industrialization and the movement of Jews to cities and new territories accelerated the erosion of traditional authority. In the cities of Russia, and in Central and Western Europe as well, new elites, many of whom had achieved success through professions outside the Jewish community, made claims to leadership. Theodor Herzl and Vladimir Jabotinsky were journalists, Chaim Weizmann a scientist, David Ben Gurion a student intellectual. The ascendancy of Theodor Herzl from assimilated circumstances to an almost messianic status was only possible as a result of the decline of the traditional leadership and the opening up of new avenues to power.

The student intelligentsia in Russia, which acquired its political education at Russian gymnasia and universities, is another example of the rise of new leaders. These Jewish revolutionaries frequently started their careers with no intention of returning to the Jewish people. The pogroms of 1881 shocked many students into identification with their people and, in moving pronouncements, they declared their desire to devote themselves to aiding the victims.[14] Some of these students organized the first group of pioneers to Palestine. In the

first decades of the twentieth century, those who founded the
political institutions in Palestine that later became the State
of Israel largely came from the ranks of the Russian student
intellectuals. Many of those who chose not to leave Russia
also found their way back to the Jewish people. Young Jewish
revolutionaries who were sentenced to exile in cities of the
Pale, which had a large Jewish working class, could continue
their political work only among Jews. Some of these activists,
such as J. Martov, who was later to lead the Menshevik Party,
formed the the Jewish Workers Bund in 1897.[15]

The Haskalah had made only modest inroads at provid-
ing a substitute leadership for the rabbis; both circumstances
and its predominantly intellectual direction limited its appeal. The new political movements enjoyed much greater success. By the beginning of the twentieth century, the Bund,
perhaps the best example of a Jewish mass movement, was
able to mobilize enormous groups of Jews for economic and
political action. The leadership that such a movement provided began to displace traditional authorities, as is revealed
in this colorful account of the street meetings that Bund or-
ganizers held in Lodz in May 1905:

> People used to come for every different reason: questions of
> divorce; a dowry; business partners who had fallen out; a
> speculator who himself had been outwitted; a young woman
> who had been deceived; a quarrel in the family; maids with
> complaints against the ladies of the house—all used to come
> and one could hardly escape them by telling them that they
> should rather go to a rabbi.[16]

By 1905, many looked to the Bund, and not to the rabbis, for
communal leadership.

The behavior of these new politicians was quite different
from those of the past. It is easy to mistake Herzl and Weizmann, at first glance, for modern incarnations of the medieval *shtadlan* or the early-modern court Jew. Both sought
favors in the corridors of European capitals; Weizmann in
particular was accused by his enemies of acting like a court

Jew who had won influence as a result of his scientific work but was reluctant to forcefully confront his British patrons.[17] Despite superficial similarities to earlier leaders, these men were different. They claimed to represent a Jewish national entity that encompassed all Jews, a state-in-the-making. They demanded not privileges for the Jews, but rights—the same rights that all peoples intrinsically deserved. If Jewish politics in earlier times were based upon the assumption that the Jews were essentially different from all other peoples and that the privileges they enjoyed were a result of this difference, the new Jewish politics assumed that the Jews were a legitimate and equal nation in an international polity.

Politicians such as Herzl and Weizmann tried to show that the Jews should be taken into account in the balance of world power. Herzl argued that a Jewish state was in the interests of the European nations and even in the interests of the anti-Semites. Throughout the Middle Ages, of course, Jews had secured their positions by showing how they might serve the interests of the monarchs. Now it was argued that the Jews constituted a factor in international politics, that they might play a role in international conflicts. For instance, Weizmann cited the importance of winning Jewish allegiance to Britain during World War I as a compelling reason for the British to issue the Balfour Declaration.[18] Even before they had a sovereign state, Zionist statesmen such as Weizmann acted as if the Jews were to be taken seriously as a political people. While such arguments were not always effective, they symbolized a new type of politics based on equality rather than privilege.

The new politics relied upon the perception of the existence of an international public opinion, to which one might appeal on behalf of the Jews. The first instance of such an appeal was during the Damascus Blood Libel in 1840. Later, protests in the West against the pogroms in Russia also attempted to affect czarist policy by influencing public opinion. Such an entity as public opinion had not existed in earlier periods of history, and it is a sign of the ability of the new

Jewish leaders to adapt to modern conditions that they understood how to address it, even though they did not always succeed in swaying it.

Public opinion meant that politics had to be carried out in public. It was here that Theodor Herzl was a real pioneer. By using dramatic techniques in organizing Zionist meetings and by exploiting the anti-Semitically inspired rumors of immense Jewish power, he was able to create the illusion that he was the leader of a state-in-the-making, rather than an eccentric with a fringe band of followers.[19] In this respect, he resembled David Ha-Reuveni from the sixteenth century, but Herzl succeeded where Ha-Reuveni had failed precisely because, in the modern era of public politics, the illusion of power could more easily become the basis of real power.

Beyond the differences in ideology between Zionists, socialists, and other political movements, these tactics and assumptions gave the new Jewish politics a common character. While in the Middle Ages power was achieved or manipulated through influence and status, power in the modern world increasingly relied on mass mobilization. In the Middle Ages, the Jews had access to power in proportion to their status in society. The loss of that status during the age of absolutism meant the loss of power, but it also created the conditions for the new politics based on mass mobilization and organization. The relative powerlessness of the nineteenth century and the decline of the traditional Jewish leadership were the precondition for the quest for power at the beginning of the twentieth.

The Ideology of Normalization

Like the eighteenth- and early nineteenth-century *maskilim*, the leaders of the new Jewish movements of the twentieth century were predominantly intellectuals. For these intellectuals, action was to be shaped and guided by ideas: whether nationalists or socialists, they all believed that power came less from the barrel of a gun than from the pen of the polemicist or the mouth of the orator. This was the age of ideologies, often borrowed from other European sources but applied to the new Jewish reality. In their own day, these movements argued bitterly about what divided them; in retrospect, they had much more in common than they were prepared to admit.

The new political ideologies in many ways came out of the Haskalah. Many of the social reforms that the *maskilim* advocated, such as "productivizing" the Jewish people, became the stock-in-trade of Zionists and socialists. At an even more fundamental level, the new movements shared with the Haskalah a basic perception of exile. For the *maskilim*, Jewish life in the Middle Ages was "abnormal" and needed to be "normalized" to conform with the life of European society. The use of this particular jargon implied certain standards against which one measured normality. Medieval Jews also regarded exile as an abnormal condition, but their standard of normality was messianic: only when the Messiah reestablished the Kingdom of David, rebuilt the Temple, gathered in all the exiles, and performed a variety of other miracles would Jewish life return to its biblical "norm." The *maskilim*, on the other hand, believed that the Jews might "negate the exile" (to use the later Zionist term) by finding a home in their European nations: European nationalism became the standard for normality. In place of the heterogeneity of medieval society, the *maskilim*, borrowing from other modern European nationalists, wanted a homogeneous society in which the Jews would be distinguished only by their religion, sharing the political and cultural identity of their neighbors. This concept of normalization contradicted the old theology of the divine election of the Jews, for it presupposed that Jews and non-Jews had something essential in common: the modern state.

The political movements of the end of the nineteenth century all adopted these notions of "normalizing the Jews" and "negating the exile" from the Haskalah. They, too, implicitly rejected the theology of divine election and saw the Jews as

one national group among many, with the same national as-
pirations as all other nations. In place of the belief in Jewish
uniqueness, they wanted to make the Jews "like all the other
nations" (ke-khol ha-goyim).

As a result of the wave of anti-Semitism that swept Europe from the 1870s to the 1890s, many of these new leaders
rejected their own societies as the standard of normality.
Jewish liberals, nationalists, and revolutionaries, who differed on everything else, all agreed that the societies of Europe in their contemporary form were inhospitable to Jews.
Only by changing society in some way or by changing the
Jews' relationship to it could the problems of the Jews of
Europe be solved. The Zionists proposed to take the Jews out
of Europe and create a new society; the territorialists suggested reordering European societies so that the Jews might
have full political and cultural autonomy, reminiscent of the
Middle Ages but on a nonreligious basis; the socialists and
liberals proposed their own versions of reordered societies.
"Normality" now signified social experiments, utopian ideals
that had never existed.

The political biography of Theodor Herzl is a striking
example of the way the concept of normalization might be
transformed into a revolutionary theory.[20] Before discovering
Jewish nationalism as a solution to the Jewish question,
Herzl proposed leading the Jews in a ceremony of mass conversion to Christianity. When he became a convert to Jewish
nationalism, he envisioned creating a European-style state
for the Jews outside of Europe. The goal remained the same:
to abolish Jewish uniqueness. Only the geographical location
now shifted. The fate of the wealthy Jews in both schema
demonstrates the remarkable similarity between Herzl's pre-
Zionist and later Zionist programs: in the first, the rich would
remain Jewish while the poor would convert; in the second,
the assimilated rich (converted or not, as they chose) would
stay in Europe while the impoverished masses would remain
Jewish but go to Palestine. The wealthy had no need to become "normal" in the sense that Herzl understood it, reli-

giously or nationally, since integration was not a problem for them.

The new political movements shared the Haskalah's veneration of the state. They looked to state structures as instruments of reform; despite their opposition to policies of individual states toward the Jews, they all accepted the assumption that any change would have to occur within the context of the modern state. The diplomatic activities of Herzl and Weizmann were based on this belief in the state; even the revolutionary activities of the Bund presumed that a socialist state was the key to solving the Jewish question in Russia.

It is important to bear in mind that, whatever the substantive differences between the movements, they all shared a common revolutionary intent: to change the political status quo. The *maskilim* a century earlier had turned the pragmatic medieval alliance between the Jews and the state into an object for celebration; the new Jewish politics made the state a target for reform or revolution.

Belief in the state as the vehicle for solving the problems of the Jews points to another characteristic common to the new political movements: in contrast to the earlier *maskilim*, all recognized the Jews as a collectivity requiring collective solutions. The Haskalah had attempted to dissolve the Jewish corporation and replace it with a collection of individuals. The new movements, reflecting the new national consciousness of the Jews, sought to reconstruct the medieval collectivity of the Jews on a new, secular basis. This collectivity might take the form of a Jewish state in Palestine or autonomous communities in Eastern Europe. Even Jewish liberals, who favored the integration of Jews as individuals into society, saw the need for collective organization and action as a means toward their goals.

Ideologies of Power

With the new political movements came an explicit recognition of the importance of power for the Jews. The new ideologies believed that, despite the evident impotence of the Jews, the modern world had created the conditions for empowering them in revolutionary ways. For instance, the socialist Zionist theoretician Ber Borochov used Marxist theory to demonstrate the inevitability of Zionism. The forces of industrialism had created a Jewish proletariat which would be forced out of the advanced capitalist countries and eventually to Palestine, where it would recreate the class struggle taking place elsewhere. Capitalism made Jewish nationalism and eventually Jewish socialism inevitable. In a very different way, Vladimir Jabotinsky, the founder of the antisocialist Revisionist Zionist movement, argued that modern nationalism furnished the Jews with the "will to power" lacking in their earlier history. He borrowed the symbols of this "will to power"—uniforms, military pageantry, and patriotic rituals—from European nationalist movements, including even Italian fascism.[21]

Theodor Herzl was perhaps the most confirmed believer in modernity as the source for solutions to the Jewish problem. He insisted that his treatment was not utopian but thoroughly realistic. The modern world had created both the Jewish problem in its contemporary form and the solutions to it. His task, as he saw it, was not to dream up new schemes but rather to show how conditions must lead to the logical conclusion of a Jewish state.

Modern anti-Semitism, Herzl argued, is fundamentally different from the medieval variety. It is a product of the entry of the Jews into the European middle class and the economic conflict between them and the non-Jewish bourgeoisie. But the new middle-class status of the Jews also gave them the power to create a state of their own, to emancipate themselves outside of Europe. Herzl repeatedly suggests that this power comes from modern technology, and his writings are replete with mechanical metaphors:

> We now possess slave labor of unexampled productivity, whose appearance in civilization has proved fatal competition to handi-

crafts; these slaves are our machines. . . . Everyone knows how steam is generated by boiling water in a kettle, but such steam only rattles the lid. The current Zionist projects . . . are tea kettle phenomena of this kind. But I say that this force, if properly harnessed, is powerful enough to propel a large engine and to move passengers.[22]

Jews were now in a position to harness these modern forces, perhaps as a result of their scientific and economic power. Herzl himself proposed a variety of visionary technical schemes for his Jewish state (one of them, a canal from the Mediterranean to the Dead Sea, is actually on the drawing boards in Israel today).

Politically, too, the new Jewish state that Herzl proposed was modeled on modern lines. Herzl was not a radical democrat, and his state has been described as something like a constitutional monarchy or aristocratic republic. But in terms of the role of religion and the definition of citizenship, the society he described in his utopia, *Altneuland*, was to be governed on thoroughly secular principles with equal rights for all, including the Palestinian Arabs.[23] In an ironic way, Herzl was perhaps the originator of the idea of a "binational" state in Palestine, since his notion of a Jewish state certainly did not entail special rights for its Jewish citizens. What Herzl envisioned was an entirely new Jewish polity, bearing no resemblance to anything in the Jewish past but with distinct similarities to those being formulated by the liberal and secular political theories current in fin-de-siècle Europe.

Herzl seems to have believed that the financial power of the Jews was enormous and that it could bring about the technical miracles he foresaw. His exaggeration of Jewish power was something that he shared with the anti-Semites of his day, and for that reason he may have been given a more receptive hearing than would have been the case if he had been more accurate. Here is another case where common misperceptions of power actually created new sources of power.

In a similar way, Herzl's political theory of the Zionist movement attempted to conjure up hidden sources of power. One of the keys to his success was his ability to project a sense that his movement represented the whole Jewish people, when, in fact, it consisted of only a small group of individuals. Not only did Herzl employ theatrical tactics to create this illusion; he also developed a theory to justify it. He borrowed a principle from Roman law (the *negotiorum gestio*) according to which an agent (*gestor*) may save an endangered property if its rightful owner cannot do so. Since the Jewish people cannot act to save itself, it is legitimate for an agent (the Zionist movement) to act for it. The state the Zionists would create takes its legitimacy not from a social contract based on a referendum of all members of the Jewish people, but from the necessary action of the *gestor*:

> A State is created by a nation's struggle for existence. In any such struggle, it is impossible to obtain proper authority in circumstantial fashion beforehand. In fact, any previous attempt to obtain a regular decision from the majority would probably ruin the undertaking from the outset. . . . We cannot all be of one mind; the *gestor* will therefore simply take the leadership into his hands and march in the van.[24]

What Herzl proposed, only a few years before Lenin's doctrine of the Bolshevik Party as the vanguard of the revolution, was a theory of the Zionist movement as a vanguard of the Jewish people. This theory of a small group as the avant-garde, chosen not by democratic vote but by historical necessity, was to be adopted by later Zionist and non-Zionist parties, from the socialist Zionist *halutzim* (pioneers) to the militaristic nationalist Betar to the anti-Zionist Bund.

A Counterhistory of Power

The Haskalah had defined the Jews as a nonpolitical, spiritual people who in no way considered themselves a "state within a state" and would have no difficulty accepting citizenship in the European nations. Many of the new political activists, and especially the Zionists, adopted this view of Diaspora Jewish history—but they found no virtue in it. In their desire to create a new political community, they saw the Diaspora as the opposite of their goals, an era of passivity and impotence. They projected back onto all of Jewish history the image of the deteriorating Jewish community at the end of the nineteenth century. As a result of their powerlessness, the Jews did not make their own history. The Hebrew writer Haim Hazaz has the protagonist of his story "The Sermon" declare: "Because we didn't make our own history, the *goyim* made it for us."[25] The task of Zionism was to "return the Jews to history," to turn them into active subjects rather than passive objects.

Some critics cast this view of the Jewish past in athletic and sexual metaphors. Max Nordau, one of the founders of the Zionist movement, catalogued the "degeneration" of Diaspora Jewish life and argued that the palliative to the Jewish *luftmensch* (the unproductive and impotent Jew who "lives from the air") was "Judaism with muscles."[26] In a similar vein, Vladimir Jabotinsky charged that Diaspora Judaism "despised physical manhood, the principle of male power as understood and worshiped by all free peoples in history. Physical courage and physical force were of no use, prowess of the body . . . an object of ridicule."[27] Such masculine virtues would find expression in military prowess. The creation of a Jewish army during World War I therefore became a high priority for Jabotinsky. The hostility of the Arabs to Zionist settlement in Palestine created in his eyes an opportunity to refute the legacy of Jewish passivity by making armed self-defense a necessity.

One of the first extensive analyses of the powerlessness of the Jews was by Leo Pinsker, a founder of the Hibbat Zion, a Russian Zionist movement in the 1880s that preceded Herzl's political Zionism. Contrary to Herzl's belief in hidden Jewish power, Pinsker defined Diaspora Jews as an impotent "ghost people" since they had no territory. He argued that the irrational fear that ghosts and other spirits conjure up lies at the heart of "Judeophobia." Pinsker called anti-Semitism a "psychic aberration . . . a disease transmitted for two thousand years." Without land, the Jews lost their vitality: "But after the Jewish people had yielded up its existence as an actual state, as a political entity, it could nevertheless not submit to total destruction—it did not cease to exist as a spiritual nation. Thus, the world saw in this people the frightening form of one of the dead walking among the living."[28] For Pinsker, as for many others, the Jews bore responsibility for anti-Semitism; the anti-Semites merely reacted in a natural and predictable fashion to the Jewish stimulus.

Interestingly enough, modern anti-Semites typically see the Jews in exactly the opposite terms to those used by Pinsker. Instead of describing the Jews as powerless, anti-Semites endow them with superhuman power. This observation does not contradict Pinsker's analysis, for it is psychologically convincing that people might attribute enormous "secret" power to that which appears insubstantial, such as ghosts and demons. Nevertheless, the apparent contradiction between Pinsker and the anti-Semites suggests the radical difference between how Jews and their enemies might evaluate Jewish power. This discrepancy had no precedent in the Middle Ages, when Jews and Gentiles tended to see the power of the Jews in much more similar terms.

The perception of Jewish powerlessness prompted outcries against a "Diaspora mentality" of passive suffering and martyrdom. The Hebrew poet Hayyim Nachman Bialik was dispatched to gather evidence after the Kishinev pogrom of 1903, but instead of writing a report, he penned a devastating epic poem, *Ir Ha-Harega* ("The City of Slaughter"). In this extraordinary work, Bialik employed the medieval language of martyrdom, but stood it on its head: instead of a *kiddush ha-shem* (see p. 74) serving to praise God, the death of the pogrom victims was a testimonial to a despicable mentality of passivity. Paying scant attention to the perpetrators of the pogrom, Bialik hurled stinging accusations at the victims.

For Bialik, the whole medieval ethos of the Jews stood condemned at Kishinev.[29]

Against the overwhelmingly negative characteristics they perceived in Diaspora life, Jewish critics at the turn of the century constructed a counterhistory of Jewish vitality in order to inspire a national renaissance: if mainstream history was a record of impotence and passivity, there was also an "underground" tradition throughout Jewish history of small groups struggling against the passivity of the established leaders.[30] For these writers, this tradition served as an inspiration for the contemporary avant-garde in its rebellion against the weight of history. They celebrated the rebels against Greece and Rome, naming their athletic clubs after the Maccabees and Bar Kokhba. Messianic adventurers such as Sabbatai Zevi became heroes. There was hope for a different future because, despite the passive mentality that the Jews had acquired during the Diaspora, they retained a more aggressive spirit, hidden away like a recessive gene.

One writer who systematically developed such a counterhistory was Micha Yosef Berdichevsky, who was born in Russia in 1865 and died in Germany in 1921. He argued that Judaism was not a monolithic religion consisting of one normative tradition but was rather torn from its earliest days between two contradictory forces: the Book and the sword. Throughout Jewish history, these two tendencies fought against each other. Indeed, the conflict began, according to Berdichevsky, with Moses and Joshua, the first representing the "ethical" revelation at Mount Sinai and the second representing the military tradition of the conquest of the land of Canaan. Later on, the ethical religion of the Prophets opposed the vitalistic nationalism of the ancient Hebrew warriors. During the Great Revolt against Rome, the Zealots championed the sword while Rabbi Yohanan Ben Zakkai continued the tradition of the Book. As we saw in chapter 1, this view of the Great Revolt is historically suspect, since the rabbis probably did not oppose the revolt altogether. With the defeat of the Zealots, however, the "sword" went underground but never disappeared. Berdichevsky found his vitalistic tradition in all the heretical and dissident—albeit unarmed—movements in medieval Jewish history, such as the Karaites (the medieval sect that rejected the Talmud), the Sabbatians, and the Hasidim. In order to escape from impotent spirituality, it was incumbent on the Jews to recover this hidden dissident tradition. From his perspective, the Judaism of the Book—the belief in study and contemplation as opposed to nationalist action—was responsible for all the ills of the Jews in his day.

The thrust of this view of Jewish history was militantly secular: the Jewish religion was a curse that bred impotence and passivity. In its hostility to the normative Jewish religion, the new counterhistory expressed its rejection of the traditional Jewish community in general. It envisioned an apocalyptic break between medieval, Diaspora history and the new era, whether it be the era of Jewish nationalism or of socialist revolution. It was a view of history guided by the desire for radical change rather than continuity. In a memorable phrase, Berdichevsky posed the choice: "We are the last Jews—or we are the first of a new nation."[31]

Not all Jews swept up by the new politics shared this historical vision. A notable exception was Simon Dubnow, the great Polish Jewish historian who was also one of the leading activists in the territorialist party. Dubnow argued that medieval Jewish autonomy was a form of limited political sovereignty and that it permitted the Jews to retain their national identity throughout the centuries of Diaspora. He charted the geographical wanderings of these centers of substitute sovereignty in his historical writings, and he pioneered the study of the East European Jews whom earlier Jewish historians such as Graetz had regarded with contempt. Dubnow's philosophy of Jewish history had its political analogue in his leadership of the territorialist movement, which sought to recreate the medieval political and cultural autonomy of the Jews in Eastern Europe on a modern, secular, and national basis.[32]

Dubnow's was a minority view. For most, the Diaspora was divorced from political life. Even those who rejected Zionism or revolution and desired a return to the Jewish tradition often adopted this view of Jewish history. For example, the German Jewish existentialist Franz Rosenzweig argued that Judaism's uniqueness consists in the fact that it is a religion "outside of history." The very timelessness of Judaism, as opposed to Christianity, made it possible for the modern Jew to find links to his tradition. In his desire to construct a nonpolitical Judaism, Rosenzweig turned the historical criticisms leveled by the Zionists into virtues.[33] For both Rosenzweig and the Zionists he opposed, traditional Judaism was devoid of a this-worldly political consciousness. Such a consciousness might perhaps be found in certain heretical or forgotten movements in Jewish history, but it would require an act of revolutionary rebellion, led by an avant-garde, to resurrect it in modern times.

Holocaust and History

The Holocaust put a decisive end to the era of politics that had begun in the 1880s. No longer was there a Jewish "nation" in Europe; no longer did solutions within Europe seem remotely relevant. From now on, Jewish politics would have to take place on a new basis, in locations outside of Europe.

The Holocaust, despite its completely unprecedented nature, reinforced the nineteenth-century argument of the fundamental powerlessness and apolitical character of the Jews. Trapped in Europe and made the target of a campaign of extermination that took precedence over Germany's war effort, the Jews were truly impotent victims during the war years. From the perspective of 1939–45, all of Jewish history appeared to be a tale of passivity and impotence. In a famous, if extreme, statement of this position, the historian Raul Hilberg asserted that the failure of the Jews to resist the Nazis was a result of an "alleviation-compliance response" which "is part and parcel of ghetto life" and dates back "to pre-Christian times."[34] In a similar way, Hannah Arendt castigated the Jews of the Holocaust period for their lack of resistance and argued that this was a consequence of the apolitical character of earlier Jewish history.[35] These writers were severely attacked for their criticism of Jewish behavior during the Holocaust, but on one point they concur with a widely held opinion: that the impotence of the Jews during the Holocaust was the culmination of two thousand years of political powerlessness.

The belief that the Holocaust represents a continuation, if in a much more extreme form, of previous Jewish history was reinforced by the way the Nazis appropriated medieval symbols of oppression. They repealed the citizenship of German Jews, thus revoking emancipation and turning the wheel of history back to the Middle Ages. They drove the Jews out of the arts and those professions, such as law, academics, government, and journalism, that symbolized their integration into society. After the outbreak of the war, they required Jews to wear a yellow star, reminiscent of medieval marks of segregation. And, finally, they locked their victims up in ghettos, the term itself taken from the later Middle Ages. In a grotesque way, the "autonomy" of the Jewish community within the ghetto resembled that of the Middle Ages, since the community council (Judenrat) functioned as a form of city government; once the deportations to the extermination sites began, it even exceeded the authority of the medieval community in its power to decide who would live and who would die. This "autonomy" and "power" were, of course, an utter sham, since the Judenrat was totally under the control of the Nazi authorities, and the leaders had no influence over the ultimate fate of the Jews.

These superficial similarities between the ghettos of the Holocaust and the communities of the Middle Ages should not mislead us, as they often succeeded in misleading the Jews of Nazi Europe. The Nazis created the illusion of turning back the clock to lull their victims into a sense of complacency: the worst that might happen, the Jews thought, would be a return to their medieval status. In reality the Nazis were preparing the way for extermination, which was unheard of in the Middle Ages. The worst official policy to which the Jews were subjected in earlier times was expulsion or forced conversion, never government-organized massacre. The experience of the Holocaust was unique in Jewish history; hence the Jewish response to the Holocaust cannot be compared to responses to earlier persecutions.

The relative passivity with which the Jews met their fate, even when it became known to them, had nothing in common with their medieval behavior. We have seen that during the Middle Ages they mobilized all of the possible means of defense at their disposal, including armed resistance. Although their objective weakness often proved too great, they were never passive in the face of danger: survival, even if not raised to the level of ideology, always informed both Jewish theory and practice during the Middle Ages.

For the Jews of the Holocaust, especially in those countries ruled directly by the Germans, such as Poland, the conquered areas of Soviet Russia, Holland, and Germany itself, the system allowed virtually no escape: the vast majority were killed, quite regardless of whether or not they suffered from a "Diaspora mentality."[36] If the Jews failed to believe the reports of the fate the Germans had planned for them, it was less a result of a historical mentality of passivity than of a thoroughly modern faith in the state, a faith they shared with all other people.[37] This belief in the state had its origins for Jews in the Haskalah, but it was just as much the legacy of the rise of state nationalism throughout Europe in the nineteenth century. For the medieval Jew, as for medieval people in general, the state was never the object of unquestioned faith; it was at best an uneasy ally, a possible source of protection. Only with the modern period did people begin to see the state as the sole object of loyalty. It was this new patriotism that made the genocidal fury of the Nazis so incomprehensible.

The relevant question is not why the European Jews did

not resist more or whether there is something in Jewish history that prevented resistance. Our concern ought to be with what the Jewish experience can teach us about the effect that totalitarian systems have on all people. The nature of totalitarian states is to suppress utterly the kind of political organization and activity that are necessary for resistance. The fact that more people were put to death in the 1930s in Soviet Russia than were killed by the Nazis in the camps should give us pause before we accept a myth of the passive Diaspora Jew; Soviet totalitarianism was even more effective in subduing any possibility of resistance, and it scarcely mattered who the victims were. The Jews of the Holocaust, rather than representing the culmination of a history of passivity, are rather a symbol of the helplessness of the individual in face of the modern state gone mad. The specific ways the Nazis treated the Jews may have been unique in history, but the Jewish experience in general, tragically, has too much in common with that of others in our century.

With the Holocaust, the attempt to find a solution to the Jewish question in the states of Europe suffered a death blow; only the search for a life outside of Europe remained viable. With the destruction of the secular ideologies that had worked to transform the Jews into a "normal" nation, all that remained was a belief in the continuity of a unique Jewish fate. A new ideology of survival revived the old theology of divine election as the basis for Jewish life, decisively altering the Jewish politics of the new state of Israel and the Diaspora community in America. In the wake of the Holocaust, the myth of historical powerlessness, which had evolved during the preceding century, became the central justification for the quest for Jewish power.

VI

Israel and the Meaning of Modern Sovereignty

NO single event has so concentrated the attention of Jews on the question of power as the creation of the modern state of Israel. Just as the Holocaust has come to represent the powerlessness of the Diaspora, so the return to political sovereignty symbolizes for many the negation of the Diaspora and the first real embodiment of Jewish power in two thousand years. That the same generation experienced the extremes of power and powerlessness has had a profound effect on the ways Jews regard political sovereignty.

The impact of Israel on Jewish ideas about power both today and in Jewish history is the result of the normative position that Zionism has in contemporary Jewish ideology: Zionism—or at least the defense of the right of the Jews to political sovereignty—is the one belief to which virtually all Jews today subscribe. As such, the conclusions drawn from its history in the last one hundred years have been accepted by many as universally true for all Jews at all times. Zionism was but one of many competing movements in the years before World War II, and frequently one of the smaller movements, yet it survived the Holocaust in which other ideologies perished. Precisely because it preached a solution for the Jews outside of Europe, it was able to assert its claim when the European possibilities had been destroyed.

The impact of the Holocaust and the circumstances under which Israel has had to fight for its survival have also dramatically colored the understanding of power and history held by most Jews today. As a result of the continuing conflict with the Arabs, the Zionist hope to create a "normal" nation has receded and been replaced by what I shall call an "ideology of survival." This new ideology has increasingly become the governing political theory of the Jewish state in the years following the Six Day War of 1967. In this theory, Zionism no longer constitutes a break with Jewish history, but is rather its continuation under different conditions. Since anti-Zionism, it is believed, has become the new form of anti-Semitism, hatred of Jews remains a problem unsolved. Instead of sovereignty turning the Jews into a nation like all others, the Jewish state has become a new expression of the separation between the Jews and the rest of the world. Instead of sovereignty bestowing a sense of security, it has led to contradictory feelings of inflated power and exaggerated fear.

The Political Theory of Classical Zionism

In the preceding chapter, we saw how the Zionists followed the lead of the nineteenth-century *maskilim* in portraying Jewish history after 70 C.E. as a period of passivity and impotence; unlike the *maskilim*, however, they found no spiritual virtue in this long era of exile. The powerlessness of the Diaspora was primarily the fault of the Jews themselves, for they had deliberately abdicated the vitality necessary for national life. The Zionists searched for their models in the more distant past, in the Bible and the militant revolutions of the Roman period. Zionism was to return this impotent people of the Book to nature and the virtues of self-defense. The "new Hebrew man" would take the place of the weak and apolitical

Jew. Jewish sovereignty in the Land of Israel would become the antidote for the ills of the exile.

This view of Jewish history, developed during the Second and Third Aliyot (the pioneering immigrations to Palestine of 1905–14 and 1918–21), was to have a formative influence on the identity of Israelis after the Jewish state was established in 1948. Perhaps the most extreme expression of Israel as a revolution in Jewish history appeared in the 1940s and 1950s in the literary movement known as the Canaanites.[1]

The Canaanite movement remained a tiny group of intellectuals, but its ideas had an influence on many more moderate Israelis. According to the Canaanites, the new Hebrews, as products of the new society of the Land of Israel, would renounce all ties to the historical Jews and to Judaism as the religion of exile. They would then rediscover their Middle Eastern heritage, the pagan culture of the Canaanites, which the movement believed was the true culture of the Bible (they held that the Bible had been rewritten during the Babylonian exile in order to suppress its Canaanite elements). In its radical interpretation of Jewish history, the Canaanite movement owed much to Berdichevsky's writings, (see above, pp. 139–40).

Not content to reject the Jewish religion, these writers even labeled Zionism as a Diaspora creation and therefore a product of the mentality of exile. Once the new Hebrew society cut its connections to the Diaspora, it would be able to integrate itself into the Middle East. Here the movement split between those, like Uri Avneri, who conceived of a peaceful "Semitic" confederation of Jews and Arabs, and an imperialistic wing, led by Yonatan Ratosh, which saw Israel as the force of secular modernism that would subdue the medieval Muslims and create a new Hebrew empire.

The mainstream culture of the new state of Israel did not accept such extreme positions. Following Herzl's theory of the Zionist movement as the avant-garde of the Jewish people, the state wished to be accepted as the agent of all

Jews, the majority of whom still lived in the Diaspora. But many elements of this rejection of the Diaspora and the search for new myths played an important role in the process of building the new Israeli state. The Bible became the standard text taught to schoolchildren for nationalistic purposes, while Diaspora history received short shrift at best. The Bible served different purposes for different branches of the Zionist movement. The socialist pioneers, or *halutzim*, who established the kibbutz movement adopted the biblical metaphors of nineteenth-century Hebrew literature and saw their agricultural settlements as the reincarnations of the agrarian society of the Bible. Such pastoral ideals were very much in vogue in the European *völkisch* movements of the early twentieth century, which rebelled against industrialism, but they were less out of place in Palestine, a country that lacked an industrial infrastructure.

The Bible also furnished sagas of military exploits and of a powerful Jewish empire, the Kingdom of David. Examples of military heroism from ancient history, such as the revolts of the Maccabees, the Zealots, and Bar Kokhba, were exaggerated out of all historical proportion and turned into staples of a national myth.[2] The final defeat of the Zealots at Masada, where, according to Josephus, the rebels took their own lives rather than surrender to the Romans, became a metaphor for the modern Jewish state surrounded by bitter enemies. Indeed, as the state of Israel was increasingly forced to define itself around national defense, the early myth of biblical pastoralism gave way more and more to the use of biblical and postbiblical history as sources for military myths.

The Zionists imagined the biblical state to be fully autonomous and an ancient model for the modern nation-state. Although only a few extremists advocated reestablishing the ancient monarchy or creating an empire the size of David's, the ideology of Israel portrayed the new Jewish state as the resurrection of its biblical ancestor. The real character of the biblical state—disunited and externally dominated for most of its existence—played no role in this memory.

The Zionists imposed an anachronistic interpretation on the biblical period as a result of the nineteenth-century definition of state sovereignty. For European nationalists, national sovereignty promised almost unlimited possibilities. The creation of nation-states out of the weak and fragmented principalities of the Middle Ages would unleash enormous creative energies. Sovereignty meant the abolition of the multiple allegiances of the Middle Ages and the creation of one political authority. For the Zionists, this new concept of sovereignty promised to solve the problem of Jewish identity in the nineteenth century: while the Jews in the Middle Ages had a single identity as members of the Jewish corporation, their identity in the modern world had become fragmented. Political sovereignty promised to solve this problem by imposing, once again, a single identity, defined now by the category of national citizenship rather than of religious corporation. Whether secular or Orthodox, middle-class or proletarian, western or eastern, all Jews might find a common identity as citizens of the state of Israel.[3]

Just as the Zionists hoped that sovereignty would revolutionize the Jew internally, so they expected that a Jewish state would radically change how the nations treated the Jews. Theodor Herzl, in particular, had high hopes that the adoption of a European model of state sovereignty would solve the problem of anti-Semitism. Precisely because the Jews established a state like all the European states, they would be accepted as equals in the family of nations. If the Jews could not lose their "foreignness" in Europe, they could do so in their own state outside of Europe. If they could not assimilate as individuals in Europe, their state could assimilate in a world of states.

Despite the influence of European ideas of national sovereignty, many of the early Zionists, including most of the socialist pioneers, had no explicit intentions of founding a state at all. Some of these settlers were ideological anarchists, such as the mystic A. D. Gordon, whose philosophy of work played a central role in the evolution of the pioneering culture.[4] For

Gordon, the Jewish settlement in Palestine was a rebellion against modern technological values, including the state. It was left to Vladimir Jabotinsky to articulate a philosophy of state power for Zionism, but Jabotinsky was rejected by the mainstream of the Zionist movement and took refuge in his own Revisionist Party.

For the Zionists, Jewish history was therefore divided into two periods: the biblical period served as a model for a golden age of Jewish sovereignty, while the nearly two thousand years since the defeat of Bar Kokhba were ignored or dismissed. Rejecting medieval Judaism as a fundamentally apolitical and subservient culture, the founders of modern Israel sought a synthesis between the image of ancient Israelite power and the lessons of European nationalism. But the latent tensions between the political legacy of Jewish history and the dictates of modern theories of sovereignty came to the surface soon after Israel became independent.

The Theory of Statism

The founders of Zionism had envisioned establishing a homogeneous Jewish society: overwhelmingly secular, composed primarily of European Jews, and certainly with few or no Arabs. When the Zionists argued that the Jews are a nation, they had in mind the mass of Jews in Eastern Europe at the end of the nineteenth century. That nation was decreased by emigration to America and largely destroyed by the Nazis. The state of Israel, as it finally emerged after 1948, was far less unified and homogeneous. It comprised the remains of the European Jews, the "unknown" Jews of the Arab world, who emigrated in large numbers following the War of Independence, and the Palestinian Arabs. Like many of the other new nation-states that arose out of the wreckage of the old colonial empires, the state of Israel is not composed of one ethnic group. But the picture is complicated even more by the divisions among Jews from different parts of the world and by the conflicts between secular and religious Jews. No modern nation is free from ethnic and religious conflicts, but the tensions among secular and Orthodox Jews, Ashkenazic and Oriental Jews, and Jews and Arabs never figured into the utopian blueprints of the Zionist founders.

These tensions have in turn augmented the conflicts of the East European Jewish politics that Israel inherited, producing a political system that seems ready at any moment to shatter into dozens of competing factions. Instead of sovereignty solving the problem of Jewish identity, it has reproduced old conflicts and created new ones: despite the existence of a Jewish state, the Jews in Israel appear to be less of a natural nation today than they did before the Holocaust. If it is true that only the situation of constant warfare has kept Israeli society together and imposed a certain communal solidarity, then it is the *abnormality* of Israel's situation rather than its intended normality that has forged the nation.[5]

David Ben Gurion, the first prime minister of Israel, was quick to recognize that the reality of the new state contradicted the dreams of classical Zionism. The first problem was that the primary loyalty of some Israelis was to their political parties, some of which had private militias, rather than to the state. During the War of Independence, he did not shrink from pushing the new nation to the brink of civil war by confronting the Irgun, the underground army of the Revisionists, and forcing it to surrender to the will of the government. Later, he disbanded the Palmach, the elite military force of the left-wing kibbutzim. These measures were intended to subordinate the Israeli army to the government of the state rather than to the political parties.[6]

Ben Gurion's creation of an army responsible only to the state symbolized the larger political theory he attempted to impose on the new society. Zionism had started its career as a revolutionary movement in opposition to Jewish life in Europe; in Palestine itself, it continued its oppositional stance as it came into conflict with the British Mandate power. But following the establishment of the state of Israel, Ben Gurion declared the revolutionary period of Zionism was over: the movement had won and become the "establishment." As it shifted from opposition to state-building, Zionism followed the pattern of many revolutionary movements, undergoing its own version of the Thermidor of the French Revolution (the counterrevolution that ended the reign of the Jacobins). Ben Gurion's new ideology came to be called "statism" (*mamlakhtiyut*).[7] The state was to inherit the mantle of the Zionist movement and become the sole focus of loyalty and the sole source of identity, superseding all the Zionist and pioneering institutions that had preceded it. Ben Gurion saw the state not as the reflection of the various conflicting interests in society—a theory that would correspond to American democracy—but as the embodiment of the "general will," a force greater than Israeli society, a secular version of God's will. In this way, the state might force unity on a fractious society and also serve as the sole voice of the Jewish people throughout the world. The perennial question "Is it good for the Jews?" became a matter of *raison d'état:* what is in the interest of the state of Israel is in the interest of the Jewish people.

The unending conflict with the Arabs forced the Zionists to give up much of their early pacifism. Since they could not create their state peacefully, they were compelled to do so with "blood and iron." Defense of the state became an end in itself, and military virtues came to be considered virtually identical to Zionism. The army became a source of national admiration and, as a people's army, was regarded as the embodiment of the "general will" much more than the political system, which naturally tended to reflect all the continuing tensions in society. In this way, Jabotinsky's Zionism, which glorified military values, surreptitiously became the ideology of the new state, even as Ben Gurion reviled Jabotinsky's disciples in the Herut Party as "fascists."

As Yeshayahu Leibowitz, an Orthodox critic of Ben Gurion's statism, has pointed out, elevating the state to a value in itself has no basis in Jewish tradition and reflects the impact of modern European theories of state sovereignty.[8] In a more

general sense, Leibowitz's argument against statism highlights the conflict between Israel as a continuation of Jewish
history and as a rebellion against it. Although Ben Gurion's
statism was supposed to replace Zionism, it shared with classical Zionism a certain hostility to Jewish history. A new
secular Israeli identity, based on the modern concept of "citizenship," was to replace Jewish identity and serve to weld a
new nation out of the diverse groups that made up Israeli
society.

At the same time, however, the leaders of the new state
wanted to emphasize its continuity with Jewish tradition.
Despite their secular bent, they included some of the Orthodox political parties in the governing coalitions. In the 1950s,
an Israeli "civil religion" began to emerge, consisting of Jewish holidays and other institutions such as Holocaust memorial days which sought to connect the cultural life of the state
with the Jewish past, or at least a Jewish past with which
most Israelis could identify.[9] Archaeology became a national
mania as Israelis literally dug for the roots of their past.

This ambivalent relationship to the Jewish past also
finds expression in the ongoing conflict between defining Israel as a "democratic" state and a "Jewish" state. These two
terms act as code words for a whole set of contradictory values. A "democratic" state suggests a secular, pluralistic polity in which Jew and Arab are political and social equals, and
religion and state are separated. A "Jewish" state means a
polity in which the Orthodox tradition plays a primary role in
state affairs, Arabs are a tolerated minority (or, in more extreme versions, expelled), and the differences between Ashkenazic and Oriental Jews are resolved by a common Jewish
heritage.

We have seen that democracy played little part in Jewish
tradition: a Jewish state based on the traditions of biblical
and medieval political theory would have to be either a monarchy or some form of theocracy ruled by the rabbis on the
basis of Jewish law. The founders of modern Israel rebelled
against these traditions and established a state rooted in lib-

eral and socialist models. Given the weakness of democratic traditions in Jewish history and in the East European states from which the Zionists came, it is virtually a miracle that Israel remains as strong a democracy as it is. One might contrast it favorably to the fate of Russian social democracy following the Russian Revolution.

Yet, neither did the founders of Israel adopt a purely democratic model, for Ben Gurion's version of statism tried to find a balance between democratic and Jewish models: the political system was democratic but ethnic, and religious interests dictated some state policies. Orthodox Jewish law governs marriage, divorce, and inheritance, and rabbinic courts adjudicate disputes in these matters. The official status of the Orthodox rabbinate conflicts with the freedom of religion that the democratic character of the state otherwise guarantees.

Israel's Arab citizens also did not benefit fully from democratic principles. They were given full political rights but were kept under military rule until the 1960s. To this day, they are not drafted into the army; they do not benefit from governmental programs for army veterans or from the programs of the Jewish Agency, which became a quasi-governmental body for development of the Jewish sector of Israeli society. The status of the Arabs contradicts the political theory of statism, according to which all of Israel's citizens should have equal benefits and duties.[10]

The tension between a modern democratic state and a Jewish state is also a product of the *millet* system which Israel inherited from the Ottoman Empire via the British Mandate. Israel took over sovereignty of Palestine from the Ottoman Turks, since the British were merely temporary governors of Palestine and not sovereign rulers. In doing so, it substantially preserved the Turkish law pertaining to the autonomy of religious communites. In terms of the power of religious authorities over matters of personal law (marriage, divorce, and inheritance), the state of Israel is much closer to its Ottoman predecessor (and to the medieval Jewish community) than it is to any modern democratic state. The persistence of the Ottoman system is a symbol of the continuity between the modern state of Israel and the Jewish Middle Ages: by preserving the power of religious law, even if in only limited areas, Israel has become functionally the modern version of the medieval community, a continuation of rather than a break with Diaspora Jewish history. And the struggle between religious and secular Jews in Israel is but one more battle in the war between the *maskilim* and the Orthodox that began in Eastern Europe in the last century for control of the *kahal.*

Israel's Ottoman heritage also has implications for the status of the Arab minority in Israel. In the Ottoman Empire, Muslims were the political rulers while Jews and Christians were tolerated minorities. In contemporary Israel, the tables have been turned and Arabs (both Christian and Muslim) are considered a national minority, even though those within the pre-1967 borders possess full political rights. Minority religions retain control over personal law, just as they did under the Ottomans and just as the Jewish majority continues to do. In its self-definition as a "Jewish" state with an Arab minority, Israel has perhaps inadvertently created a modern form of the Ottoman *millet* system, modern in that the Arabs have the formal rights of citizens but medieval in its definition of minorities as separate and outside the identity of the state. There is an inherent tension, if not a contradiction, between this Ottoman legacy and democratic, statist principles that would require treating the Arabs as fully equal citizens.

The question of the democratic character of modern Israel is connected to the question of Israel's legitimacy as a state. In terms of international law, Israel draws its legitimacy from the United Nations declaration partitioning mandatory Palestine, and it is therefore as legitimate as any of the states that succeeded the colonial empires. The problem lies rather in its internal legitimation. The Zionist movement, as we have seen, claimed to speak for all the Jewish people based on Herzl's doctrine of *negotiorum gestio.* Its institutions in Palestine were recognized by the British as the representatives of the Palestinian Jews, and these institutions became the government of the new state in 1948. Yet, the Constituent Assembly elected at the beginning of 1949 never drafted the constitution for which it had been elected and instead simply declared itself the first Knesset (parliament) of the state. The government of the state therefore rests on the shaky ground of its prehistory in the Mandate period and of the unilateral assumption of power by the Constituent Assembly. There is no formal "social contract" in the sense of a written constitution, no declaration of which traditions are to govern the state. Israel's Declaration of Independence, which is often referred to as a kind of pseudolegal basis for the state's identity, contains thoroughly contradictory principles, asserting the equality of all religions in the state but at the same time declaring Israel a "Jewish" state. Rather than solving the problem of a "democratic Jewish state," the Declaration of Independence only drew further attention to it. Without a constitution, the state of Israel lacks the coherent identity that Jewish political theory provided to the medieval Jewish community and remains torn by contradictions between differing interpretations of the meaning of Jewish sovereignty.

The Holocaust and the Ideology of Survival

Ben Gurion's statism failed to unify the new Israeli nation to the extent that he had hoped. Many of the Jews from Arab lands did not accept the Labor Party leadership and regarded the government with ever greater hostility and alienation. In the mid-1960s, the economy went into a deep recession and emigration from the country exceeded immigration. A pervasive sense spread that not only had Zionism run its course, but that statism had also failed to produce an enduring solution for all the Jewish people. Then, the Six Day War of 1967 transformed the identity of the state of Israel and created a "new Zionism."[11] Just as statism had adopted and altered some old themes from classical Zionism, so the new

Zionism represented not an entirely new political theory but rather a renewal of certain tendencies in much more explicit terms. The 1967 war left Israel in control of most of the biblical Land of Israel, namely, the West Bank of the Jordan River (referred to in antiquity as Judaea and Samaria), and the Golan Heights, in addition to the whole Sinai Peninsula. Having defeated all the Arab armies, many Israelis considered themselves a major military power.

In the 1950s and early 1960s, Ben Gurion had been acutely aware of the limitations on Israel's power and of her dependence on the major powers. In both 1948 and 1956, he responded quickly to Western pressure and withdrew from the Sinai Peninsula. Although his favorite saying was "Don't listen to what the Gentiles say, look at what the Jews do," he nevertheless always sought international approval for Israel's actions. It is significant that Ben Gurion's was a lone voice calling for Israeli withdrawal from the conquered territories after 1967, arising out of his fears for what a prolonged occupation might do to both Israel's international standing and her internal unity.

In the wake of the 1967 war, however, the "small" Israel of Ben Gurion's era vanished and was replaced by a vastly enlarged nation harboring a sense of omnipotence. Although the governing Labor Party never took a clear position on the newly occupied territories, strong annexationist forces were soon at work, uniting secular and religious nationalists from a variety of political parties, including the Labor Party itself. These forces saw Zionism as a movement of expansion and settlement. Since the pioneering movement of the pre-state era had glorified these values, the "new Zionism" claimed to be fulfilling old Zionist goals rather than creating new ones. Since Israel now ruled over a million Arabs—residents of the new territories who did not possess Israeli citizenship—the pre-1967 conflict between the "Jewish" and "democratic" character of the state became much more acute. Now in possession of the biblical Land of Israel, many Zionists felt a renewed sense of connection to Jewish history, and the tendencies toward an ethnically exclusive "Jewish state" accelerated.

The new feelings of power were accompanied, paradoxically, by increased feelings of insecurity. On the eve of the Six Day War, many Jews both in Israel and elsewhere felt that Israel, surrounded by mobilized Arab armies on all sides, faced annihilation; this sense continued even when, a few days later, the Israeli army had produced the greatest Jewish military victory of modern times. The 1973 Yom Kippur War and Israel's increasing isolation in the world community added to these feelings of weakness.

The new fears of isolation and impending catastrophe found expression in the increased use of Holocaust metaphors. In 1948, when Arab armies had invaded Israel from all sides and her military situation had been infinitely more precarious, the Holocaust was invoked much less as an image representing her position. In part, the events in Europe were too recent and too painful to be fully assimilated. More importantly, the Zionist view of Jewish history created a distance between the Diaspora Jews of Europe and the "new Hebrews." As a result, Israeli commemorations of the Holocaust focused primarily on acts of resistance, like the Warsaw Ghetto uprising, emphasizing the difference between those who took up arms against the Nazis (typically identified incorrectly as only Zionists) and all the other Jews, led, according to the slogan, like "sheep to the slaughter." The ideological assumption behind this distinction was the belief in the historical passivity of the Diaspora Jews and the role of Zionism as a revolt against passivity.

In the 1960s, however, first the Eichmann trial and then the Six Day War forced Israelis to identify much more with all the victims of the Holocaust. The sense of encirclement preceding the war and the abandonment by Israel's Western allies caused many who had hitherto scorned Diaspora history to describe their situation in terms of the Holocaust: they perceived themselves facing a "second Auschwitz." This new connection with the Holocaust prompted a new image of the relationship of Israel to Jewish history, an increasing identification with what was called "Jewish fate" (*ha-goral ha-yehudi*).[12] This Jewish fate was understood to be eternal isolation, unending anti-Semitism, and a continual threat to Jewish survival. Jews now possessed the weapons to resist this fate, but not to change or eliminate it. The 1973 war added substantially to this sense of an eternal Jewish fate as Israel faced extreme condemnation throughout the world and Arab armies, for the first time since 1948, seemed on the verge of victory.

The sense that only the Diaspora Jews could be counted on to defend the Jewish state contributed to the new connection drawn to the Diaspora and its history. The centrality of Israel in Jewish history, a cardinal Zionist principle, now meant that while the Jewish communities of Western Europe and North America enjoyed a temporary reprieve from the Jewish fate, it was Israel that carried the burden of persistent threats to survival. Israel's importance to the Jews was no longer its presumed "normality" but rather its abnormality, the degree to which it confronted directly the eternal fate of the Jews.

These tendencies were strengthened and elaborated as a result of the change in political leadership that took place in 1977. The earlier Labor Party politicians were, for the most part, pioneers who had left Europe as teenagers, rejecting entirely the European Jewish experience. They were well established in Palestine by the time of the Holocaust. They were not survivors since, as they saw it, they had anticipated the catastrophe before it struck. Although many of them lost families to the Nazis, they were separated from the events engulfing Europe.

Menachem Begin, the leader of the Herut Party who became prime minister in 1977 after decades in opposition, was, on the other hand, a product of Polish Jewish politics and spent the first part of the war in Eastern Europe.[13] Begin was the first Israeli leader to come from the world of the Holocaust and to view it as the fundamental event in both his own life and in Jewish history. Many of his opponents accused him of suffering from a "ghetto mentality" of paranoia, but his world view was shaped not so much by the medieval ghetto as by Poland on the eve of the Holocaust. Begin transplanted the sense of desperation that characterized Jewish politics in Poland of the 1930s to the state of Israel. While he was elected in 1977 as a result of the declining popularity of the Labor Party and the disenchantment of Israelis from North Africa and, to a lesser extent, other Arab lands, he symbolized something beyond the internal dynamics of Israeli politics, namely, the feeling that Zionism was not so much a negation of the Diaspora as a continuation of its fate in a new way. With Begin, the experience of the Holocaust survivors became the ethos of the state.

Begin's ideology claimed that all Jews have in common the experience of persecution and can therefore overcome their religious and ethnic differences. His success in attracting Israel's Jews from North Africa to vote for his party lay in part in this appeal. It is significant that Begin, who perhaps did the most to connect the Holocaust with contemporary Israel, was able to make the Holocaust a symbol for the persecutions suffered by the Middle Eastern Jews, who otherwise typically resented the obsession Ashkenazic Israelis have with the fate of their European cousins. Begin's success with these Jews had much to do with their hatred of the socialist establishment, but it was also the result of treating Jewish persecution as more than a European experience. For Begin, all Jews are united by the hostility of the non-Jewish world, a hostility at once historical and contemporary.

According to Begin and his followers, the state of Israel seemed condemned to repeat the experience of the ghetto, as a pariah among nations. "The whole world is against us" were the words that began a popular song from this era. But the image of the ghetto was taken less from the historical ghetto of the late Middle Ages than from the ghetto of the Holocaust period. Jews increasingly conceived of the state as an armed Warsaw Ghetto and the Arabs—particularly the

Palestine Liberation Organization—as reincarnated Nazis. The Holocaust increasingly became the historical justification for Israel's military actions. During the 1982 siege of Beirut, Prime Minister Begin discussed the ethics of bombing a city with a large civilian population in terms of the Holocaust: would it have been justified to destroy a house of innocent people if Hitler were holding them hostage?[14]

The Masada metaphor now converged with the Warsaw Ghetto in a kind of telescoping of Jewish history. Where previously the Zealots were seen as the opposite of the "ghetto Jews," the differences now seemed less obvious, for all of Jewish history became the chronicle of a surrounded people battling for its life and prepared to commit suicide rather than surrender. Another historical metaphor was that of Samson: the state of Israel, capable of building atomic weapons, might "die with the Philistines," taking all the world with it if threatened with extinction. No longer a normal state "like all the other nations," Israel became the embodiment of persecuted and desperate Jewry. The Jew remained a victim, but now a victim with an army.

These newly articulated connections between Israel and the Holocaust found expression in the May 1985 ceremonies marking the fortieth anniversary of the liberation of the concentration camps from the Nazis. The central feature of the commemoration, which attracted Jews from all over the world, was military demonstrations by the Israeli army. At the same time, Dov Shilansky, the Knesset member who chaired the event, proposed a bill in the Knesset to make the six million Jewish victims of the Nazis posthumous citizens of the state of Israel, as if their status as victims identified them more closely than other Jews with Israel.

The new Zionism replaced the utopian dreams of the early twentieth-century political movements with one obsession: survival. It asserted that Jews had been victims in the past because they did not make survival their cardinal commandment; they did not pursue power with the single-mindedness necessary for survival. The Holocaust was a watershed in Jewish history because it decisively shattered all illusions and focused the Jews on their physical survival, which, for the proponents of this ideology, meant the survival of the Jewish state. In the words of Emil Fackenheim, a Canadian philosopher now residing in Israel and one of the foremost exponents of the ideology of survival, Auschwitz presents the Jew with a "614th Commandment: not to render to Hitler a posthumous victory." As the expression of the divine commandment of collective Jewish survival, the state of Israel assumes religious meaning.[15] The implication of Fackenheim's position for the interpretation of Jewish history is that only in the wake of the Holocaust have the Jews taken up the political task of survival. The title of one of his books, *The Jewish Return into History*, succinctly expresses this view.

In its emphasis on survival, the new Zionism substantially transformed the revolutionary doctrine of "normalization." Early twentieth-century Jewish politics had imagined a normal people to be something like the Swiss: no longer the focus of the world's attention and allowed to pursue its destiny on the fringes of history. Herzl could envision a utopia in his *Altneuland* precisely because it was so far from the maelstrom of the world's power struggles. Similarly, the utopian visions of the socialist pioneers relied on leaving a corrupt Europe for a *terra rasa*, a land presumably empty and ready to be shaped. The new ideology sees the relationship of the Jews to the rest of the world in a thoroughly different way. Zionism has failed to solve the problem of anti-Semitism because anti-Semitism is endemic to the non-Jew. Moreover, the world will never allow the Jews to leave the center stage of history. Jews will continue to have the status of pariahs, but now as a pariah state among the nations of the earth.

Since they are unable to become a normal people, the experience of the Jews remains unique. No other people attracts persistent animosity, quite independent of objective reality. The Holocaust itself demonstrates the uniqueness of the Jews, for never before had there been an attempt to eradicate a nation so utterly. The argument has become a secular version of the chosenness of the Jews: the Jews have suffered a unique fate and therefore the struggle for Jewish survival draws its meaning and justification from this uniqueness. The very choice of the term Holocaust in the 1960s as the principal designation of the murder of the European Jews suggests the theological overtones of the new ideology. The Jews, like Isaac in the Book of Genesis, have become the sacrificial victims on the altar of their own history. Their modern fate is the culmination of their eternal destiny. In its rejection of the quest for normalization and its affirmation of the uniqueness of the Jewish experience, the new ideology represents a return to the old theology of divine election.[16]

The doctrine of chosenness in the past gave a theological dimension to perceptions of Jewish power. In the biblical period, it bestowed a sense of centrality on a marginal and weak people and was used to justify revolts against the empires. In the wake of defeat, it gave a theological significance to exile and served to rationalize the powerlessness of the Jews. The secular version of the uniqueness of the Jews feeds at one and the same time feelings of power, represented by Jewish sovereignty, and feelings of impotence, represented by the Holocaust. Israel is a continuation of the unique Jewish fate of anti-Semitism, but it is also a miraculous manifestation of power; the very legacy of powerlessness bestows a unique power on the state. That these contradictory feelings could coexist was demonstrated during the Lebanon War when Ariel Sharon, on the one hand, asserted that Israel could act as the greatest power in the Middle East, while Menachem Begin compared the PLO's threat to the Jewish people with that of the Nazis.[17] The ideology of survival oscillates between these extreme feelings of power and powerlessness.

Curiously enough, the sense of impotence that marks one pole of the ideology of survival is the mirror image of how Israel's enemies perceive the conflict: they typically see themselves as impotent and Israel as omnipotent. Thus, there is a symmetry between the views of Jews and Arabs: each suffers from the same disjunction between images of itself and the other. In a similar way, modern anti-Semites, including the Nazis, often viewed the Jews as all-powerful (the "Elders of Zion") at a time when their political power was in fact at a nadir. It is out of just such illusory perceptions of oneself and one's enemies that political conflicts become mythologized and their resolution grows increasingly remote.

At the same time that the nationalist ideology of survival argues for the continuing uniqueness of the Jewish experience, it reinterprets this persistent abnormality as a form of normality. Many Jews now argue that the essence of national life is warfare and the struggle for elemental survival. The Holocaust, rather than an extreme aberration in history, is representative of the behavior of nation-states toward those without power. Israel must become "normal" and therefore safe by using the same physical methods that nations have always used when their existence was threatened. This kind of survivalism was, to be sure, a natural corollary of Ben Gurion's statist philosophy, but the perceived continuum between Diaspora Jewish history and the sovereign state of Israel is new. And while Ben Gurion's sense of Jewish power was always tempered by an equal sense of the limitations on Israel, the new *realpolitik*, exemplified best by Ariel Sharon's plan for the invasion of Lebanon, seeks power without restraint. (Israel's disastrous experience in Lebanon has now focused considerable criticism on this concept of power).

The continuing war with the Arabs has therefore brought the Holocaust home to Israel in a way never imagined by the founders of the state. Out of a new ideology of survival, the battles of the state have become the culmination of a centuries-long Jewish struggle against anti-Semitism. Anti-Zionism has become the new form of anti-Semitism, and Israel feels herself to be a ghetto among the nations. Between the Jew as victim and the Jew as military hero, the ideal of the Jew as a normal human being has begun to disappear. A legacy of powerlessness becomes the justification for the exercise of power.

The New Messianism

Menachem Begin's six years in power marked a major watershed in Israeli politics. For twenty-nine years, Israel was essentially a one-party state, even though the Labor Party could only rule in coalition. Begin's election was the first swing of the democratic pendulum and it gave a sense of enfranchisement to large groups of voters who had previously felt alienated from the political system. Yet, at the same time that it furthered Israeli democracy, it also created the atmosphere for the rise of extreme antidemocratic forces drawn from the ranks of the Orthodox, such as the Gush Emunim (Bloc of the Faithful) and the extremist followers of Meir Kahane. In their demands for a messianic state, these movements have drawn attention more boldly than ever before to the potential contradictions between a Jewish and a democratic state.

The new form of nationalism represented by Menachem Begin was much more consciously and explicitly connected to Jewish history than was the Zionism of Herzl and the socialist pioneers. In the years after the Six Day War, the sense of return to Jewish tradition found particular expression in a messianic Zionism, articulated by militant religious nationalists: for these Jews, Zionism represents the fulfillment of the millenarian promise of Jewish history. This radical byproduct of religious Zionism argues that the commandment to settle the Land of Israel, including the retention of all the territories occupied in the 1967 war, takes precedence over all other divine commandments and is the true justification for Zionism.

The Gush Emunim, a group of young Orthodox Israelis, pioneered in the initially illegal settlement of the captured territories. Despite its relatively small numbers, it found a sympathetic hearing in the Begin government and was able to strike up an alliance with secular nationalist forces.[18] The

Gush bases its Zionism on a nationalist interpretation of traditional Judaism. Zionism is the fulfillment of biblical promises, a theme that had always been present in Zionist ideology, but not with the same degree of Orthodox conviction. In this religious-nationalist hybrid, Zionism becomes the realization of traditional messianism rather than a revolution against tradition, and the religion of Judaism is turned into a political ideology.

Although the activist messianism of the Gush Emunim departs from the more cautious nationalism of older religious Zionists, it represents the logical culmination of the tradition of political messianism discussed in chapter 2. This type of messianism, originating in the Talmud but articulated most cogently by Maimonides in the twelfth century, claimed that human action can precipitate the coming of the Messiah. In the late eighteenth and nineteenth centuries, a number of Orthodox authorities developed this doctrine further. The circle around the Vilna Gaon argued that a Messiah son of Joseph (a figure mentioned in the Talmud) would reestablish the Jewish community in the Land of Israel and prepare the ground for the coming of the Messiah son of David. They considered this first Messiah to be a military leader and associated him with the war of Gog and Magog (Ezekiel 38–39). Some of these messianists emigrated from Lithuania to Palestine, where they were involved in a millenarian movement around the year 1840. At about the same time, Zvi Hirsch Kalischer, an important Polish rabbi, called for the renewal of some of the ancient sacrifices in Jerusalem as a prelude to the coming of the Messiah.[19]

All these ideas belong much more to the history of Jewish messianism than they do the prehistory of political Zionism, but they were to have an important impact on religious Zionists in the twentieth century. Rabbinical authorities such as Abraham Isaac Kook, the chief rabbi of Palestine from 1921 to 1935, and Menachem Kasher, a noted Israeli talmudic scholar, revived this tradition by interpreting the Zionist settlement in Palestine as a fulfillment of messianic theory.

Kook held that the secular pioneers unwittingly served God's messianic plan by settling the land and that after they accomplished their mission, the Orthodox would inherit political power. Kasher argued that the Six Day War (and, later, the Yom Kippur War) was the War of Gog and Magog prophesied in the Bible. The Gush itself, which regards Kook and Kasher as its foremost teachers, relies heavily on the messianic tradition that these authorities have emphasized. It sees the wars of Israel as messianic wars and the politics of the state of Israel as preparations for the coming of the Messiah.[20]

Given the Gush Emunim's definition of Zionism as a messianic movement, it is no surprise that it has little commitment to Western democratic values. Since the Gush considers democracy to be foreign to the Jewish tradition, messianism takes precedence over democracy. The discovery in 1984 of a Jewish terrorist underground whose members were drawn from the Gush proved that these messianists consider their religious goals to supersede the laws of the state. For the members of the movement, if Zionism is to be the fulfillment of Jewish history, Israel must sever its ties to alien Western traditions.

The Gush's synthesis of messianism and Jewish nationalism has led to a new understanding of the use of power and military force. Rabbi Eliezer Waldman, one of the spiritual leaders of the Gush, argues that the Lebanon War was part of the messianic process, since, "when there is a war in the world, the power of the Messiah is aroused."[21] Waldman sees the exercise of power by the Jews as part of Israel's election, its mission to the nations of the world. He views the exile as a time of physical weakness when the Jews could not fulfill this mission:

> For thousands of years in exile we were oppressed. In those years we maintained our purity, but we could not influence others and could not be a light unto the nations. We sent forth only the light of weakness. The wisdom of the victim is a wisdom which is despised. Light shines forth only from heroes, only from those who struggle, who do not submit to others; only

this light possesses the power to influence the nations. Thus, in the process of return [to Zion] we must ascend in stages and be ready to fight wars.[22]

Adopting the Zionist view of the Diaspora and linking it to messianism, Waldman proposes a new version of the chosenness of the Jews in which the exercise of sovereign power and the initiation of wars serve as a "light to the nations," the slogan used by nineteenth-century Reform Jews to advance an "ethical" and antinationalistic interpretation of Judaism. No matter how unpopular these wars may be in the eyes of the world community, they will help bring the Messiah and will therefore ultimately make the nations of the world respect and admire the Jews. According to Waldman, the Jewish mission to the world is not peace but war, not democracy but a messianic state.

The question of how the state of Israel relates to Jewish history therefore remains crucial to the debate over the nature of power in the Jewish state. First, if Israel is a Jewish state in the sense dictated by the Orthodox tradition, can it also be democratic? The freedom promised by emancipation meant freedom not only from arbitrary gentile rule but also from the authoritarian rule of the medieval Jewish communities. Would an Orthodox state mean that Israel will become little more than a resurrected version of the medieval community? Yet, if Israel adopts an entirely modern ideology of democratic individualism and true equality between Jews and Arabs, it may lose its self-identity as a Jewish state, particularly if it retains the large Arab populations of the territories occupied in 1967. Second, if Israel represents a fundamental shift in Jewish history from exile to sovereignty, is it in the direction of "normality" or messianism, a state like all others or a fulfillment of the eschatological dreams of the Jewish tradition?

The Zionist movement gave to the Jewish people a new political vocabulary. By its very nature, the movement was composed of an avant-garde with a utopian vision of a unified and homogeneous Jewish state. This political vocabulary could have little relevance for the state of Israel as it actually came into being, a state torn by divisions among Jews and between Jews and Arabs. The task for contemporary Jewish political theory is therefore not to try to resurrect a "classical" Zionism but rather to forge a new vocabulary based on contemporary realities.[23]

The Limits of Modern Sovereignty

Political Zionism was based on late nineteenth-century notions of sovereignty that are less and less relevant to today's world. The "spring of small nations" in Eastern Europe after World War I infected the Zionist quest for power. Yet, just as these hopes were dashed in Eastern Europe by the Nazis and the Soviets, so the dream of full Jewish sovereignty today has had to accept severe limitations. Despite the proliferation of small independent countries since World War II, the world is increasingly dominated by the large powers and by a widening network of international corporations. Even nations blessed with strategic resources cannot escape the entanglements of the world political economy: sovereignty for small nations too often means dependence on the major powers.[24]

Israel's geographical position has compounded the problem of being a small nation. Israel is the product of the European age of nationalism, but she sought to realize her ambitions outside of Europe and thus came into conflict with Third World nationalism. Israel falls in the crack between the developed and the underdeveloped worlds, neither Western nor Middle Eastern. She fails to fit neatly into the categories of colonialism and imperialism, just as the Jews in all ages have defied ordinary definition. As her attempts to become a member of the community of "nonaligned" nations were frustrated by Arab oil and propaganda, Israel was forced to identify with the West; and as the Arab-Israeli conflict imposed enormous financial and military burdens, she turned to Western sources for assistance.

The restrictions imposed on the sovereignty of small states have forced Israel to relate to the non-Jewish powers in ways similar to those adopted by the medieval Jews. In order to assure its survival, the state must follow a medieval strategy of alliance with those in power. In the modern world, this means alliance with one of the superpowers. The state would have probably been aborted at the outset without the convergence of interests between the major powers in supporting its creation. In the 1950s, it was France that became Israel's patron, but for most of the history of the Jewish state, it is the alliance between Israel and the United States that has ensured survival. To be sure, diplomacy between two sovereign states is not the same as the politics of *shtadlanut* of the Middle Ages, but the argument by Israel and its Jewish supporters to demonstrate that Israel serves American interests strongly resembles the contentions medieval Jews made for royal protection.[25] If Israel is by no means the only small state forced into this client relationship with one of the superpowers, the legacy of Jewish history makes her dependence all the more painful.

Just as disturbing, the problems faced by the Israeli economy have eroded the financial autonomy upon which sovereignty must be based, for Israel has now become totally dependent on American credits and grants to avoid economic collapse. Suggestions to convert the Israeli economy to the American dollar symbolize this loss of sovereignty, for in the modern world, as in ancient and medieval times, the right to mint one's own coins is a sign of national independence. Here again, the politics of survival have necessarily eroded the hopes for full Jewish sovereignty.

Israel's reliance on outside protection and aid highlights one of the cardinal ambiguities of her power. While her military prowess makes her the most powerful state in the Middle East, her size, economic fragility, and diplomatic isolation limit that power. Israel is at once a world power and a very small power indeed. This duality has undoubtedly fed the contradictory senses of power and powerlessness that have characterized Israel's self-conception since the Six Day War. We have already observed some of the consequences of this dilemma in relation to the Yom Kippur War of 1973 and the Lebanon War of 1982–85. In the latter case in particular, Israel's attempt to act like a major power exposed all too painfully the political limitations on military might, a reality confronted by America in Vietnam.

Perhaps most importantly, the threat of nuclear war and the utter destruction of the human race has undermined the old definitions of sovereignty and power for all nations. Those who possess nuclear weapons are, theoretically, the most powerful but they are muscle-bound by their own strength. Dependent on one of these nuclear powers and opposed by the clients of another, Israel's ability to act autonomously is severely restricted. If Israel herself acquires nuclear arms—as some argue she already has—she too will confront this paradox of the powerlessness of nuclear power.

In the light of these realities, it may be that Zionism succeeded too late on the world stage, for it sought to build a small, Western-oriented nation in an area singularly hostile to such undertakings. Yet the Jewish quest for power through a nation-state has by no means been a failure. The notion of a sovereign state as a kind of ghetto with an army has distorted the very real achievement of Zionism: to turn defense against persecution into a matter of politics and statecraft. An Israeli soldier who dies on the border is fundamentally different from a Jewish martyr in the Crusades, even if the latter died with a weapon in his hand. The Israeli soldier dies, in Clausewitz's definition, as an instrument of "diplomacy carried on by other means," while the martyr dies precisely because his diplomatic or political options have been exhausted. The death of the first is a sacrifice in defense of a collective, while that of the second is an admission that the collective can no longer defend itself. A nation-state does not only increase quantitatively and organizationally the means of defense: it transforms the very meaning of defense from desperation to statecraft.

Indeed, in terms of defense, Israel is much more secure today than at any other time in her history. She is the greatest military power in the region and has been so since 1967. Despite the apparent threat of the Arabs to Israel's existence in 1967 and 1973, the Israeli Defense Forces repeatedly defeated Arab armies decisively; in retrospect, the outcome of these wars proves that from a purely military point of view there was little real danger of the Arabs overrunning the country, as there may have been in 1948. Although future wars may be even more devastating in terms of human losses, Israel does not face imminent annihilation. The Jewish state remains at war with all her neighbors except Egypt, but the deep-rooted fears of a second Holocaust have no current military basis.

Even if the state of Israel has not been able to abolish anti-Semitism and has, on the contrary, given it a new and focused target, it has transformed the whole meaning of the conflict between the Jews and their enemies. Anti-Zionism employs many of the same arguments and images as anti-Semitism, and this has led many to equate the two. But the very existence of a state turns the opponents of the Jew from persecutors into enemies also carrying on diplomacy by other means. Even if the intention of the Arabs is really genocide, they are forced into a political relationship with their Israeli adversaries by the fact that the Jews have a state. It is this changed circumstance that holds open the possibility, however remote it may seem, for eventual peace between Arab and Jew. It is therefore a tribute to the success of Zionism that anti-Zionism, no matter how virulent and irrational, cannot be fully equated with anti-Semitism.

Although the Zionists intended to save the Jews by fleeing from Europe, the presumed center of world history, they now find themselves—to their surprise—still very much in the center. This unexpected centrality to world history has brought with it severe problems for the Jewish state, but it is also one of the reasons the state has succeeded to the extent that it has. Israel's rapid economic and military development is a result of the Arab-Israeli conflict. Had the state been established without a struggle, it is possible that the tremendous energies unleashed by the condition of permanent war would have remained bottled up and Israel would today be a backwater republic. And had Israel not been established in such a geopolitically sensitive area and become embroiled in a conflict with threatening implications for world peace, she might never have won the support from America that helped turn underdeveloped Palestine into the industrialized nation of today. Thus, the inability of Zionism to realize some of its original goals may have been unwittingly the impetus for the Jews to build a modern state. In a paradoxical way, the failure of Zionism to achieve a normal relationship with its neighbors (surely an essential aspect of the normalization of the Jews) has had unanticipated positive consequences.

The various limitations the modern world in general and the Jewish situation in specific have imposed on the state of Israel give a different, more modest meaning to Jewish sovereignty than that which the founders of Zionism envisioned. The state of Israel has not provided a total solution to either the "problem of the Jews" or the "Jewish problem." These, in their late nineteenth-century versions, no longer exist, in part because there is a Jewish state but in larger measure because of the end of European Jewish history. But new problems have taken their place, whether of new forms of anti-Jewish sentiment or of new conflicts among Jews. As in antiquity, sovereignty has fallen short of bestowing on Jews total control over their fate—a utopian quest, perhaps, but one that has defined Jewish political thought throughout Jewish history.

Israel and Jewish History

We have seen that both the classical theory of Zionism and the newer ideology of survival have defined themselves in relation to Jewish history, the first as a revolution and a return to biblical sources, the second as a fulfillment of Jewish fate and of traditional messianism. These ideologies mine history for usable models, or "monuments," as Nietzsche called them. But history cannot provide programmatic answers to contemporary problems: its role is to serve rather as a warning and a caution, not as a myth to be fulfilled or negated.

With the modern state of Israel, many themes in Jewish history come full circle. The struggle for Jewish sovereignty in the modern world strikingly resembles the dilemma of ancient Israel, caught between the great imperial powers of that distant age. While the geographical position of biblical and Second Temple Israel meant conquest and submission, it also meant centrality to world history and thus a certain kind of power. That only the Jews among all ancient Middle Eatern peoples survived may owe something to this curious double-edged heritage. Modern Israel falls in this same dialectic between power and danger in a world of nationalism and global powers. In this respect, those who see Zionism as a continuation of Jewish history, rather than a revolutionary escape from it, may well be right.

After two thousand years without a sovereign state, Jews are obsessed with the problem of reconciling might with right, power with morality. Many assume that only a powerless people can afford a moral stance and that the price of power is relinquishing absolute principles. In confronting this problem and the larger question of survival in the modern world, the experience of the Jews in the period between the destruction of the northern Kingdom of Israel in 722 B.C.E. and the destruction of the Kingdom of Judah in 586 C.E. may provide a valuable model. The destruction of the Kingdom of Israel brought home what it meant to live in a world of ruthless imperialism. Having experienced something like a holocaust in their own time and fearing the destruction of their state, the Judaean political thinkers evolved a sophisticated political response. With extraordinary realism, they warned that sovereignty could only be maintained by a prudent sense of the limitations on Jewish power and by tempering power with restraint: military force is not the only means to political ends. The key to their teaching was an attempt to bring perceptions of power in line with the realities of power: the Jews were neither as powerless as they might fear nor as powerful as their theology had led them to believe.

Internally, ancient Judaean society was perhaps no less divided than is modern Israel, and the Prophets strove mightily for a vision of social justice that could unite the ancient Israelites. Despite the moral tone of their political philosophy, men such as Isaiah and Jeremiah were neither the pacifists nor the naive moralizers that some imagine them today: they were nationalists with a firm grasp of the meaning of political power in a hostile world. Morality, they argued, does not contradict politics; might is not the enemy of right. On the contrary, justice is pragmatic, for it guarantees a healthy body politic. In the end, their advice was ignored and the Kingdom of Judah was destroyed.

The history of the Second Temple can also provide a useful caution. We recall that the reestablishment of full sovereignty under the Hasmoneans—an event often compared to the success of Zionism— had unexpectedly negative consequences. Instead of firmly uniting the nation, the Hasmoneans fostered sectarianism. With their fall and the disastrous reign of King Herod, the fragile institutions of Jewish politics were further weakened, leaving an untended field in which the most extreme sects flourished. It was these sects, together with the conflicts between the Jews and other ethnic groups in Judaea, that pushed the Second Temple state into its fatal war with the Romans. Today, too, the creation of a sovereign state has both united the Jews and created deep new divisions. The conflicts among different types of Jews, as well as between Jews and non-Jews thrown together in a society still in formation, raise troubling questions that echo with resonances from the distant past: how can a unified Jewish state allow the variety of Jews and the varieties of Judaism to thrive without destroying it?

The melancholy fate of Jewish sovereignty in antiquity provides no concrete answers to these problems of contemporary Jewish politics. If the blessings of sovereignty have proven more modest than ideology and theology promised, they have not been insignificant either. The task the Jews of today face—a task perhaps as difficult as that of their biblical ancestors—is to reconcile the desire for state power with the limitations on modern sovereignty. If Jewish sovereignty is to endure, Jews must find a way of navigating a middle course between dreams of boundless power and nightmares of historical powerlessness.

VII

American Jews and Contemporary Diaspora Power

THE Holocaust marked the end of the long era of European Jewish history. With the destruction of two-thirds of the European Jews, the new communities of Israel and America became the centers of Jewish life, not only numerically but politically as well. Both communities were products of the great wave of emigration which started in the 1880s, although both were built on the foundations of small settlements of Jews already in existence. Israel and the American Jewish community represent politically the movement of Jews from the peripheries of world power—the underdeveloped areas of Eastern Europe and the Middle East—to centers of power. These two new foci of Jewish power had a common origin and they remain politically interdependent, strengthening each other in ways not foreseen by classical Zionist theory or by theories of Jewish assimilation in America.

It has been argued that the American Jewish community is at once the freest and the most powerful Diaspora community in Jewish history. Today, this community has access to the highest corridors of power and possesses considerable ability to influence, if not always decisively, the government of the United States in favor of Jewish interests, especially in support of the state of Israel. It is a community with extensive financial resources which it contributes generously to Israel and other foreign Jewish communities, as well as to numerous political and cultural causes in America. Although anti-Semitism still exists in American society, there has never been a Diaspora community in modern times that has faced less discrimination. Jews no longer encounter significant economic or occupational barriers, and there are far fewer social barriers than in any Diaspora community in history. Never has a Jewish community of such size been so well integrated into the life of a non-Jewish society.

Yet, Jewish power in America cannot be facilely compared with that of other Diaspora communities. The nature of power in a pluralistic democracy necessarily differs from power in other types of polities of the past. The very existence of a sovereign Jewish state also alters the exercise of power by a Diaspora community. If power means, as I have previously defined it, "the ability of a people to control its relations to other peoples as well as its own internal political, cultural, religious, economic, and social life" (p. 7), the American Jewish community is a very powerful community indeed, but not without qualification. I suggested further that power is a measure of the "exercise [of] strength and authority within a collective framework, informed by conscious political goals" (p. 7). The integration of Jews into American society has enhanced their power as individuals, but frequently at the expense of communal cohesiveness. The very success of American Jews in entering the power structure in America has therefore both strengthened and weakened their ability—and desire—to act as a collectivity in the historical sense of the word. These new and, for the most part, unprecedented circumstances suggest that it may be necessary to revise old definitions of power in favor of new ones still in the making.

The Social Basis of American Jewish Power

The ability of Jews to influence the societies in which they live has typically been a measure of their involvement in the highest levels of government. In societies governed from above, such as the European absolutist states, a very small number of court Jews might have disproportionate influence, although such influence was fragile since it depended on the whim of the autocrat. Where power in society was fragmented, such as in the medieval corporate state, the Jews might achieve a measure of power as a special group under the protection of the monarch. Jews played a role in the elites of all the premodern societies in which they lived, and their power stemmed from their involvement with the governing elite. But in all these premodern examples, the Jewish elite comprised a very small percentage of the Jewish population and in fact owed its position to the lack of general participation in government.

Power in the modern democracies—and particularly in the United States, which has fewer traditional elites than do the European countries—tends to be diffused among a relatively large group comprising a wide range of professions. Since society has come to rely increasingly on technology and "expert" knowledge in general, this elite includes professionals, technical experts, and intellectuals: lawyers, doctors, economists, scientists and engineers, university professors, writers, and artists. Before World War II, educational and occupational barriers prevented Jews from entering many of these fields. Indeed, those Jews—one thinks immediately of Felix Frankfurter, Louis Brandeis, Henry Morgenthau, Bernard Baruch, and Stephen Wise, to name but a few—who were influential in American political life in the first half of this century were on the whole exceptional individuals, drawn primarily from the well-established German Jewish community, and did not represent a more widespread penetration of Jews into the circles of power. Similar to the court Jews of an earlier period, these men represented an older form of Jewish power. Nevertheless, even in the years before World War II, Jews were politically active in large numbers, especially in the Democratic Party, and thereby laid the groundwork for later achievements. After World War II, as discriminatory barriers fell, Jews entered the American power structure in disproportionate numbers. Although Jews are generally wealthier per capita than the average American, much of the real wealth of the country continues to be controlled by industrialists and bankers whose ranks include relatively few Jews, so the Jewish role in the American elite is only partly a function of money. It is perhaps more a function of knowledge: the proportion of Jews in scientific and intellectual fields has given larger numbers of them greater access to political and cultural institutions than in any previous period of history.

It is not difficult to substantiate the degree to which Jews have entered those professions that open up the doors of government. For example, the percentage of Jews employed as faculty members at the top-ranked universities in America is 20.9 percent, some seven times their number in the population. A study in the 1970s that identified 545 leaders in government, business, labor unions, and other areas of importance in American society found that 11.4 percent were Jewish, nearly four times their percentage of the population. The highest Jewish participation (25.8 percent) was in the media.[1] Jews are disproportionately represented in both houses of Congress and in the high levels of the bureaucracy. Their involvement in American political parties on both the national and local levels remains possibly higher than that of any other ethnic or religious group.

Although individual Jews previously possessed considerable power in their societies, never has such a large number of the Jewish people in any one country of the Diaspora been counted as part of the elite. What their financial and commercial assets did for the power of Jews in a much smaller way in the Middle Ages, their intellectual and professional achievements have done for them in the last generation.

The movement of Jews into the American political elite marks one of the most radical social transformations in Jewish history and probably, for that matter, in history in general. The Jews of Eastern Europe, the group from which most American Jews came, were impoverished by the end of the nineteenth century. Many of them had become an urban proletariat, and this was the economic class they entered when they came to America. The first generation of immigrants found conditions in the slums of the great American cities that were not substantially better than in Eastern Europe. Anti-Semitism remained a potent roadblock to many professions for the first half of the twentieth century, although probably not to the same degree as in Europe. It took two full generations for most of these immigrants to move into the middle class, despite the prevailing myth that it happened much more rapidly. By the post–World War II period, this poor, urban proletariat had acquired enough wealth and education to change its occupations to commerce and the professions and its address to the suburbs.[2] In a remarkably short time, less than a century, the Jews went from premodern small merchants and artisans to industrial workers and then to middle-class Americans.

America and other Western democracies such as England were not the only countries in which this revolutionary change occurred in the twentieth century. The Jews of the Soviet Union also underwent a dramatic transformation, from impoverishment in the czarist Pale of Settlement to a disproportionate force in the technical intelligentsia of the Soviet state. Yet, whereas American Jews have parlayed their social and occupational integration into political power, Soviet Jews were compelled to renounce any Jewish identification as the price for entering the power structure. Today, those who wish to assert their Jewish identity are driven out of their positions; under Stalin, many of them were killed. The social basis for the power of Jews in America is the extraordinary integration of Jews into American society, an integration that does not require assimilation or the renunciation of Jewish identity.

It might be objected that the Jews of Weimar Germany were almost as well integrated into the culture and politics of their country, yet as Weimar collapsed, their position did not protect them from Nazi anti-Semitism. If the collective interests of the majority of society, or of a new governing elite, become explicitly hostile to those of the Jews, no degree of involvement in the old power elite will suffice. The chances of this happening in America since World War II are, of course, vastly less than in Weimar Germany. American Jews can be found throughout most of the political spectrum and, with the exception of a few right-wing and left-wing extremists, anti-Semitism is a taboo word in the political vocabulary. Even those who genuinely hold anti-Semitic opinions generally feel constrained to suppress them in public or to apologize for them. There is no broadly accepted political philosophy in America in which anti-Semitism serves a key symbolic function; the Ku Klux Klan, neo-Nazis, and certain radical black nationalists remain on the lunatic fringe. Anti-Semitism does not function as a "cultural code" in America as it did in Germany, signifying a whole set of political beliefs such as antimodernism, antirepublicanism, and imperialist nationalism.[3] Lacking such a tradition, American anti-Semitism, even if it should increase to pre-World War II levels, is unlikely to become the core of a successful political ideology.

Social anti-Semitism, although it may be perceived as a sign of more dangerous tendencies, does not threaten the physical safety of American Jews, and it now impinges on their economic and social well-being only to a very limited extent. Indeed, the disabilities arising from it have been sharply reduced in many areas of American life by the activities of Jews, in concert with others, to break down discrimination against blacks, women, and other minorities in such areas as jobs, clubs, and education.

It is less anti-Semitism than the inevitable consequences of success that can undermine the relative power of the American Jews. For a community to integrate fully means that avenues are open to individuals to leave the community. American Jewish power derives from the degree to which American Jews have become part of America, but if integration becomes full-fledged assimilation—the renunciation of any ties, whether religious, cultural, or political, to the Jewish people—the cohesion of the community is threatened demographically and culturally. The rate of intermarriage between Jews and non-Jews in America has been estimated at around twenty-five percent, but it may be much higher. There is considerable dispute among demographers about the actual danger that intermarriage poses to the Jews, and there are some who argue that intermarriage may even *increase* the Jewish population through conversions and raising the children of such marriages as Jews.[4] If the pessimists are right, however, intermarriage and other forms of assimilation could decrease both the absolute and relative size of the community, thus lessening the population base which is surely one important factor in political power in a democracy.

Whether or not the actual size of the Jewish community changes, the more the Jews succeed in entering American society, the less they may identify with collective Jewish issues and the less they may be inclined to use their positions to further specifically Jewish interests. At the same time, the more Jews feel themselves to be accepted in America, the less pressing are such Jewish issues and the greater the extent to which they become general issues. For instance, prayer in public schools and affirmative action—two questions on which Jews have been particularly vocal—are less Jewish concerns than they are representative of broader political ideologies. Indeed, the gradual disappearance of issues demanding a specifically Jewish politics is a sign of the integration of the Jews and thus of their power in American society, although a very different sort of power than at any other time in Jewish history.

Israel as a Source of American Jewish Power

An indigenous American Jewish politics has existed since the first part of the twentieth century. In New York City during the first decade of the century, Jewish organizations united in a *kehilla*, a political umbrella representing the entire community modeled in a loose way on the medieval Jewish communities.[5] Although the Kehilla lasted for only a few years, it served as an impetus for later attempts at uniting Jewish communities in welfare federations. A variety of political organizations such as the American Jewish Committee, the American Jewish Congress, and the B'nai Brith Anti-Defamation League took on the struggle for defense of Jewish interests in America: the fight against anti-Semitism, quotas at universities, and other forms of religious or cultural discrimination against Jews.[6]

By the 1950s and early 1960s, Jews had been sufficiently accepted in America that much of the impulse behind this political life vanished. Yet, it was precisely at the time when collective Jewish politics seemed headed for the museum that it was regenerated by the cause of Israel. American Jewish organizations had lobbied for the creation of Israel in 1948, but support for Zionism was by no means a consensus within the community; a vocal opposition to Jewish nationalism could be found in many quarters, especially the Reform Movement.[7] Following the establishment of the state, American Jews paid little attention to Israel; few visited it as tourists and fewer still emigrated there. Leon Uris' popular novel *Exodus*, published in 1958, awakened a certain pride in Israel among American Jews, but it had no political ramifications.

With the Six Day War, however, defense of Israel gave unprecedented cohesion and purpose to Jewish political activity. Israel not only provided a focus for the exercise of Jewish power but also enhanced that power to a significant degree: as we shall see below, American Jews had to be accepted into the national councils dealing with foreign policy, and this gave added strength to the pursuit of collective Jewish interests in America. Yet American Jews would have been unable to provide political backing for Israel had it not been for their earlier entrance into the American power elite, which coincided with the first decades of Israel's existence.

Much of the earlier political activity of American Jews had also revolved around defense of Jews elsewhere in the world.[8] As early as 1840, Jews persuaded the Van Buren Administration to send a note of protest to Turkey over the Damascus Blood Libel (see p. 97). In the period after the Civil War, American Jews repeatedly sought expressions of concern for the plight of foreign Jews. Following the Kishinev pogrom in 1903, American Jewish political activity reached a new level of intensity, in part due to the pressure of the recent East European Jewish immigrants. Enormous protest marches were staged and, between 1911 and 1914, a struggle was waged to abrogate the commercial treaty with Russia. Jewish pressure was also important at the Versailles peace conference after World War I in obtaining the clauses protecting national minorities in the new states of Eastern Europe.

These achievements of earlier Jewish politics were largely symbolic and legalistic, with perhaps some impact on American foreign policy but much less on the actual treatment of Jews in foreign countries. In particular, American Jews failed to force the American government to open the gates to refugees from Germany and Eastern Europe in the 1930s and during the Holocaust.[9] This failure had to do in part with the Jews' fear of anti-Semitism, which was still a real force at that time, but it was also a result of the fact that ethnic politics were less legitimate than they became after the war, and particularly in the 1960s. One wonders whether the fate of the European Jews might have been significantly different if defense of ethnic self-interest had been as widely accepted in the 1930s and 1940s. Yet the failures of earlier Jewish politics in defense of foreign Jews were not without positive consequences. Even if many of these efforts bore little fruit, they established patterns of political behavior that shaped the more successful activities of Jews on behalf of Israel, as well as other Jewish communities such as the Soviet Jews.

The cause of Israel has transformed the nature of American Jewish politics. There is a qualitative difference between the defense of oppressed Jews in distant lands and the politics of support for Israel. As a nation-state, Israel furnishes American Jews with a new kind of pride and patriotism. Its political and diplomatic representatives serve as agents for organizing American Jewish political activity on its behalf.

It is also Israel's importance in world politics that has empowered American Jewish organizations by opening the highest corridors of American power to them in a way that was known only to individual Jews previously: where Stephen Wise might try to use his personal relationship with Franklin Delano Roosevelt to save Jews during the Nazi period, American Jewish organizations speaking for Israel have won an audience for more purely political reasons. This influence stems from more than just the voting power of Jews in congressional and presidential elections. Since Israel is locked in a struggle with clients of the Soviet Union, her actions—or her response to Arab actions—can potentially involve the United States in dangerous global conflicts. Given the close ties between the American Jewish community and Israel, the American government needs the goodwill of the community as part of its relationship with Israel; the community, insofar as it seeks to defend Israel, has become a direct party to superpower geopolitics. Precisely because Israel has been forced to become a major military power, American Jewish organizations have received a hearing in matters of foreign policy to a much greater degree than ever before.

The American Jewish "Israel lobby" has developed since the Six Day War into one of the most sophisticated and effective lobbying organizations in the United States Congress. It has done so in part by developing a national network of Jewish Political Action Committees for contributing campaign funds to congressional candidates based on the criterion of support for Israel.

As important as the lobbying of American Jews is for Israel, they do not, of course, determine American policy in the Middle East. Many domestic political and international geopolitical factors combine in the formation of policy, and these are not susceptible to the influence of any one lobby or ethnic interest.[10] American Jews have sustained significant defeats over issues they have defined to be in Israel's interest, such as the sale of AWAC planes to Saudi Arabia. Access to those who wield power is not necessarily the same as power, and the connection of American Jews to Israel can just as easily work the other way: if United States policy swings against Israel, American Jews automatically lose power as well. Yet, as opposed to the Jews of Europe during the Holocaust, the state of Israel has armed divisions and cannot be ignored. Just as it would be a mistake to exaggerate the power of American Jews in influencing policy toward Israel, so it would be incorrect to underestimate it. Especially with respect to the Congress and to a lesser degree in relation to the President, Jewish support for Israel is an important factor in the American political equation.

The transformation of Jewish politics can be seen within Jewish communal organizations as well. Fundraising for Israel, although based on a long tradition of philanthropy for foreign Jews, underwent a quantitative and qualitative jump after 1967. Not only were the amounts of money raised much greater than ever before and not only did many Jews who had previously not contributed become involved, but fundraising as such became increasingly the hallmark of Jewish identification. Involvement in the activities of the United Jewish Appeal became many people's most important Jewish commitment. The Jewish philanthropic federations became not just institutions for raising and disbursing charity; they are increasingly perceived as political bodies speaking for the Jewish community. The General Assembly of the Council of Jewish Federations has come to be considered by those involved in Jewish politics as the yearly national congress of American Jews. While the funds raised by these organizations do not all go to Israel, it is clearly the cause of Israel that has made fundraising so central to American Jewish life.

By virtue of Israel's simultaneous strength and vulnerability, the political influence of American Jews has been enhanced beyond anything in the past. Israel has provided the stage for American Jews to exercise collectively the power they have achieved in American society. This development of the last two decades has had a decisive effect on domestic Jewish political activity, for it has made Jews more willing to assert themselves politically on other issues as well. Identification with Israel has created a sense of Jewish nationalism largely absent from American Jewish identity before 1967.

Not all American Jews regard Israel as the focus of their Jewish identity. Certainly, very few American Jews have been inclined to move to Israel. For most, a sovereign Jewish state is a necessity for the Jewish people as a whole, but not for them personally; like the Jewish aristocracy in Herzl's vision of Zionism, American Jews remain in the Diaspora while Israel is supposed to solve the problem of the poor Jewish masses from elsewhere. Yet, for the organized Jewish community, lack of support for Israel is tantamount to treason. If in the Middle Ages obedience to Jewish law and to the will of the Jewish community defined a Jew, today, when self-identifying Jews take radically different positions on all other religious, cultural, and political questions, Israel is the one issue over which lack of belief is treated as heresy. Even those who are critical of Israel cannot hope to have a discourse with the established Jewish community if they do not accept the basic right of the Jews to statehood.

The Orthodox Jewish community has not been immune to this development. Most Orthodox authorities were suspicious of or even opposed to Zionism in the years before the Holocaust. Since the establishment of the state, and particularly since Israel conquered the biblical territories of Judaea and Samaria in the Six Day War, Orthodox Jews have become vociferously nationalistic, with the exception of the Satmar Hasidim, an ultra-Orthodox sect located in Brooklyn. The new messianism among the Orthodox in Israel has found a ready audience among Orthodox American Jews as well. A large number of Orthodox Americans have emigrated to Israel to join the West Bank settlements, and some have been among the most visible supporters of the most extreme Israeli political parties, including Meir Kahane's Kach.

The ideological hegemony that Zionism has achieved in the organized American Jewish community in the last two decades has had the effect of stilling debate about many of the specific policies of the Israeli government. Fear for Israel's existence has created caution among American Jews about openly discussing the political issues that are raging within Israel itself: the future of the West Bank and other foreign-policy questions on which the American Jewish community feels called upon to lobby the American government. Many American Jews who hold liberal views in America supported the Lebanon War, which they would probably have opposed had they lived in Israel; some of these people continued their support long after the war had become thoroughly unpopular in Israel itself. Thus, in embracing the political identity that the cause of Israel has bestowed on them, some American Jews have unwittingly divorced their political principles from their Jewish commitment.

In part, this tendency to support the policies of whichever Israeli government is in power reflects not so much the hegemony of Zionism as a Diaspora version of Israeli statism. The Zionist movement in its classical pre-state period was not a dogmatic movement with a party line; if anything, it is a miracle that such a contentious group of factions ever created a state. The vitality of ideological debate among the parties of classical Zionism, from Revisionists to left-wing socialists, finds little resonance among American Jews, for whom Israel represents an achievement that must be defended at all costs, a metaphor for their own acquisition of power in American society. The politics of opposition and revolution that characterized the Jews of the turn of the century have given way to a defensive politics, just as in Israel itself statism replaced revolutionary Zionism.

It is, however, a measure of the impact of Israel on American Jews that this defensiveness and dogmatism have begun to change. Political conflicts in Israel are being reproduced in America. Every shade of the Israeli political spectrum comes to the American Jewish community for financial and political support. The Israeli peace movement, Peace Now, has its American Jewish support groups, as does the messianic Gush Emunim. Orthodox rabbis take out ads in Jewish newspapers in America defending Israeli Jewish terrorists, while left-wing American Jews publicly criticize the Israeli government from their own point of view. Issues hotly debated in Israel—such as the definition of who is a Jew—have involved Diaspora organizations in Israeli political discourse and have also prompted healthy debates among Jews in America. On more and more questions, Jewish communities around the world are behaving as if they are one political body. The vital political life of Israel, for all its failings, has begun to invigorate the communal politics of American Jews. Perhaps in this way, the legacy of East European Jewish politics, which has persisted in Israel but disappeared in America after World War II, may still be resurrected in the New World.

Zionism, more in its contemporary Israeli incarnations than in its classical form, has become the underlying ideology of the Diaspora Jews—an ironic success, since classical Zionism argued for the "negation of the Diaspora" (*shelilat hagolah*). Without Israel, especially since 1967, it is possible that the political identity of the American Jewish community would have attenuated and the forces of assimilation would have overwhelmed the desire for a collective Jewish politics. By strengthening the political identity of American Jews, Israel has inadvertently undermined its own aspiration to "gather in all the exiles." The necessary alliance between Israel and the American Jewish community has increased the power of both, thus confounding the Zionist ideology that denigrated the Diaspora for its intrinsic apolitical impotence.

The Self-Perceptions of American Jews

The largely unprecedented nature of Jewish power in America is reflected in the self-perceptions of American Jews, the ideologies they have evolved to explain their relationship to America. Compared to the other countries to which the Jews have migrated in their long history of wandering, America meant something very different to many Jewish immigrants. For example, in the late Middle Ages, German Jews moved to Poland; Spanish Jews, expelled from their land in 1492, migrated to the Ottoman Empire, Italy, and Amsterdam. Despite the favorable welcome they received in these countries, however, they did not see them as anything but refuges from persecution and poverty. Jewish immigrants to America, on the other hand, frequently saw their destination in messianic terms: not just as a refuge, but as a land in which the endemic problems of exile might find a permanent solution. Although devoid of many of the traditional characteristics of Jewish messianism (the return to the Land of Israel, the reestablishment of the Kingdom of David, and the rebuilding of the Temple), this messianic vision of America shared with traditional messianism a profound desire to put an end to exile.

Through newspaper accounts and letters, Jews in Eastern Europe developed a myth of the *goldene medine* ("golden country"), which had strong idealistic overtones beyond the purely material advantages that America had to offer.[11] Here the Haskalah's ideals of the integration of the Jews into society might finally be realized. Although the primary cause of emigration from Europe was economic, Jewish memory has insisted on the importance of the East European pogroms, thus suggesting that America meant salvation from political persecution even more than it meant prosperity.[12] Even though economic conditions were extraordinarily difficult for the new immigrants, the rate of return to Europe was much lower among Jews than among any other immigrant group. While the social backgrounds of the immigrants may have accounted in part for these differences (Jews from the cities of Russia had an easier time adapting to American cities than did Italian peasants), America as a messianic land for the Jews played a major role: many of them viewed it as the end of the European exile. They had come to America to stay.

The perception of America as a messianic country coincided remarkably with the image that America had of itself, an image going back to the original Puritan settlers. The pilgrims were also victims of religious persecution. They developed a myth of the New World as a messianic destination, calling themselves the "chosen people," destined to build a "city on the hill." This founding myth could theoretically include the Jews in a way that the myths of national origins of the European nations could not. Just as the pilgrims saw themselves as reincarnations of the biblical Hebrews, so, when Jews arrived from Germany in the middle of the nineteenth century, they began to define themselves not as Jews but as Hebrews, as the names of some of their institutions attest: Hebrew Union College, Hebrew Free Loan Society, Hebrew Immigrant Aid Society. The implication of these names was that the Jewish community in America was not a continuation of European Jewish history but a return to biblical models in a new land. America could become a Promised Land for the Jews because it already saw itself as such.

The self-definition of America as a "chosen land" laid the basis for an ideology of Jewish identification with America, but it also posed a fundamental challenge to Jewish identity. It was one thing to see oneself as the Chosen People in Europe, where Jews were segregated to one degree or another. While neither Christians nor Muslims saw the Jews as still elected by God, the special status they imposed on the Jews reinforced the Jews' own sense of themselves as chosen. But Jews would have a much more difficult time considering themselves chosen in the traditional sense in a land where everyone was, at least theoretically, chosen. As the historian Arnold Eisen has shown, this paradox forced many Jews to redefine the doctrine of chosenness.[13] In the Reform Movement, chosenness came to mean the mission of the Jews toward the rest of the world, a mission identified with universalist ethics. In the more radical reinterpretation of Mordecai M. Kaplan, the founder of Reconstructionism, the Jews were not chosen at all, because there is no such thing as a God who chooses. By rejecting the traditional theology of the Chosen People, these movements constructed ideologies stressing what the Jews had in common with other Americans, ideologies that could function to help the Jews integrate into America.

These reinterpretations of the doctrine of divine election bear a great similarity to the doctrines of "normalization" of the Jewish people that characterized the Haskalah. The way in which German Jews defined themselves as "German citizens of the Mosaic persuasion" and tried to demonstrate the similarities between "Jewishness" and "Germanness" foreshadowed the American Jewish experiment. Just as the Haskalah searched for a basis for integrating the Jews into the nations of the world, so American Jewish ideologies searched for points of identification between Jewish and American self-understandings. The chosenness of the Jews, according to these ideologies, lies not in their differences from others but in their similarities.

One of the major differences between American Jewish ideologies and their European predecessors, however, is that American Jews sought to change the way America defined itself. While the reasons for America becoming a more open society, particularly in the years since World War II, are many, and most have little to do with the Jews directly, the Jews and other immigrant groups did not wait passively to be accepted. American Jews not only fought for acceptance in America on America's terms, they contributed significantly to America's own self-definition through the variety of ideologies we will turn to now. The degree to which Jews helped shape America's understanding of itself is a measure of their power in American society; their acceptance in America is in part a consequence of their ideological contribution to America's pluralistic identity.

American Jewish ideologies have undergone significant changes over the last hundred years, but they retain a common thread: the desire of Jews to identify with the ethos of America, as they have understood it and sometimes redefined it. The "melting pot" theory of American society, according to which all immigrant groups would surrender their identities in favor of a common American identity, is now long out of vogue.[14] But in its heyday, during the first half of this century, Jews were among its most fervent advocates. It was a Jewish poet, Emma Lazarus, who wrote the words on the Statue of Liberty, thus turning the immigrant experience of the Jews into a definition of America as a refuge for all immigrants. The schoolteachers who insisted most vociferously that their immigrant pupils abandon the languages and cultures of their origins were typically Jews. No other immigrant group learned English as fast as the Jews, and no other immigrant group was as quick to enter into the cultural life of America.

It was not only in assimilationist ideologies that the Jews demonstrated their identification with America. Even their fervent support for left-wing movements of opposition, such as socialism and communism, flowed from a profound Americanism. Although the Jews brought socialist ideas from Eastern Europe, they developed them along specifically American lines.[15] It is astonishing with what incredible self-confidence the Jewish immigrants professed a revolutionary ideology in America. It was as if they assumed that socialism was not at all foreign to the American dream and that immigrants might boldly assert its claim upon their new home. Similarly, American Communists, many of whom were Jews, identified almost fanatically with their myth of America, even as they followed the party line from abroad.

With the movement of the Jews out of the working class and out of the cities in the years since World War II, the socialist and communist ideologies of the first half of the century became less central to Jewish self-understanding, although radicalism remained an important component in the identity of many Jews. Three other ideologies, whose origins lie in the prewar period, became crucial for the way Jews saw themselves—and continue to see themselves—in relation to America: a religious ideology that hails Judaism as one of the three great American religions, a political ideology that defines Judaism as intrinsically equivalent to this or that American political philosophy, and a cultural ideology that sees Jews as one ethnic group in a pluralistic society.

All these ideologies are "beyond the melting pot" in the sense that they affirm a legitimate public role for the Jews as Jews. To be Jewish means to announce oneself as Jewish in public, whether religiously, politically, or ethnically. It no longer matters what one does in private; in fact, most American Jews do not live in their homes differently from other Americans of similar classes. In the years since World War II, American Jews have reversed the formula of the Enlightenment that said: "Be a Jew at home and a man in the street." For those who celebrate the identity of America and the Jews, the slogan now reads: "Be a Jew in the street and an American at home."

The first of these three ideologies is based on the notion, initially formulated by the Jewish writer Will Herberg, that America contains "three great religions": Protestantism, Catholicism, and Judaism.[16] Despite the fact that Jews are numerically less than three percent of the American population, Herberg's formula turns them mythically into thirty-three percent! From a tiny minority, the Jews become one of the three custodians of America's religious identity. America is no longer a Christian country, for Christianity as such no longer exists, having been transmuted into Protestantism and Catholicism, which share equal billing with Judaism.

To claim a place in America, which remains a fundamentally religious society, the Jews therefore claim an equal religious identity. Yet they insist strongly on the separation of church and state and on the toleration of all religious beliefs, since they perceive any use of government for religious purposes as detrimental to the Jews as a religious minority. It was probably this fear of politicizing religion that led over sixty percent of Jewish voters in 1984 to vote against Ronald Reagan, in defiance of what many assumed to be a conservative trend among Jews.[17] For most Jews, religion should play a public role only to the extent that it advances common values; at the point where differences become salient, religion should remain private.

Orthodox Jews have come to assert their own claims in American politics, based on a variant of this ideology. Parallel to the rise of Christian fundamentalism as a political movement, they have claimed a public role for traditional Judaism. Like the Agudat Israel in Poland, they advance their interests in the political arena. In their strong proclamations of patriotism and in their voting patterns, which are more conservative than those of other American Jews, Orthodox Jews have demonstrated their integration into the American political system: their identification with the state divorces them radically from their medieval forebears. Orthodox Jews have created their own version of an American Jewish identity in which Jews benefit not from American secular traditions but from the equally strong persistence of religion in American society.

The second ideological strategy argues that Jewish values are identical to American political values. For most of the last half-century, especially since the presidency of Franklin Roosevelt, the political values adopted by the advocates of this ideology were those of liberalism.[18] According to this theory, Jews are liberals because their tradition predisposes them to value social justice and democracy: the Jewish community of the Middle Ages was inherently democratic, and traditional philanthropy was a symbol of the Jewish commitment to the underprivileged. Some of these ideas are myths: the Jewish community of the Middle Ages was hardly a model of democracy, and the philanthropy of the time served to support the rigid class differences in Jewish society. Yet, this myth of Jewish liberalism made possible the expression of Judaism for the secular Jew through social activism, a position inherited from Jewish socialism. One could, for example, be a good Jew by working for the civil rights of blacks or by organizing workers in labor unions. Liberal arguments are also important on behalf of Israel: Jewish liberals argue for an intrinsic alliance between Israel and the United States based on their common democractic values.[19] Jewish liberalism therefore constructs positions that allow for full participation in American life without renunciation of a Jewish identity.

With the challenge to liberalism posed by the so-called neoconservatives in the 1970s and 1980s, a new ideology of American-Jewish symbiosis has emerged. Jewish neoconservatives argue that the conservative agenda corresponds to the contemporary interests of Jews, such as supporting Israel as part of the struggle against Soviet Communism. In addition, they claim that the present economic and social position of the Jews makes their old alliance with the Democratic Party outdated. Like the Jewish liberals, the neoconservatives argue that traditional Jewish values are identical to their political values: for instance, Jews have always believed in rewarding merit and so are naturally opposed to affirmative action. Although the content of neoconservative ideology is radically different from that of the Jewish liberals or the earlier Jewish socialists, it shares with them the penchant for asserting the identity of American and Jewish interests and values, as each defines them.[20]

The third ideology is a cultural argument with important political ramifications: the doctrine of ethnic pluralism. As the belief in America as a "melting pot" eroded in the 1950s and 1960s,[21] Jews, like blacks, Latin Americans, and other ethnic groups, have redefined themselves in ethnic terms, that is, according to their national origins before immigration.

Israel has played an important role in the Jewish claim to be one of these ethnic groups, for, like other ethnic groups, the

Jews have their own nation, even if it is a substitute for their actual nations of origin. While every other ethnic group in America identifies to a greater or lesser degree with the country of its origin, most Jews no longer have such an ancestral home. The adoption of the cause of Israel by American Jews, although occasioned by the struggles of an embattled Jewish state, also represents the search for a substitute homeland.

Significantly, the doctrine of ethnic pluralism as the cardinal definition of America was originally advanced by a Jewish writer, Horace Kallen, in 1920.[22] Like the definition of Judaism as a religion, it has the power to deny the absolute numerical inferiority of the Jews by substituting a different criterion for significance in American society. Jews are not a tiny minority in America, but one of the most important and successful of the immigrant communities. This definition of America allows the sense of nationhood that developed among Jews in Eastern Europe at the end of the nineteenth century to continue in the New World.

The ideologies that American Jews have evolved serve to create a Jewish identity that is equally American. They are reflections of the social integration of American Jews and of their involvement in the American political system. For some, the success of the American Jewish community is cause for celebration in virtually messianic terms: as opposed to all other Jewish communities, the Jews of America no longer live in exile. The degree to which they have been accepted in America has made it possible, in the words of Charles Silberman, to "speak truth to power."[23] For those who subscribe to this position, the ethos of America and the essence of Judaism have become virtually identical.

The Holocaust in American Political Thinking

Despite the tangible achievements of the American Jewish commmunity and despite the ideologies proposing a vision of America in which Jews have considerable power, many American Jews regard their power with considerable uneasiness and even pessimism. Regardless of what the actual statistics may say, some consider the rates of intermarriage and assimilation as portents of a cultural and demographic disaster, and there are those who predict that the American Jewish community may disappear almost entirely in a century. Even as economic and military aid for Israel rises from year to year, American Jews fear that the United States commitment to the defense of Israel remains skin-deep and that Jews around the world are imminently in danger of finding themselves isolated and without allies. For some, the memory of the Holocaust has created fears of the possibility of a second holocaust in America or elsewhere. American Jews consistently perceive anti-Semitism to be more endemic to American society than the objective indices, such as public opinion polls, say it is.[24] In fact, even to remark on the relative political power of the American Jewish community—whether of the Israel lobby in Washington or of Jewish influence in domestic affairs—arouses fear in some quarters of giving ammunition to the anti-Semites. To criticize Israeli policies in public raises similar kinds of fears. It is almost as if memories of powerlessness have created an embarrassment over power, so that the subject cannot be discussed above a whisper.

Paradoxically, such fears have grown together with the growth in American Jewish power in the last two decades. While American Jews had good cause for concern over anti-Semitism and discrimination before World War II, these issues are no longer as pressing. Although Israel was in much greater danger in 1948, it is her situation since 1967 that has caused the greater concern. In contrast to the fears of earlier generations, the present anxiety takes the form of a virtual ideology: an ideology of survival with strong similarities to the Israeli ideology of survival discussed in chapter 6.[25] If the ideologies asserting the identity of American and Jewish interests represent a sense of American Jewish power, the new ideology of survival, which is at once more nationalistic and more pessimistic, resurrects historical feelings of powerlessness.

As in Israel, consciousness of the Holocaust plays the critical role in the ideology of survival, but it is the Holocaust intertwined with feelings about the state of Israel. During the two decades after the end of World War II, the destruction of the European Jews had little impact on American Jewish life. Few courses on the Holocaust were taught in American universities and few books were published on the subject, most of them being scholarly works with limited audiences. The very term Holocaust came into common usage only in the 1960s. The Eichmann trial was of some importance in bringing the Holocaust to the attention of American Jews, but its effect was transitory. A *Commentary* symposium on the state of Jewish belief in 1966 elicited virtually no mention of the Holocaust as an influence on Jewish thinking.[26]

Only with the Six Day War did American Jews begin to confront the Holocaust. The real fear that Israel might be annihilated opened up a floodgate of associations with the Holocaust and a much greater sense of identification with the Jewish state than had been true in the period since the establishment of Israel in 1948. Perhaps some mechanism of repression was at work after the Holocaust that prevented Jews from confronting fully what had actually happened in Europe; by 1967, Jews were prepared to express their sense of collective trauma, and the war in the Middle East triggered a delayed reaction. Similarly, only after the state of Israel had existed for close to thirty years could American Jews come to identify fully with it—and then only when its very existence seemed threatened. The often exaggerated sense of guilt that American Jews today feel over their failure to save the European Jews reflects their fear for Israel, just as their fear for Israel feeds their consciousness of the Holocaust. In their association of the Holocaust with the state of Israel, American Jews have come to see Israel as a second chance to defend what they failed to save forty-five years ago.

The works of two men, Elie Wiesel and Emil Fackenheim, whose books became exceptionally popular in the post-1967 period, demonstrate this new connection between the Holocaust and Israel. Wiesel as a novelist and Fackenheim as a theologian tried to come to terms with the Holocaust, an event both experienced. Wiesel had written some of his most important books before 1967, but he was only "discovered" as a result of the new interest in the Holocaust sparked by the Six Day War. In a number of books written after the war, such as *A Beggar in Jerusalem*, Wiesel explicitly connected the Holocaust with the state of Israel. Fackenheim, who had devoted himself to Hegelian philosophy until the late 1960s, introduced the theme of the Holocaust in his *God's Presence in History*, published in 1970. In that work, he asserted that the survival of the Jewish state is a divine commandment issued by the "Commanding Voice at Auschwitz." For both of these writers and for the audiences that received them with such acclaim, the Holocaust and the state of Israel were the two poles of the new Jewish identity.

The Holocaust has become the primary historical event around which the American Jewish community unites. In media events such as the television series "Holocaust," in the proliferation of books published on the subject, and in the disproportionate popularity of college courses, Jewish identity in America has been tied to the Holocaust, perhaps to a greater degree than in the state of Israel. The establishment of a Presidential Commission on the Holocaust during the Carter Administration demonstrated at once the centrality of the event for American Jews and the willingness of the American political establishment to acknowledge the Holocaust experience in the cause of domestic politics. It is remarkable testimony to the contemporary political power of American Jews that the Holocaust has acquired virtually sacred status in the vocabulary of American politics forty years after World War II, during which neither the government nor the media made more than perfunctory mention of it.

American Jews have also succeeded in linking the Holocaust to foreign policy by making it a weapon in the propaganda war for Israel: lack of support for Israel is portrayed as a denial of the lessons of the Holocaust, just as lack of recognition of the Holocaust appears to connote lack of support for Israel (those who deny that the Holocaust ever happened are driven by a similar desire to connect the two issues, for the primary motivation behind their historical "revisionism" is anti-Zionism: the state of Israel cannot claim that the Holocaust justifies its existence since the Holocaust never took place). Just as Israel was probably the main catalyst for the belated Jewish attention to the Holocaust, so the American relationship to Israel has given the Holocaust a political role forty years after the event.

The paradox of the introduction of the Holocaust into American Jewish political thought is that it is through identification with the most powerless Jews in all of history that American Jews have asserted their collective power: they have turned the experience of powerlessness in Europe into a potent political weapon. In projecting their fears about themselves onto the Holocaust and onto Israel, American Jews have stumbled on a particularly successful strategy that has in fact enhanced their power. It may be that the preoccupation of American Jews with the Holocaust and the state of Israel represents a "vicarious identity," based on the experience of Jews in other places and other times.[27] But it is an identity that has produced considerable if unintended political dividends.

America and the History of the Diaspora

The Holocaust is a metaphor for the uneasiness of the American Jewish community, for its difficulty in coming to terms with the actual power Jews possess today, both in Israel and in the Diaspora. Historical fear and embarrassment over power have created a chasm between perceptions and reality. The relative power of American Jews, like the power of the sovereign state of Israel, stands in striking contrast to the powerlessness of the European Jews. Clearly, no one would advocate that the Holocaust should not be remembered, for it is unquestionably the most important event in recent Jewish history. But there is a difference between remembrance and constructing a collective identity around an event and an experience alien to the realities of American Jewish life.

The unavoidable confrontation with the Holocaust needs to be tempered with a broader view of Jewish history. The American Jewish community is in many ways one of the most powerful in all of the history of the Diaspora, yet by comparing it with other communities we can arrive at a balanced view of both its power and its weaknesses. For example, the current obsession with the demography of the Jewish community and with its possible effect on communal survival appears in a different light when we look at other eras. As the history of the Jews of the Middle Ages attests, the size of a community does not necessarily determine its quality. The communities of the Rhineland were extraordinarily vital and influential even though they were extremely small; so were the Polish Jewish communities of the sixteenth century. Although political power in a democracy has much to do with sheer numbers, the power of the Jews owes more to nonquantitative factors: education, organization, and ideological commitment, as well as the role of the Jews in society. Even if the prophets of demographic doom are correct and the American Jewish community loses half or more of its members in the next century, it will be its inner political and cultural strength that will shape its external power.

No medieval analogy will be very helpful in evaluating the American Jewish community, since at no time then did a sovereign Jewish state exist in the Land of Israel, and, as I have argued, the state of Israel is a fundamental factor in the contemporary power of American Jews. Perhaps one possible analogy might be the Babylonian Jewish community, which rivaled the Palestinian one in political power and talmudic learning, just as, today, it might be claimed, the American

Jewish community is becoming the equal of the state of Israel.

The Babylonian example is not, however, that useful either. The Babylonian Jewish commmunity began its rise as the Palestinian Jewish community declined in the third century C.E., while the power of the American Jewish community, as we have seen, derives in part from the ascendance of the state of Israel. In the Babylonia of late antiquity, Jewish learning took place in the framework of a powerful political system of internal self-government, recognized by the gentile state. In America, such a strong set of autonomous institutions is lacking; for all their communal organizations, American Jews do not possess the partial sovereignty that characterized antiquity and the Middle Ages. Despite signs of Jewish creativity, the American Jewish community has not produced a major contribution to Jewish thought, let alone a modern equivalent of the Babylonian Talmud. For all the power of the American Jews, an argument could be made that the Babylonian Jewish community was more powerful, certainly in its governance of its own members and perhaps even in its relationship to the non-Jewish power structure.

A better analogy, perhaps, is the Alexandrian Jewish community of the first century C.E. The Jews of Alexandria enjoyed extensive rights and considered themselves the equals of the Hellenized aristocracy. Individuals could rise to positions of great power and become Roman citizens, although the community as a whole did not have citizenship status. The community was closely tied to the Second Temple state, sent contributions to the Temple in the manner of the United Jewish Appeal, and defended its Judaean brothers in the Roman court. Some of the extreme sects in Judaea, such as the Essenes, had their counterparts in Egypt. As opposed to Babylonia, where the rabbis imposed their interpretation of Judaism on the Jewish population, the Judaism of first-century Alexandria was pluralistic and included an ancient version of Reform Judaism. Assimilation was a common phenomenon (a nephew of the Alexandrian Jewish philosopher

Philo even became a general in the Roman army that destroyed the Temple!). Yet it was this community that rose in revolt against the Romans in 115–117 C.E. and proved to be as militant as the Jews of Judaea. Like the Jews of today, the Jews of Judaea and Alexandria lived in a world in which the sovereignty of small nations suffered under severe constraints. As today, the Jews of both communities responded then by imitating the culture of the larger world but also by asserting their national identity.

The Alexandrian analogy, regardless of its imperfections, raises some cautionary questions. That community had its own identity, independent of the Second Temple state, yet it declined as the ancient Jewish state lost power. Today, too, one might wonder what the future of the American Jewish community would be, not so much if Israel were to disappear, but if, on the contrary, genuine peace were to come to the Middle East and Israel were to establish herself on a firm economic footing. If Israel at war has been an important factor in motivating the American Jewish community, what effect would an Israel at peace—a "normal" Israel—have on the political identity of American Jews? Will the concern of Jews as Jews with domestic issues continue to furnish a framework for a vital Jewish politics?

These remain hypothetical questions. Yet, in searching for an understanding of their present power, American Jews should consider the whole panoply of Jewish history, not so much to find precise analogies as to correct the misperceptions that the legitimate immersion in the Holocaust necessarily creates. Both the achievements and failures of past communities can shed light on the power and vulnerabilities of the American Jewish community. The exercise of collective power in a pluralistic democracy is indeed new in Jewish history. Yet, for all that the journey to America meant a break with the past, American Jews must, if they wish to remain Jews, analyze their experience in terms of their whole history.

Epilogue
The Political Legacy of Jewish History

THE Jews have chosen the modern nation-state, whether in the form of the state of Israel or American democracy, as the best guarantee for their survival. That they have identified with the nation-state is no surprise, for they have always demonstrated a shrewd understanding of the political forms of each age, from partial sovereignty in imperial antiquity to corporate power in the Middle Ages. Identification with the state is the modern version of Jewish politics; different strategies pertained in the past. To suggest that modern Jews should adopt some other strategy for survival—to argue that nationalism or democratic pluralism are foreign to Judaism—is to ignore the political legacy of Jewish history, a persistent tradition of political imitation and accommodation, but never of passivity or retreat from politics. Zionism and Diaspora nationalism in their modern forms may be new in Jewish history, but they represent no more and no less than the latest incarnation of this political tradition.

These contemporary strategies for survival, for all their limitations and failures to fulfill messianic expectations, have still proven to be largely successful. The Jews of Israel and the

Western Diaspora face less of a threat to their physical survival than at any other time since the end of the Holocaust and certainly less in comparison to the Jews of Europe before the Holocaust. To say that these Jews are secure would be foolhardy in light of Jewish history, but they are certainly more secure than many allow themselves to believe.

The discrepancy between contemporary Jewish power and the insecurity many Jews feel owes much to the inverted image that modern anti-Semites have of Jewish power. If Jews typically see themselves as less powerful than they really are, anti-Semites, since the nineteenth century, portray them as much more powerful: a secret cabal in control of the world. The state of Israel has not diminished this paranoia; on the contrary, anti-Semites now see Zionism as a force equal to twentieth-century imperialism. Afraid of feeding these bizarre delusions, many Jews shrink from acknowledging the actual power they possess. The reality, as I have argued throughout this book, lies somewhere between Jewish fear and anti-Semitic fantasy.

Traumatic historical memories play as great a role in the Jews' misperception of their contemporary power. Every nation labors under the burden of its own history, caught in the tensions between its understanding of history and current political realities; these tensions are often the cause of misguided political decisions. The United States, torn between conflicting legacies of isolationism and interventionism, and fearful of being perceived as a "paper tiger," became entangled in Vietnam. The Soviet Union, invaded repeatedly by the West, holds tenaciously to the countries of Eastern Europe as a buffer against imagined Western threats. The Germans, fearful of their neighbors and obsessed with national unification, repeatedly launched wars against the rest of Europe, only to find themselves after World War II permanently divided and the most likely battlefield for a war between East and West; by succumbing to paranoid fears and messianic appetites, the Germans brought down on themselves exactly the situation they most dreaded.

None of these examples sheds direct light on the dilemma of the Jews, for no other nation has a history analogous to theirs. But each of these cases suggests that the burden of history is a problem common to all nation-states, even as the shape and content of the burden differs. For Jews, contemporary political problems return inevitably and fatefully to the Holocaust, the final denouement of European Jewish history. The Jews have classically defined their history as unique, and in many ways it is. Their victimization by the Nazis revived anew this sense of uniqueness, at a time when ideologies of "normalization" had begun to undermine the concept of a Chosen People. For many, the return of the Jews to sovereignty could be understood only against the backdrop of the Holocaust, the epitome of the powerlessness of a powerless people: the Holocaust became a metaphor for the special character of all of Jewish history, and only Jewish sovereignty could be a response to this condition of impotence. I have argued that the extremes represented by the boundless terror of the Holocaust and by the victories of the state of Israel should not distort our perception of the Jews' relationship to power throughout Jewish history; neither should they blur our vision of politics today. To see both past and present realistically without forgetting or suppressing the memory of the Holocaust remains the Jews' particular burden from history.

When they consider their past, the Jews have no choice but to grapple with the Holocaust. But the Holocaust may also convey a different message with respect to the future: it may signify that the fate of the Jews is no longer unique, becoming instead a symbol for the fate of all mankind. In the twentieth century, the promise of the nation-state, which the European Enlightenment believed would free mankind, has been irrevocably compromised. With the murder of the Jews, the nation-state went mad, reducing some of its subjects to powerless pawns and, finally, corpses. The Nazis were by no means the only twentieth-century rulers to terrorize and murder those they ruled, but they did so with a systematic efficiency and industrial rationality never imagined before.

The total deprivation of human rights and utter degradation suffered by the Jews are not a closed chapter buried in history. Throughout the world today, dictatorships of widely different ideological persuasions have remembered the lessons of the totalitarian regimes of the 1930s and 1940s. In the atrocities committed by governments against their own citizens, the terrifying legacy of the Holocaust lives on. The very powerlessness of the Jews under the Nazis is a warning of the possible fate of human beings anywhere in the world.

The powerlessness of the Jews during the Holocaust also points to the fate of all humanity in the face of nuclear war. It is now possible for governments to deliver the ovens of Auschwitz to all corners of the earth, to make a holocaust of all mankind. Like the Jews of Nazi Europe, the people of the world will be utterly impotent in such a war, neither soldiers nor even innocent bystanders, but, again like the Jews, intentional victims.

As a metaphor for a new politics of irrationality, the Holocaust contains a message of inescapable relevance for a nuclear world. For the first time in human history, a government sought to eradicate a whole people from the earth for reasons that had nothing to do with political realities. In a similar way, the idea of nuclear war lacks the most elementary political rationality, for it would necessarily destroy everything it meant to save: it would take genocide, invented in its most systematic form by the Nazis, to its global and ultimately suicidal conclusion.

Post-Holocaust Jewish nationalism—the accepted ideology of many of the world's Jews—derives its logic and its legitimacy from both the modern history of the Jews and the modern history of the world. From this point of view, Jewish nationalism is the irrefutable answer to the powerlessness of the Holocaust. At the same time, as a prefiguration of the terrors of contemporary politics, the Holocaust has thrown a dark shadow over the future of the nation-state as such, diminishing the promise of modern nationalism for the Jews as for all other peoples.

The urge toward a normal existence in a Jewish state grew out of a profound desire to escape the "unique destiny of a unique people." Yet, if a "normal existence" today means confronting the terror of global nuclear genocide, then instead of the Jews escaping their historical destiny, it is the world that has become Jewish; the Jews have entered the world of nations only to discover that all mankind faces the holocaust they themselves already suffered. In this world, power is no longer a complete antidote to powerlessness. Possessed of the power to destroy this world, the nations of the earth have become the prisoners of their own might, limited in their sovereignty by forces of their own making: power has created its own vulnerability.

In this dialectic between power and vulnerability, the long history of the Jews may unexpectedly serve as a beacon to the nations. From biblical times to the present day, the Jews have wandered the uncertain terrain between power and powerlessness, never quite achieving the power necessary to guarantee long-term security, but equally avoiding, with a number of disastrous exceptions, the abyss of absolute impotence. They developed the consummate political art of living with uncertainty and insecurity; their long survival owes much to this extraordinary achievement. Jews today must struggle to come to terms with this history in light of their present power, to see both past and present through a realistic lens, neither inflating their power nor exaggerating their powerlessness. The lessons this history can teach are necessary for their own continued existence and are equally relevant to the continued existence of mankind.

Notes

Preface

1. Bernard Avishai has now treated this subject in *The Tragedy of Zionism* (New York, 1985).

2. *Gershom Scholem: Kabbalah and Counter-History* (Cambridge, Mass., 1979).

3. Amos Funkenstein, "Passivity as the Characteristic of the Diaspora Jews: Myth and Reality" (Hebrew), Tel Aviv University School of Historical Studies, 1982.

Introduction

1. David Ben Gurion, "The Imperatives of the Jewish Revolution," in Arthur Hertzberg, ed., *The Zionist Idea* (Philadelphia, 1959), 607.

2. Hannah Arendt, *The Origins of Totalitarianism* (Cleveland and New York, 1958), 8.

3. Michael Selzer, *Zionism Reconsidered* (New York, 1970), x. For a fuller explication of Selzer's views, see his *Wineskin and the Wizard* (New York, 1970).

4. If this is still the most commonly accepted view of Jewish history, it is not necessarily accepted by all historians. In 1928, Salo Baron criticized what he called the "lachrymose" view of Jewish history, meaning the idea that the Diaspora is one long period of persecutions and suffering. See "Ghetto and Emancipation," *Menorah Journal* 14 (June 1928): 515–26; see further his *History and Jewish Historians* (Philadelphia, 1964), 65–106. Baron's own reading of Jewish history can be found in his great multivolume work, *The Social and Religious History of the Jews*, 18 vols. (New York, 1967). He also wrote a study of the structure and authority of the Diaspora

Jewish communities, *The Jewish Community* (Philadelphia, 1942). Two other distinguished historians who have espoused a similar view of the history of the Diaspora are Simon Dubnow and Haim Hillel Ben-Sasson. See Dubnow's *Nationalism and History*, ed. Koppel Pinson (Philadelphia, 1958), and Ben-Sasson's contribution to *A History of the Jewish People*, ed. H. H. Ben-Sasson (Cambridge, Mass., 1976), section on the Jewish Middle Ages. The work of these and other historians on which I have drawn is cited in the notes of the relevant chapters below.

5. There are two important recent essays that make this argument and to which I am indebted. They are Amos Funkenstein's Hebrew lecture "Passivity as the Characteristic of the Diaspora Jews" and Ismar Schorsch's "On the History of the Political Judgment of the Jew," Leo Baeck Memorial Lecture 20 (1976).

6. For a historical treatment of concepts of power and legitimacy, see Reinhard Bendix, *Kings or People: Power and the Mandate to Rule* (Berkeley and Los Angeles, 1978), 16. A further theoretical discussion can be found in Brian Barry, ed., *Power and Political Theory* (London, 1976).

7. Yosef Hayim Yerushalmi, *Zakhor: Jewish History and Jewish Memory* (Seattle, 1982), especially chap. 4.

Chapter 1

1. Josephus Flavius, *The Jewish Wars*, trans. G. A. Williamson, (London, 1959), 360.

2. Translated in James Pritchard, ed., *Ancient Near Eastern Texts* (Princeton, N.J., 1958), 231.

3. For a good integration of biblical history with the history of the ancient Middle East, see John Bright, *A History of Israel*, 3d ed. (Philadelphia, 1981).

4. For a discussion of the Persian and Hellenistic periods, see Elias Bickerman, *From Ezra to the Last of the Maccabees* (New York, 1962); Victor Tcherikover, *Hellenistic Civilization and the Jews* (Philadelphia, 1961); and Solomon Zeitlin, *The Rise and Fall of the Judaean State*, 3 vols. (Philadelphia, 1962).

5. On the legal status of the Jews in the Diaspora, see Tcherikover, *Hellenistic Civilization*, and Mary Smallwood, *Jews under Roman Rule* (Leiden, 1976). Smallwood includes a discussion of the revolts of 115–117. Additional primary sources translated into En-

glish can be found in V. Tcherikover and A. Fuks, *Corpus Papyrorum Judaicarum* (Cambridge, Mass., 1957–64).

6. See, for instance, Isaiah 30:15.

7. On Manasseh, see II Kings 21. A more sympathetic history of his reign can be found in II Chronicles 33, which claims that Manasseh repented after having been imprisoned by the Assyrians.

8. See Jeremiah 4.

9. An example of this position can be found in Michael Avi Yonah, *The Jews under Roman and Byzantine Rule* (New York, 1984), 12, where he argues curiously that "this period of political atrophy . . . was a time of economic and demographic consolidation," as if economic prosperity is possible without an active political order.

10. Josephus, *Antiquities*, trans. W. Whiston (Philadelphia, 1888), 12, chap. 3. For commentary including earlier interpretations, see Tcherikover, *Hellenistic Civilization*, 73–89.

11. See Elias Bickerman, *The God of the Maccabees*, trans. Horst R. Moehring (Leiden, 1979). For a discussion of the historiography and one further interpretation, see Tcherikover, *Hellenistic Civilization*, 152–203.

12. On Herod, see Josephus, *Antiquities*, 15 and 16. See further Abraham Shalit, *Hordus ha-Melekh* (Jerusalem, 1960); Samuel Sandmel, *Herod: Profile of a Tyrant* (Philadelphia, 1967); and Michael Grant, *Herod the Great* (New York, 1975).

13. *Tosefta Menahot* 13:20. See further Babylonian Talmud (henceforth BT), Gittin 55b–56a and Shabbat 119b.

14. Gedaliah Alon, *Jews, Judaism and the Classical World*, trans. Israel Abrahams (Jerusalem, 1977), 269–313.

15. Alon compares the relevant sources and concludes that the midrash on Lamentations (1:51) is more historical than the oft-quoted passages from *Avot de-Rabbi Natan*.

16. Jacob Neusner, *A Life of Yohanan ben Zakkai*, 2d ed. (Leiden, 1970). See also his *From Politics to Piety* (New York, 1979), especially 146–54, in which he argues for the political astuteness of the Pharisees. Neusner does not adopt Alon's position on the meaning of Yohanan ben Zakkai's move to Yavneh, but his argument tends in the same direction.

17. On the Bar Kokhba Revolt, see Yigal Yadin, *Bar Kokhba*, (London, 1978).

18. See Avi Yonah, *Roman and Byzantine Rule*, chaps. 2 and 3.

19. Origen, *Epistula ad Africanum*, par. 14.

20. BT, Shabbat 33b.

21. Origen, *Contra Celsum*, trans. Henry Chadwick (Cambridge, 1965), 6.78 (p. 391); see also 4.36 (p. 214).

22. On the '*apiru*, see Bright, *History of Israel*, 94; Moshe Greenberg, *The Hab/piru* (New Haven, Conn., 1955); and Roland de Vaux, "Le problème des Hapiru après quinze années," *Journal of Near Eastern Studies* 27 (1968): 221–28. Greenberg demonstrated the lack of linguistic connection between the Hebrews and the '*apiru*, but the possibility of some historical connection remains nevertheless.

23. On the Israelite conquest, see G. E. Mendenhall, "The Hebrew Conquest of Canaan," *Biblical Archaeologist* 25 (1962): 66–87, and Albrecht Alt, "The Settlement of the Israelites in Palestine," in his *Essays on Old Testament History and Religion*, trans. R. A. Wilson (Garden City, N. Y., 1967), 173–222.

24. See Martin Noth, *Das System der zwoelf Staemme Israels* (Darmstadt, 1966).

25. Max Weber suggested the idea of the system of the Judges as one of "charismatic" leadership. See his *Ancient Israel*, trans. Hans Gerth and Don Martindales (New York, 1952), 90–95, and his *Sociology of Religion*, trans. E. Fischoff (London, 1965), 2, 3, 55.

26. On the unique political status of Moses, see David Rapoport, "Moses, Charisma and Covenant," *Western Political Quarterly* 32 (Summer 1979): 123–53 (including critical responses). Rapoport argues that Moses was the only creative charismatic figure, while all other such biblical figures, such as the Judges, hearken back to the political doctrines Moses established. He also correctly (as opposed to Weber) shows that biblical charisma does not stand by itself but stems from the notion of covenant.

27. Psalm 89:4–5, 28. The psalm ends with an amendment obviously added after the Babylonian exile that laments the destruction of the Davidic monarchy and asks how God could have forsaken His vow to establish the line of David forever. The transmutation of Davidic theology into messianism was the answer to the psalmist's perplexity. For a further example of Davidic political theology, see II Samuel 7:13–16.

28. Isaiah 9:5–6, 11:1–5; Micah 5:1–6.

29. Zechariah 4:1–3, 14. For the Dead Sea texts, see Geza Vermes, ed., *The Dead Sea Scrolls in English* (Baltimore, 1965), 106 (from the "Damascus Covenant") and 121 (from the "Messianic Rule"). See further J. Liver, "The Doctrine of the Two Messiahs in

Sectarian Literature in the Time of the Second Commonwealth,"
Harvard Theological Review 52 (1959): 149–85.

30. Isaiah 10:5.

31. The viewpoint of the Book of Kings appears first in the
debate preserved in I Samuel 8–12 over the establishment of the
monarchy. It is generally assumed that the antimonarchical position
in this text belongs to that of the editor of Kings, although it may
also reflect actual opposition to the monarchy at the time of Samuel.
The law of the king appears in Deuteronomy 17:14–20.

32. Jeremiah 29:5–7.

Chapter II

1. A recent example of this position is Gershon Weiler,
Te'okratiyah Yehudit [Jewish Theocracy] (Tel Aviv, 1976). Weiler
tries to show that the claims of the present-day Orthodox in Israel to
establish a state grounded in *halakhah* are not based on a correct
historical understanding of Jewish law, which is unsuited to the
political life of a state. An answer to Weiler's argument that there is
no rabbinic political theory is Daniel Elazar and Stuart Cohen, *The
Jewish Polity* (Bloomington, Ind., 1984), which tries to apply some
rabbinic political concepts to all of Jewish history. This attempt to
unify all of Jewish history under a presumed rabbinic "constitution"
is severely flawed by the mechanical and unhistorical way in which
the authors try to find these concepts operating in every period and
in every Jewish community.

2. For some of the theologies of exile, see the article "Galut" by
H. H. Ben-Sasson in the *Encyclopedia Judaica* (Jerusalem, 1972). See
further Yitzhak F. Baer, *Galut* (New York, 1947).

3. *Mekhilta de-Rabbi Ishmael*, ed. J. Lauterbach (Philadelphia,
1949), 1:114ff. See also BT, Megillah 29b. For a discussion of the
concept of *shekhinah* (the aspect of God that "dwells" among the
Jewish people), see E. E. Urbach, *The Sages: Their Concepts and Beliefs*, trans. I. Abrahams (Jerusalem, 1975), chap. 3.

4. BT, Yoma 69b. The present discussion of the rabbinic concepts of God's power and the election of Israel is not intended to
exhaust the subject but merely to point out some new, peculiar features. For a comprehensive discussion, see Urbach, *Sages*, 255–85,
525–41.

5. On the Lurianic Kabbalah, see Gershom Scholem, *Major Trends in Jewish Mysticism*, 3d ed. (New York, 1961), chap. 6.

6. BT, Yoma 9b, Sanhedrin 11a, Sotah 48b. These texts allow for a heavenly voice (*bat kol*) to take the place of prophecy. But see against even this intervention BT, Baba Metzia 59b (infra, n. 31).

7. See Shlomo Eidelberg, ed. and trans., *The Jews and the Crusaders: The Hebrew Chronicles of the First and Second Crusades* (Madison, Wis., 1977), and the anonymous text published in *Hebrew Union College Annual* 12–13 (1937–38): 435ff.

8. See Judah Ha-Levi, *Sefer ha-Kuzari*, trans. H. Hirschfeld (New York, 1964), 4:22 and 1:113, for his use of the concept of *humilitas*. An acute analysis of Ha-Levi's doctrine of passivity can be found in H. H. Ben-Sasson, "The Uniqueness of the Jews in the Mind of the Twelfth Century" (Hebrew), *Perakim* 2 (1971): 155–64. Ha-Levi's argument implicitly turns the *galut* into a positive religious experience. In eighteenth-century Hasidism, Dov Baer, the Maggid of Mezeritch, argued that only in exile can the Jews find and defeat the forces of evil, a mystical version of Ha-Levi's argument.

9. Judah Loew ben Bezalel, *Netzah Yisrael* (Tel Aviv, 1964), chap. 1.

10. Ben-Sasson has collected the sources supporting this second approach to *galut* in "Uniqueness of the Jews," 165ff. He argues that this position was the dominant one, at least in the twelfth century, and that Ha-Levi's passivity was in the minority.

11. For a survey of rabbinic attitudes, see Urbach, *Sages*, 649–90, and Abba Hillel Silver, *The History of Messianic Speculations in Israel* (New York, 1927).

12. For a discussion of rabbinic statements on Bar Kokhba, see Richard Marks, "The Image of Bar Kokhba in Jewish Literature up to the Seventeenth Century—False Messiah or National Hero" (Ph.D. diss., UCLA, 1980). See further Urbach, *Sages*, 673–76. For an examination of the impact of Bar Kokhba on subsequent Jewish ideology, see Yehoshafat Harkabi, *The Bar Kokhba Syndrome*, trans. Max Ticktin (Chappaqua, N.Y., 1983).

13. See Neusner, *Yohanan ben Zakkai*.

14. The only treatment of monarchy in the rabbinic sources is Gerald Blidstein, "The Monarchic Imperative in Rabbinic Perspective," *Association of Jewish Studies Annual Review* 7–8 (1982–83): 15–40. No comparable comprehensive study exists for the Middle Ages.

15. BT, Sanhedrin 97b.

16. BT, Ketubot 111a and Shir Ha-Shirim Rabba 2:7.

17. Joel Teitelbaum, *Va-Yoel Moshe* (Brooklyn, N.Y., 1959–61). See further Allen Nadler, "Piety and Politics: The Case of the Satmar Rebbe," *Judaism* 31 (1982): 135–51.

18. See Marks, "Image of Bar Kokhba," especially 43–94.

19. Amos Funkenstein, "Maimonides: Political Theory and Realistic Messianism," *Miscellanea Mediaevalia* 11 (1977): 81–103. On Maimonides' political theory, see also Leo Strauss, "Maimonides' Statement on Political Science," *Proceedings of the American Academy for Jewish Research* 22 (1953): 115–30.

20. BT, Sanhedrin 99a.

21. *Mishneh Torah*, Hilkhot Melakhim, chaps. 11, 12.

22. Ibid., 1:9.

23. Ibid., Hilkhot Sanhedrin.

24. BT, Sanhedrin 98b.

25. Nissim of Marseilles, *Ma'ase nissim*. See Baron, *Jewish Community*, 1:176.

26. BT, Gittin 62a. See Jacob Neusner, *A History of the Jews in Babylonia* (Leiden, 1966–70), 3:75–81.

27. See Ben-Sasson, *History of the Jewish People*, 595, 598.

28. Nathan of Hanover, *Yeven Metzula* (Tel Aviv, 1945), translated in Bernard Weinryb, *The Jews of Poland* (Philadelphia, 1972), 173.

29. See Gerson D. Cohen, "The Story of the Four Captives," *Proceedings of the American Academy for Jewish Research* 29 (1960–61), and Abraham ibn Daud, *Sefer ha-Qabbalah*, ed. and trans. Gerson D. Cohen (Philadelphia, 1967), 263–89.

30. Translated in Yitzhak F. Baer, *History of the Jews in Christian Spain*, 2 vols. (Philadelphia, 1961), 2:77.

31. BT, Baba Metzia 59b. See further E. E. Urbach, "Halakhah and Prophecy" (Hebrew), *Tarbiz* (1947), and idem, *Sages*, 118–19.

32. Translated in Baer, *Jews in Christian Spain*, 2:77.

33. On the political theory of the Jewish community, see Yitzhak F. Baer, "The Origins of the Organization of the Jewish Community in the Middle Ages" (Hebrew), *Zion* 15 (1950): 1–41; S. D. Goitein, "The Local Jewish Community in the Light of the Cairo Geniza Records," *Journal of Jewish Studies* 12 (1961): 141ff.; Samuel Morell, "The Constitutional Limits of Communal Government in Rabbinic Law," *Jewish Social Studies* 33 (July 1971): 87–119; Irving Agus,

Rabbi Meir of Rothenburg, 2d ed. (New York, 1970), Appendix; S. Albeck, "Sources of the Authority of the Kehillot in Spain until R. Meir Abulafia (1180–1244)" (Hebrew), *Zion* 25 (1960): 85–121; Menachem Elon, "Power and Authority: Halachic Stance in the Traditional Community and Its Contemporary Implications," in Daniel Elazar, ed., *Kinship and Consent: The Jewish Political Tradition and Its Contemporary Uses* (Washington, D.C., 1983), 183–213; and Gerald Blidstein, "Individual and Community in the Middle Ages: Halakhic Theory" in Elazar, *Kinship and Consent,* 215–56. The best general study of the structure of the Jewish community is still Baron, *Jewish Community.*

34. *Responsa of Ribash* (Riva da Trent, 1558), no. 228, fol. 155r.

35. BT, Baba Batra 8b.

36. BT, Moed Katan 17a. On this doctrine, see Gerald Blidstein, "Notes on Hefker Bet Din," *Dinei Yisrael* 4 (1973): 35–50.

37. Elijah Mizrahi, *Responsa* (Jerusalem, 1938), 145–46, translated in Elon, "Power and Authority," 189.

38. Ibid.

39. *Teshuvot Ha-Geonim Shaarei Tsedek* (Jerusalem, 1966), 125, translated in Morell, "Constitutional Limits," 88.

40. *Responsa of the Rosh,* Klal 7, par. 3, translated in Elon, "Power and Authority," 211 n. 49.

41. *Responsa of Maharashdam,* Orakh Hayyim, 37, translated in Elon, "Power and Authority," 197.

42. See the discussions by Morell, "Constitutional Limits," and Blidstein, "Individual and Community."

43. Menachem Meiri, *Beit Ha-Behirah al Baba Batra,* ed. A. Sofer (New York, 1956), 59ff., translated in Morell, 106.

44. See H. H. Ben-Sasson, *Hagut ve-Hanhagah* (Jerusalem, 1969), chap. 12.

45. See, for example, Irving Agus, "Democracy in the Communities of the Early Middle Ages," *Jewish Quarterly Review* 43 (1952–53): 153–76, and idem, *Meir of Rothenburg.*

46. On monarchy and democracy in the Middle Ages, see F. Kern, "The Divine Right of Kings and the Right of Resistance in the Early Middle Ages," in *Kingship and Law,* trans. S. B. Chrimes (Oxford, 1956), and Otto Gierke, *Political Theories of the Middle Ages,* trans. F. W. Maitland (Cambridge, 1922), especially chap. 10.

47. On Meir and Isserles, see Morell, "Constitutional Limits."

48. See Gil Graf, "Separation of Church and State in Thought

and Practice: Application and Extension of Dina de-Malkuta Dina in Jewish Law, 1750–1848" (Ph.D. Diss., UCLA, 1982; publication forthcoming), 31–32.

49. BT, Yevamot 90b.

50. Rab, for example, was said to have flogged a man who betrothed a woman with a myrtle branch, which was theoretically legal but violated the spirit of the marital laws. See BT, Kiddushin 12b, for this and other similar examples.

51. Maimonides, for instance, advocated capital punishment for heretics such as the Karaites (the sect that rejected the Talmud), even though Jewish law stipulates no punishments for different beliefs. See his *Perush ha-Mishnayot* (Jerusalem, 1965), Hulin, 1:2, p. 176. See further Ben-Sasson, "Uniqueness of the Jews," 190. A more extensive treatment of the actual application of capital punishment in the Middle Ages appears in the next chapter.

52. BT, Gittin 88b.

53. See Graf, "Separation of Church and State," chap. 1. The most comprehensive treatment of the principle is by S. Shiloh, *Dina de-Malkhuta Dina* (Jerusalem, 1975). For the interpretation of the doctrine in Spain, see S. Albeck, " 'The Law of the King is the Law' in the Jewish communities of Spain" (Hebrew), *Abraham Weiss Jubilee Volume* (New York, 1964), Hebrew section, 109–25.

54. BT, Nedarim 28a; Gittin 10b; Baba Kama 113a–b; Baba Batra 54b–55a.

55. BT Avodah Zara 4a.

56. Solomon ibn Verga, *Shevet Yehudah*, ed. Shaul Robinson (Tel Aviv, 1946), 2.

57. Solomon ben Adret, *Novellae to Nedarim* (Warsaw, 1902), 28a.

58. Maimonides, *Mishneh Torah*, Gezellah 5:14. See Graf, "Separation of Church and State," 16–18.

59. Ibid.

60. Meir of Rothenberg, *Teshuvot Maharam*, no. 128. See Graf, "Separation of Church and State," 19.

Chapter III

1. On the Book of Esther, see Elias Bickerman, *Four Strange Books of the Bible* (New York, 1984), chap. 4.

2. Bernard Lewis, *The Jews of Islam* (Princeton, N.J., 1984), 62.

3. For discussions of the Jews in Christian thought, see James Parkes, *The Conflict Between Church and Synagogue* (London, 1934), and idem, *The Jew in the Medieval Community*, 2d ed. (New York, 1976). For a more recent discussion of the rise of a new and more hostile Christian attitude toward the Jews in the twelfth and thirteenth centuries, see Jeremy Cohen, *The Friars and the Jews* (Ithaca, N.Y., 1982). For the Islamic attitude toward the Jews, see Lewis, *Jews of Islam*, chap. 1, and Norman A. Stillman, *The Jews of Arab Lands* (Philadelphia, 1979).

4. The most important discussions of the legal status of the Jews in the various nations of Europe are: Guido Kisch, *The Jews in Medieval Germany* (Chicago, 1949); Baer, *Jews in Christian Spain;* Weinryb, *Jews of Poland;* Simon Dubnow, *History of the Jews of Russia and Poland*, trans. I. Friedlander, 5 vols. (Philadelphia, 1916–20); and S. A. Cygielman, "The Enhanced Privilegium of the Jews of Northwest Poland as Reflected in Polish Historiography" (Hebrew), *Zion* 48 (1983): 281–314. The best comprehensive treatment of Jewish legal status is Salo Baron's *Social and Religious History of the Jews*, especially vol. 11.

5. Quoted in Baron, *Social and Religious History*, 11:10.

6. Meir ben Baruch of Rothenburg, *Responsa*, Prague ed. (reprinted Sdilkow, Russia, 1835), no. 1001. The translation is an expansion of the original text by Agus, *Meir of Rothenburg*, 141. See also Tosafot commentary to BT, Baba Kama 58a.

7. Baron, *Social and Religious History*, 11:14–17. See also Kisch, *Jews in Medieval Germany*, 139. Kisch quotes the general principle that *Stadtluft macht frei* ("city residence confers freedom").

8. Giovanni da Anagni, *In librum quintum decretalium* (Milan, 1492), fol. 63, translated in Baron, *Social and Religious History*, 11:17.

9. Eberhard Otto, *Adel und Freiheit im deutschen Staat des freuhen Mittelalters*, (Berlin, 1937) 37, translated in Baron, *Social and Religious History*, 2:9.

10. Baer, *Jews in Christian Spain*, 2:100–101.

11. On the development of the status of *servitus camerae*, see Kisch, *Jews in Medieval Germany*, 129–68, and Baron, *Social and Religious History*, 2:4–13.

12. Rimbert, *Vita Anshari*, 4th ed., ed. G. Waitz (Hanover, 1884), 24, quoted in Amos Funkenstein, "Changes in the Patterns of Chris-

tian Anti-Jewish Polemics in the Twelfth Century" (Hebrew), *Zion* 33 (1968): 128.

13. Al-Qalqashandi, *Subh al-Asha*, (Cairo, 1913–19), 11:390–91, translated in Stillman, *Jews of Arab Lands*, 270.

14. See Neusner, *Jews in Babylonia*, vols. 1–6, passim, and Moshe Beer, *Rashut ha-Golah be-Bavel be-yeme ha-Mishnah ve-ha-Talmud* (Tel Aviv, 1970).

15. For a history of this institution, see Mark Cohen, *Jewish Self-Government in Medieval Egypt* (Princeton, N.J., 1980).

16. Kisch, *Jews in Medieval Germany*, 149.

17. Abraham ibn Daud, *Sefer ha-Qabbalah*, 73–74.

18. On Yazdagird I, see Neusner, *Jews in Babylonia*, 5:10–14. On Kasimir and Esterka, see Chone Shmeruk, *Sifrut Yidish be-Polin* (Jerusalem, 1981), 206–75.

19. Weinryb, *Jews of Poland*, 150.

20. *Seder Olam Zuta*, ed. Yair Weinstock (Jerusalem, 1957), chap. 10, pp. 131–34. See further Neusner, *Jews in Babylonia*, 5:95–105, 110–11.

21. For sources on Abu Isa, see Zvi Aescoli, *Ha-tenu'ot ha-meshihi'ot be-yisrael* (Jerusalem, 1956).

22. Meir of Rothenburg, *Responsa*, Berlin ed. (Berlin, 1891–92), no. 335. Agus' *Meir of Rothenberg*, 659, suggests that this *responsum* may not be authentic to Meir. But even if spurious, it most probably still stems from a thirteenth-century rabbi.

23. The German cases are discussed in Kisch, 111–28. The Spanish example is in Baer, *Jews in Christian Spain*, 1:234.

24. Kisch, *Jews in Medieval Germany*, 114; Ben-Sasson, "Uniqueness of the Jews," 165.

25. *Chronicle of Solomon bar Shimson*, translated in Eidelberg, *Jews and the Crusaders*, 30. See further Kisch, *Jews in Medieval Germany*, 114.

26. Kisch, *Jews in Medieval Germany*, 123–24.

27. See Jacob Katz, "Between 1096 and 1648" (Hebrew), *Yitzhak Baer Seventieth Jubilee Volume* (Jerusalem, 1961), 318–37.

28. Quoted in Ben-Sasson, *History of the Jewish People*, 655.

29. Nathan of Hanover, *Yeven Metzula* (Tel Aviv, 1945). See further Weinryb, *Jews of Poland*, 191–92.

30. Translated in Stillman, *Jews of Arab Lands*, 254.

31. Menachem Mendel b. Abraham, *Zemach Zedek* (Amsterdam, 1675), no. 111.

32. *Memoirs of Ber of Bolechow,* trans. M. Vishnitzer (New York, 1922), 97–98.

33. Adolph Neubauer, "Documents Inédits," *Revue des Etudes Juives* 10 (1885): 98.

34. Nicholas de Nicolay, *Navigations* (Antwerp, 1576), 246. See Lewis, *Jews of Islam, 134–35.*

35. Samuel Ha-Nagid, *Diwan, Ben-Mishlei,* 239, par. 988, trans. in Ben-Sasson, *History of the Jewish People,* 457. On Samuel, see L. J. Weinberger, ed. and trans., *Jewish Prince in Moslem Spain: Selected Poems of Samuel Ibn Nagrela* (University, Ala., 1973).

36. Baer, *Jews in Christian Spain,* 2:323.

37. Jacob Katz, "A State within a State: The History of an Antisemitic Slogan," in his *Emancipation and Assimilation* (Westmead, England, 1972), 47–76.

38. Baron, *Social and Religious History,* 11:21.

39. See Neusner, *Jews in Babylonia,* vols. 1–6, passim.

40. Baer, *Jews in Christian Spain,* 1:234.

41. M. Balaban, "Die Krakauer Judengemeinde-Ordnung von 1595 und ihre Nachtrage," *Jahrbuch der Jüdisch-Literarischen Gesellschaft* 10 (1913): 296–360; 11 (1916): 88–140.

42. Baer, *Jews in Christian Spain,* 1:235.

43. One major source for permission to flog for rebelliousness is Maimonides, *Mishneh Torah,* Hilkhot Sanhedrin, 24:4.

44. *Pinkas Medinat Lita,* ed. S. Dubnow (Berlin, 1925), 43.

45. BT, Sanhedrin 27a–b and Nidah 49b. See the discussion of capital punishment in talmudic times in Neusner, *Jews in Babylonia,* 4:187–89.

46. *Mishneh Torah,* Hilkhot Hovel u-Mazik, 8:11. On Maimonides' approval of the death penalty for heretics, see above, chap. 2, n. 51. A later text confirming Maimonides' observation is in the statutes of the synod of Castilian Jews from 1432. See Louis Finkelstein, *Jewish Self-Government in the Middle Ages* (New York, 1964), 362–63 (translation of text).

47. *She'elot u-Teshuvot ha-Rosh* 17:8, quoted in Abraham Neuman, *The Jews in Spain* (Philadelphia, 1942), 1:138–39.

48. Baer, *Jews in Christian Spain,* 1:233.

49. Ezekiel Landau, *Noda Be-Yehudah,* 2d ed. (Prague, 1811), question 23.

50. Ben-Sasson, *History of the Jewish People,* 679.

51. Ben-Sasson, *Hagut,* chap. 13.

52. Israel Yuval, "An Appeal Against the Proliferation of Divorce in Fifteenth-Century Germany" (Hebrew), *Zion* 48 (1983): 177–216.

53. Ben-Sasson, *Hagut*, chap. 12.

54. For general discussion of this controversy and a bibliography of the details of charges regarding Sabbatianism, see *Encyclopedia Judaica*, s.v. "Emden, Jacob" and "Eybeschuetz, Jonathan."

55. On the ordination controversy, see Jacob Katz, "The Ordination Dispute Between Rabbi Jacob Berav and Levi Ben Haviv," *Zion* 16 (1950): 28–45.

56. The source for this story is Josephus, *Antiquities*, bk. 18, chap. 9. See further Neusner, *Jews in Babylonia*, 1:54–57.

57. On the Khazars, see D. M. Dunlop, *The History of the Jewish Khazars*, (New York, 1967).

58. Arthur J. Zuckerman, *A Jewish Princedom in Feudal France* (New York, 1972). Zuckerman's contention that the princedom was authentic has been refuted by Jeremy Cohen, "The Nasi of Narbonne: A Problem in Medieval Historiography," *AJS Review* 2 (1977): 45–76.

59. See the letter of Nathan of Gaza to Raphael Joseph translated in Gershom Scholem, *Sabbatai Sevi: The Mystical Messiah*, trans. R. Zwi Werblowski (Princeton, N.J., 1973), 270–75 and especially 273–74.

60. Gershom Scholem argues that the main cause for the virtually worldwide Jewish fascination with Sabbatai Zevi was the acceptance of the Lurianic Kabbalah, which was the mystical system used by the Sabbatian propagandists to justify Sabbatai Zevi's actions. See ibid., chap. 1.

61. Heinrich Graetz, *The Structure of Jewish History and Other Essays*, trans. and ed. Ismar Schorsch (New York, 1975), 136.

Chapter IV

1. On the theory of a *nova lex*, see Amos Funkenstein, "Changes in the Patterns of Christian Anti-Jewish Polemics," 125–44. On the mendicant orders, see Jeremy Cohen, *Friars and the Jews*. On changes in papal policy, see Kenneth Stow, *Catholic Thought and Papal Jewry Policy, 1555–1593* (New York, 1976). On the effects of the Reformation, see H. H. Ben-Sasson, *Encyclopedia Judaica*, s.v. "Reformation."

2. On the Marranos, see Cecil Roth, *A History of the Marranos* (New York, 1974). Two excellent case studies of the Marranos are Y. H. Yerushalmi, *From Spanish Court to Italian Ghetto—Isaac Cardoso* (New York, 1971), and Joseph Kaplan, *Me-Natzrut Le-Yahadut: Hayyav u-Po'alo shel he-Anus Yitzhak Orobio de Castro* (Jerusalem, 1983). The thesis of the impact of Sabbatianism in undermining rabbinic authority has been advanced by Jacob Katz in his *Tradition and Crisis* (New York, 1961), 213–24, and is based on the arguments of Gershom Scholem in his studies of Sabbatianism and its aftermath. For a summary of Scholem's position, see my *Gershom Scholem*, chap. 7.

3. See Ben-Sasson, *History of the Jewish People*, 764–67.

4. See Bendix, *Kings or People*. An excellent case study of early absolutism is Thomas Curtis Van Cleve, *The Emperor Frederick II of Hohenstaufen* (Oxford, 1972).

5. The best study of Prussian absolutism remains Hans Rosenberg, *Bureaucracy, Aristocracy, and Autocracy: The Prussian Experience, 1660–1815* (Cambridge, Mass., 1958).

6. On Jews in the Prussian absolutist state, see Selma Stern, *Der preussische Staat und die Juden*, 4 vols. (Tubingen, 1962–75).

7. See Israel Halpern, "Panic Marriages in Eastern Europe" (Hebrew), in his *Yehudim ve-Yahadut be-Mizrah Europa* (Jerusalem, 1969), 289–309.

8. On the ideology of Russian absolutism under Nicholas I, see N. V. Riasanovsky, *Nicholas I and Official Nationality in Russia, 1825–1855* (Berkeley and Los Angeles, 1969). The best history of the Jewish policy of Nicholas is Michael Stanislawski, *Tsar Nicholas I and the Jews: The Transformation of Jewish Society in Russia, 1825–1855* (Philadelphia, 1983). Stanislawski emphasizes the importance of absolutist ideology over anti-Semitism in explaining the policy of Nicholas' government.

9. Christian Wilhelm von Dohm, *Ueber die buergerlich Verbesserung der Juden* (Berlin, 1781). An English translation of a section of this essay appears in Paul Mendes-Flohr and Jehuda Reinharz, eds., *The Jew in the Modern World* (Oxford, 1980), 27–34.

10. This argument about the discrepancy between the continued reality of communal power and the perception of its decline appears in Stanislawski, *Nicholas I*, 123–27. The quotation, translated in ibid., is from a letter written to Moses Montefiore and was quoted first by Azriel Shochat, "The Administration of the Commu-

nities in Russia after the Abolition of the Kahal" (Hebrew), *Zion* 44 (1979): 159.

11. See, M. Diogène Tama, *Transactions of the Parisian Sanhedrin*, trans. F. D. Kirwan (London, 1807). Large sections of this work have been reproduced in Mendes-Flohr and Reinharz, *Jew in the Modern World*, 112–123. On the Paris Sanhedrin, see Simon Schwarzfuchs, *Napoleon, the Jews and the Sanhedrin* (London, 1979). On the *consistoires*, see Phyllis Cohen Albert, *The Modernization of French Jewry: Consistory and Community in the Nineteenth Century* (Hanover, N.H., 1977).

12. See Stanislawski, *Nicholas I*, 13–34.

13. Barukh Halevi Epstein, *Sefer Mekor Barukh* (New York, 1954), 1:965 (translated in Stanislawski, *Nicholas I*, 129).

14. On the Jews in the Ottoman Empire, see Lewis, *Jews of Islam*, chaps. 3 and 4. On the Damascus Blood Libel, see ibid., chap. 4, and A. J. Brawer, *Encyclopedia Judaica*, s.v. "Damascus Affair." Documents from the affair can be found in Stillman, *Jews of Arab Lands*, 393–402.

15. See Selma Stern, *The Court Jew* (Philadelphia, 1950), and F. L. Carsten, "The Court Jews: A Prelude to Emancipation," *Leo Baeck Institute Yearbook* 3 (1958): 140–58.

16. Arendt, *The Origins of Totalitarianism*, 11–53. Arendt's argument owes something to Werner Sombart, *Die Juden und das Wirtschaftsleben* (Leipzig, 1911).

17. The Nazi film was a perversion of the historical novel by the German Jewish author Lion Feuchtwanger, *Jud Suess* (Munich, 1925), translated by Willa and Edwin Muir as *Power* (New York, 1926). On Suess Oppenheimer, see Selma Stern, *Jud Suess: Ein Beitrag zur deutschen und zur juedischen Geschichte* (Berlin, 1929).

18. For a social history of Hasidism, see Simon Dubnow, *Geschichte des Chassidismus* (Berlin 1931). Jacob Katz, in *Tradition and Crisis*, 225–44, has suggested the connection between the decline of the traditional scholarly elite and the rise of Hasidism.

19. On the conflict between the Hasidim and their opponents, see Mordecai Wilensky, *Hasidim u-Mitnaggedim* (Jerusalem, 1970).

20. On Israel Salanter (Lipkin), see Hillel Goldberg, *Israel Salanter: Text, Structure, Idea* (New York, 1982), and Emmanuel Etkes, "R. Israel Salant and the Origins of the Musar Movement" (Hebrew; Ph.D. diss., Hebrew University, Jerusalem, 1975).

21. On the German Haskalah, see Michael Meyer, *The Origins of*

the Modern Jew (Detroit, 1967). An excellent study of the connection between the ideology and social context of the German Haskalah is David Sorkin, "Invisible Community: The Subculture of German Jews, 1780–1840" (unpublished manuscript). On Galicia and Poland, see Raphael Mahler, "The Social Aspects of the Haskalah in Galicia," *YIVO Annual of Jewish Social Science* 1 (1946): 64–85, and, more extensively, his *Hasidism and the Jewish Enlightenment: Their Confrontation in the First Half of the Nineteenth Century*, trans. E. Orenstein and A. Klein (Philadelphia, 1984). On Russia, see Jacob Raisin, *The Haskalah Movement in Russia* (Philadelphia, 1915), and Stanislawski, *Nicholas I*, chaps. 3, 4.

22. For studies of Haskalah ideology, see Sorkin, "Invisible Community"; Mordecai Levin, *Erkhei Hevrah ve-Kalkalah ba-Ideologiah shel Tekufat ha-Haskalah* (Jerusalem, 1975); and Max Wiener, *Ha-Dat ha-Yehudit be-Tekufat ha-Emantzipatziya* (Jerusalem, 1974).

23. On the interpretations of *dina de-malkhuta dina* in the modern period, see Graf, "Separation of Church and State," 73–177.

24. From *Transactions of the Parisian Sanhedrin*. See Mendes-Flohr and Reinharz, *Jew in the Modern World*, 119.

25. Y. H. Yerushalmi in *The Lisbon Massacre of 1506 and the Royal Image in the Shebet Yehudah*, Hebrew Union College Annual Supplements, no. 1 (Cincinnati, 1976), 35–66. Yerushalmi may, however, have read Ibn Verga incorrectly, as Martin Kohn has argued in "Jewish Historiography and Jewish Self-Understanding in the Period of Renaissance and Reformation" (Ph.D. diss., UCLA, 1979), 52–57. If Kohn is correct that Ibn Verga was much more skeptical and satirical in his view of the relationship of monarchs to the Jews, then he would belong more to a medieval mentality.

26. David Gans, *Zemach David* (Jerusalem, 1966), 2:95. See Kohn, "Jewish Historiography," 134–43.

27. On Luzzato's economic theory, see Kohn, "Jewish Historiography," 144–86.

28. Jacob Emden, *Etz Avot*, 47. See further Azriel Shochat, *Im Hilufei Tekufot* (Jerusalem, 1960), 63–66, and Jacob Katz, *Exlusiveness and Tolerance* (Oxford, 1961), 156–68. Katz argues that the favorable attitude toward gentile regimes begins in the eighteenth century, but it would appear from the material presented here that it existed in the previous century as well.

29. *Works of Spinoza: Theologico-Political Treatise and Political Treatise*, trans. R. H. M. Elwes (New York, 1951).

30. Naphtali Herz Wessely, *Divrei Shalom ve-Emet* (Berlin, 1782). See the translation of the relevant passage in Mendes-Flohr and Reinharz, *Jew in the Modern World*, 66.

31. Translated in Mendes-Flohr and Reinharz, *Jew in the Modern World*, 312–13.

32. David ben Nathan of Lissa, Hebrew manuscript translated in ibid., 67–69.

33. For a collection of Hirsch's writings, see *Judaism Eternal: Selected Essays from the Writings of Rabbi Samson Raphael Hirsch*, ed. and trans. I. Grunfeld (London, 1956). Hirsch's main works were his "Nineteen Letters on Judaism" and *Horeb*. For an excellent study of modern Jewish views of the state, see Eliezer Schweid, "The Attitude Toward the State in Modern Jewish Thought Before Zionism," in Elazar, *Kinship and Consent*, 127–47.

34. Samuel Hirsch's main work was *Die Religionsphilosophie der Juden* (Leipzig, 1842). See Schweid, "Attitude," 136–37, and Julius Guttmann, *Philosophies of Judaism* (New York, 1964), 356–65.

35. Steinheim's main work was *Die Offenbarung nach dem Lehrbegriff der Synagoge* (Frankfurt, 1835). See further Schweid, "Attitude," 142–44.

36. Moses Mendelssohn, preface to the 1782 German translation of Menasseh ben Israel's *Vindiciae Judaeorum*. Translated in Mendes-Flohr and Reinharz, *Jew in the Modern World*, 38–42. For Mendelssohn's *Jerusalem*, see the new translation by Allan Arkush (Hanover, N.HJ., 1983). See further Amos Funkenstein, "The Political Theory of Jewish Emancipation," in *Deutsche Aufklaerung und Judenemanzipation*, supp. 3 of *Jahrbuch des Instituts fuer Deutsche Geschichte* (Tel Aviv, 1980).

37. Saul Ascher, *Leviathan oder ueber Religion in Ruecksicht des Judenthums* (Berlin, 1792). Sections translated in Mendes-Flohr and Reinharz, *Jew in the Modern World*, 89–92. See further Meyer, *Origins of the Modern Jew*, 122–25.

38. See Meyer, *Origins of the Modern Jew*, chap. 5; D. Philipson, *The Reform Movement in Judaism* (New York, 1967); and G. W. Plaut, *The Rise of Reform Judaism* (New York, 1963).

39. See Azriel Shochat, *Mosad ha-Rabbanut me-Ta'am be-Russiya* (Haifa, 1975).

40. Translated in Mendes-Flohr and Reinharz, *Jew in the Modern World*, 80.

41. Translated in ibid. 104.

42. Ibn Verga, *Shevet Yehudah*, 31.

43. For Spinoza's "Zionist" statement, see the *Theologico-Political Treatise*, 56.

44. Immanual Wolf, "Ueber den Begriff einer Wissenschaft des Judentums," *Zeitschrift fuer die Wissenschaft des Judentums* 1 (1822); trans. in Michael Meyer, *Ideas of Jewish History* (New York, 1974), 143–55.

45. Isaac Marcus Jost, *Allgemeine Geschichte des Israelitischen Volkes*, vol. 1 (Berlin, 1832). Sections translated in Meyer, *Ideas of Jewish History*, 177–84.

46. See M. Wiener, *Abraham Geiger and Liberal Judaism* (Philadelphia, 1962). On Geiger's views of the Pharisees, see his *Sadducaeer und Pharisaeer* (Breslau, 1863).

47. Translated in Graetz, *Structure of Jewish History*, 136. For Graetz's scheme of Jewish history, see "The Structure of Jewish History" in ibid.

48. Baron, "Ghetto and Emancipation."

Chapter V

1. The best attempt to treat the Jewish socialist and nationalist movements under the general heading of "the new politics" is Jonathan Frankel, *Prophecy and Politics: Socialism, Nationalism and the Russian Jews, 1862–1917* (Cambridge, 1981).

2. For a good summary of modern Jewish demography, see Mendes-Flohr and Reinharz, *Jew in the Modern World*, 525–42. The statistics quoted here have been taken from this text, which in turn gives the sources for its tables.

3. For the rise of modern Yiddish literature, see Dan Miron, *A Traveler Disguised* (New York, 1973). On "lowbrow" Yiddish literature, see David Roskies, "Ayzik-Meyer Dik and the Rise of Yiddish Popular Literature" (Ph.D. diss., Brandeis University, 1975).

4. Two histories of nineteenth-century anti-Semitism are Jacob Katz, *From Prejudice to Destruction: Anti-Semitism, 1700–1933* (Cambridge, Mass., 1980), and Paul Massing, *Rehearsal for Destruction: A Study of Political Anti-Semitism in Imperial Germany* (New York, 1949).

5. Recent scholarship tends to put greater emphasis on economic factors over persecution in causing the waves of emigration from Eastern Europe. See Simon Kuznets, "Immigration of Russian

Jews to the United States: Background and Structure," *Perspectives in American History*, 9 (1975): 35–124. For a review of the literature, see Eli M. Lederhendler, "Jewish Immigration to America and Revisionist Historiography: A Decade of New Perspectives," *YIVO Annual of Jewish Social Science* 18 (1983): 391–410.

6. On the Alliance, see Georges Ollivier, *L'Alliance Israélite Universelle, 1860–1960* (Paris, 1959), and Michael Laskier, *The Alliance Israélite Universelle and the Jewish Community of Morocco, 1862–1962* (Albany, N.Y., 1983).

7. On the Centralverein, see Ismar Schorsch, *Jewish Reactions to German Anti-Semitism, 1870–1914* (New York, 1972).

8. On the American Jewish Committee, see Naomi Cohen, *Not Free to Desist: The American Jewish Committee, 1906–1966* (Philadelphia, 1972). On the American Jewish Congress, see Frankel, *Prophecy and Politics*, 492–551.

9. Quoted in Frankel, *Prophecy and Politics*, 141.

10. See Bernard Johnpoll, *The Politics of Futility: The General Jewish Workers Bund of Poland, 1917–1943* (Ithaca, N.Y., 1967).

11. On the varieties of Jewish political activities in Eastern Europe, see Ezra Mendelsohn, *The Jews of East Central Europe Between the Wars* (Bloomington Ind., 1983). Note that the one country where Jews did not form their own political parties was Hungary, where assimilation of the urban Jews was much greater than in other East European countries.

12. On Poland, see ibid. 11–84, and idem, *Zionism in Poland: The Formative Years, 1915–1926* (New Haven, Conn., 1981).

13. On the Agudat Israel in Poland, see Gershom Bacon, "Agudath Israel in Poland, 1916–39: An Orthodox Jewish Response to the Challenge of Modernity," (Ph.D. diss., Columbia University, 1979).

14. For reactions to the pogroms and the importance of the events of 1881–82 in creating the new politics, see Frankel, *Prophecy and Politics*, 49–132.

15. On the history and ideology of the Bund, see ibid., 171–257, and Henry J. Tobias, *The Jewish Bund in Russia: From Its Origins to 1905* (Stanford, Calif., 1972). For Martov's biography, see Israel Getzler, *Martov: A Political Biography of a Russian Social Democrat* (London, 1967).

16. Aleksandr Chemerisky, "In Lodz in 1905," *Royte Bleter* 1 (Minsk, 1929): 1 Translated in Frankel, *Prophecy and Politics*, 148.

17. On Weizmann, see Jehuda Reinharz, *Chaim Weizmann: The*

Making of a Zionist Leader (Oxford, 1985), and M. Weisgal and Joel Carmichael, eds., *Chaim Weizmann: A Biography by Several Hands* (New York, 1963).

18. On the politics of the Balfour Declaration, see Leonard Stein, *The Balfour Declaration* (Jerusalem, 1983).

19. For descriptions of Herzl's theatrical approach to Zionist politics, see Amos Elon, *Herzl* (New York, 1975), and Carl Schorscke, *Fin-de-Siècle Vienna* (New York, 1980).

20. In addition to the biographies cited above, a good selection of Herzl's writings can be found in Hertzberg, *Zionist Idea* 200–231.

21. For selections of Borochov's and Jabotinsky's writings, see Hertzberg, *Zionist Idea*, 352–67, 556–71. A particularly perceptive analysis of Jabotinsky's philosophy of power can be found in Shlomo Avineri, *The Making of Modern Zionism* (New York, 1981), 159–86.

22. Theodor Herzl, *The Jewish State*, (New York, 1946), in Hertzberg, *Zionist Idea*, 208, 205–6.

23. Herzl's *Altneuland* was translated by Paula Arnold as *Old New Land* (New York, 1960).

24. Herzl, *Jewish State*, 138.

25. Haim Hazaz, "The Sermon," in *Israeli Stories*, ed. Joel Blocker (New York, 1962), 69.

26. For a translation of selections of Nordau's Zionist writings, see Hertzberg, *Zionist Idea*, 235–45. See further his *Degeneration*, English trans. (New York, 1968). On Nordau, see Steven Aschheim, *Brothers and Strangers* (Madison, Wis., 1982), 87–88.

27. From Jabotinsky's introduction to *Chaim Nachman Bialik: Poems*, ed. L. V. Snowman (London, 1924), ix–xv.

28. Pinsker, *Autoemancipation*, in Hertzberg, *Zionist Idea*, 184–85.

29. For a shrewd analysis of *Ir Ha-Harega*, see Alan Mintz, *Hurban: Responses to Catastrophe in Hebrew Literature* (New York, 1984), 129–54.

30. For a definition of the term "counterhistory" and a discussion of historical writers who made use of it, see my *Gershom Scholem*, especially the Introduction.

31. For a translation of short selections of Berdichevsky's writings, see Hertzberg, *Zionist Idea*, 290–302. On Berdichevsky, see my *Gershom Scholem*, 39–43.

32. See the English collection of Dubnow's essays, *Nationalism*

and History. Dubnow's major work on East European Jews is his *History of the Jews in Russia and Poland.*

33. See Rosenzweig's *Star of Redemption,* trans. William Hallo (New York, 1964), Part 3, Book 1. See further Alexander Altmann, "Franz Rosenzweig on History," in his *Studies in Religious Philosophy and Mysticism* (London, 1969), 275–91. I owe this observation to Ismar Schorsch; see his "Political Judgment of the Jew," 5–6.

34. See Raul Hilberg, *The Destruction of the European Jews* (New York, 1961), 16–17.

35. For her views on Jewish passivity during the Holocaust, see Hannah Arendt, *Eichmann in Jerusalem* (New York, 1964; 1983), 117–25. For an analysis of Arendt's book, with bibliography on the controversy it created, see my "Arendt in Jerusalem," *Response* 12 (Summer 1980): 33–44.

36. For a comparative discussion of how the Jews fared in different parts of Europe depending on the degree of Nazi control, see Michael R. Marrus and Robert O. Paxton, *Vichy France and the Jews* (New York, 1983), 341–72. See further Helen Fein, *Accounting for Genocide: National Responses and Jewish Victimization During the Holocaust* (New York, 1979).

37. This argument is suggested by Amos Funkenstein in his lecture, "Passivity as the Characteristic of the Diaspora Jews."

Chapter VI

1. On the Canaanites, see Ya'akov Shavit, "The Relation Between Idea and Poetics in the Poetry of Yonatan Ratosh" (Hebrew), *Ha-sifrut* 17 (Fall 1974): 66–91 (including an extensive bibliography), and "The Ideology of Israeli Anti-Zionism" (Master's thesis, Tel Aviv University, 1972). See further James S. Diamond, *Homeland or Holy Land: The Canaanite Critique of Israel* (Bloomington, Ind., forthcoming).

2. This critique of Israeli culture has been suggested recently by the retired Israeli general Yehoshafat Harkabi in *The Bar Kokhba Syndrome.*

3. For a review of the political theories of Zionism, see Ben Halpern, *The Idea of a Jewish State,* 2d ed. (Cambridge, Mass., 1969), and Avineri, *Making of Modern Zionism.*

4. On A. D. Gordon, see Eliezer Schweid, *Ha-yahid: Olamo shel*

A. D. Gordon (Tel Aviv, 1970). A selection of Gordon's writings in English can be found in Hertzberg, *Zionist Idea*, 368–86.

5. For a recent treatment of the problems of modern Israeli society, see Calvin Goldscheider and Alan S. Zuckerman, *The Transformation of the Jews* (Chicago, 1984), Part 5.

6. See Anita Shapira, *The Army Controversy, 1948: Ben Gurion's Struggle for Control* (Hebrew), 2d ed. (Kibbutz Ha-Meuchad, Israel, 1985). On the first year of Israeli statehood, see Tom Segev, *Nineteen Forty-Nine: The First Israelis* (New York, 1985).

7. For a discussion of this concept, see Avishai, *Tragedy of Zionism*, 172–203, and Charles Liebman and Eliezer Don-Yehiya, *Religion and Politics in Israel* (Bloomington, Ind., 1984), 50–52. An analysis of the concept in terms of Western political theory can be found in Shlomo Aharonson, "The Israeli Political System in Comparison to Other Political Systems" (Hebrew), *Medinah u-Mimshal* (Fall 1985).

8. Some of Leibowitz's views can be found in English in Ben Ezer, *Unease in Zion*, 177–200. See further Leibowitz's collected essays, *Yahadut, Am Yehudi ve-Medinat Yisrael* (Tel Aviv, 1975). Leibowitz goes so far as to call statism the equivalent of fascism.

9. On the concept of an Israeli civil religion, see Charles Liebman and Eliezer Don-Yehiya, *Civil Religion in Israel* (Berkeley and Los Angeles, 1983). The concept of a civil religion is taken from Robert Bellah and Phillip Hammond, *Varieties of Civil Religion* (New York, 1980).

10. The best treatment of the status of Arabs in Israel is Ian Lustick, *Arabs in the Jewish State* (Austin, Tex., 1980).

11. See Avishai, *Tragedy of Zionism*, 235–71.

12. Expressions of this sentiment by young kibbutz soldiers after the war were collected in *Si'ah Lohamim*, translated into English as Henry Near, ed., *The Seventh Day* (London, 1970).

13. For Menachem Begin's autobiography, see his *Revolt* (1948; Los Angeles, 1972). A cogent analysis of the relationship between Begin's biography and his politics is Leonard Fein's "A Man of His Words: Menachem Begin and the Golan Heights," *Moment* 7, no. 2 (January–February 1982): 24–38.

14. See the *Jerusalem Post*, August 3, 1982. See further Prime Minister Begin's letter to Senator Alan Cranston in the New York Times, October 2, 1982. For a discussion of this use of the Holocaust

and Jewish history, see Amnon Rubinstein, *The Zionist Dream Revisited: From Herzl to Gush Emunim and Back* (New York, 1984), x–xi.

15. Emil Fackenheim, *God's Presence in History* (New York, 1970), 84. For examples of Fackenheim's use of the Holocaust to give Israel a religious significance, see his "Holocaust and the State of Israel: Their Relation," *Encyclopedia Judaica Yearbook* (1974), 152–57, and, more extensively, *The Jewish Return into History: Reflections in the Age of Auschwitz and a New Jerusalem* (New York, 1978).

16. Fackenheim is, again, probably the most forceful advocate of this position, arguing for the Holocaust as a *novum* in history and, by extension, for the uniqueness of the state of Israel. For another attempt to argue the uniqueness of the Holocaust, see Steven Katz, "The 'Unique' Intentionality of the Holocaust," in his *Post-Holocaust Dialogues* (New York, 1983), 287–317.

17. For a history of the Lebanon War and especially of Ariel Sharon's theory of Israeli power, see Zeev Schiff and Ehud Yaari, *Israel's Lebanon War*, trans. Ina Friedman (New York, 1985).

18. On Gush Emunim's place in Israeli ideology, see Rubinstein, *Zionist Dream Revisited*. See further David Newman, *Jewish Settlement in the West Bank: The Role of Gush Emunim* (Durham, England, 1982).

19. On the Lithuanian circle, see Aryeh Morgenstern, "Messianic Theories and the Settlement of Eretz Israel in the First Half of the Nineteenth Century" (Hebrew), *Cathedra* 24 (1982): 52–78 (includes commentary and responses). On Kalischer, see Jody Myers, "Seeking Zion: The Messianic Ideology of Zevi Hirsch Kalischer, 1795–1874," (Ph.D. diss., UCLA, 1985).

20. Kasher was the author of a very influential book entitled *Hatekufah ha-Gedolah* (Jerusalem, 1968), which includes a late eighteenth-century messianic text, *Kol ha-Tor*, by Hillel of Shklov, one of the circle around the Gaon of Vilna. On Kasher's influence on the Gush Emunim, see Janet Aviad, "The Contemporary Israeli Pursuit of the Millennium," *Religion* 14 (1984): 199–222. On Rav Kook, see my "Mysticism and Politics in Modern Israel: The Messianic Ideology of Abraham Isaac Ha-Cohen Kook," in Peter Merkl and Ninian Smart, eds., *Religion and Politics in the Modern World* (New York, 1983), 191–202. See also my "Messianic Connection: Zionism, Politics, and Settlement in Israel," *Center Magazine* 18, no. 5 (September–October 1985): 35–45.

21. Eliezer Waldman, *Arzi* 3 (Jerusalem, 1983): 18; quoted in Aviad, "The Contemporary Israeli Pursuit," 217. The saying is taken from the teachings of Rav Kook.

22. Waldman, *Nekuda* 46 (June 8, 1982): 4; in Aviad, "The Contemporary Israeli Pursuit," 217–18.

23. In his otherwise admirable analysis of the emergence of a religious-nationalist alternative to classical Zionism, Amnon Rubinstein advocates a return to the old idea of normalization based on principles of Western liberalism, as if it were possible to turn back the clock to some mythical age in Zionist history. This nostalgia is a characteristic of contemporary socialist and liberal elements in Israel and is aptly symbolized by the tremendous success of Anita Shapira's 1980 biography of Berl Katznelson, the Labor Zionist leader who died in 1944, during the "golden age" of the pre-state settlement. See the English translation, *Berl: The Biography of a Socialist Zionist*, trans. Haya Galai (Cambridge, 1984). It is the virtue of Bernard Avishai's *Tragedy of Zionism* that he calls for a "post-Zionist" political theory, one in which Israel would presumably give up its exclusive ethnic character in favor of democratic pluralism.

24. On the problems of small nations, see David Vital, *The Survival of Small States: Studies in Small Power/Great Power Conflict* (London, 1971). Vital is also the author of an excellent two-volume history of the early Zionist movement, *The Origins of Zionism* (Oxford, 1975) and *Zionism: The Formative Years* (Oxford, 1982); it is perhaps no surprise that his interest in Zionism is connected to this interest in the fate of small nations.

25. Ismar Schorsch has also suggested this analogy between Israel and the medieval Jewish community in "Political Judgment of the Jew," 17–18. For an analysis of Israel's relationship to America, see Nadav Safran, *Israel: The Embattled Ally* (Cambridge, Mass., 1978).

Chapter VII

1. See W. D. Rubinstein, *The Left, the Right and the Jews* (New York, 1982), chap. 2. Additional statistics and discussion can be found in Charles E. Silberman, *A Certain People: American Jews and Their Lives Today* (New York, 1985), chaps. 3, 4.

2. See, for instance, Irving Howe, *World of Our Fathers* (New York, 1976), and Moses Rischin, *The Promised City* (Cambridge,

Mass., 1962). For a discussion beyond the immigrant generations, see Deborah Dash Moore, *At Home in America: Second-Generation New York Jews* (New York, 1981). See also Selma Berrol, "Education and Economic Mobility: The Jewish Experience in New York City, 1880–1920," *American Jewish Historical Quarterly* 65, no. 3 (March 1976): 257–71.

3. See Shulamit Volkov, "Anti-Semitism as a Cultural Code," *Leo Baeck Institute Yearbook* 23 (1980): 25–46.

4. For a recent discussion of Jewish demography in America and a presentation of this argument, see Silberman, *A Certain People*, chap. 7.

5. On the New York *kehilla*, see Arthur Goren, *New York Jews and the Quest for Community* (New York, 1970).

6. See chap. 5, n. 8.

7. See Yehuda Bauer, *The Jewish Emergence from Powerlessness* (Toronto, 1979), 76–77. For a discussion of the relationship of American Jews and Zionism, see Melvin Urofsky, *American Zionism from Herzl to the Holocaust* (Garden City, N.Y., 1975).

8. For a discussion of "American Power and Jewish Interest in Foreign Affairs," see Henry Feingold, *A Midrash on American Jewish History* (Albany, N.Y., 1982), 193–206.

9. See ibid., 207–20. See further Yehuda Bauer, "The Holocaust and American Jewry," in his *Holocaust in Historical Perspective* (Seattle, 1978); Arthur Morse, *While Six Million Died* (New York, 1967); Henry Feingold, *The Politics of Rescue* (New York, 1980); David Wyman, *Paper Walls: America and the Refugee Crisis, 1938–1941* (Amherst, Mass., 1968); and, most important, idem, *The Abandonment of the Jews* (New York, 1984).

10. See Steven Spiegel, *The Other Arab-Israeli Conflict: America's Middle Eastern Policy from Truman to Reagan* (Chicago, 1985).

11. On the image of America, see Howe, *World of Our Fathers*, 27 and 34–36 and Sanford Ragins, "The Image of America in Two East European Hebrew Periodicals," *American Jewish Archives* (November 1965).

12. Simon Kuznets, "The Immigration of Russian Jews to the United States: Background and Structure," *Perspectives in American History* 9 (1975): 35–124; Lederhendler, "Jewish Immigration to America."

13. Arnold M. Eisen, *The Chosen People in America: A Study in Jewish Religious Ideology* (Bloomington, Ind., 1983).

14. See Nathan Glazer and Daniel Patrick Moynihan, *Beyond the Melting Pot* (Cambridge, Mass., 1963). It is perhaps no surprise that one of the authors of this important revision, Nathan Glazer, is known as part of a circle of self-identified Jewish intellectuals.

15. On Jewish radical politics and union organizing in America, see Frankel, *Prophecy and Politics*, chap. 9; Rischin, *Promised City*, pt. 4; and Arthur Liebman, *Jews and the Left* (New York, 1979).

16. Will Herberg, *Protestant, Catholic, Jew: An Essay in American Religious Sociology* (Garden City, N.Y., 1955).

17. Silberman, *A Certain People*, 345–52.

18. For a variety of views on this subject, see the *Commentary* symposium "Liberalism and the Jews," *Commentary* 69 (January 1980): 15–82.

19. Arguments along this line have been advanced in particular by Daniel Elazar, an American Orthodox political scientist, who now teaches in Israel. Elazar's initial work was on American federalism. More recently, he has written a number of works maintaining that the Jewish political tradition contains a constitution (the laws of the Written and Oral Torah), a form of federalism (in the autonomy of communities), and a division of powers (the talmudic terms "crown of Torah," "crown of monarchy," and "crown of priesthood"). See especially *The Jewish Polity*. The underlying message of this attempt to describe the Jewish political tradition in terms of the American model and to demonstrate that the state of Israel represents a continuation of this tradition is an assertion of the political similarity between Israel and America.

20. The main forum for the Jewish neoconservative point of view is *Commentary* magazine.

21. See Eugene Litt, *Beyond Pluralism: Ethnic Politics in America* (Glenview, Ill., 1970).

22. Horace M. Kallen, *Cultural Pluralism and the American Idea* (Philadelphia, 1956). Kallen's influence was probably greatest in the 1920s.

23. Silberman, *A Certain People*, 360–66.

24. Ibid., 107–9 and 328–29.

25. See Jonathan Woocher, "Jewish Survivalism as Communal Ideology: An Empirical Assessment, *Journal of Jewish Communal Service* 57, no. 4 (Summer 1981): 291–303, and Deborah Lipstadt, "From Noblesse Oblige to Personal Redemption: The Changing Pro-

file and Agenda of American Jewish Leaders," *Modern Judaism* 4, no. 3 (September 1984): 295–305.

26. *Commentary*, August 1966. On the Holocaust in American Jewish consciousness, see Silberman, *A Certain People*, 183, and Deborah Lipstadt, "The Holocaust: Symbol and 'Myth' in American Jewish Life," *Forum on the Jewish People, Zionism, and Israel*, no. 40 (Winter 1980/81): 73–88.

27. See Jacob Neusner, *Stranger at Home: "The Holocaust," Zionism, and American Jews* (Chicago, 1981).

Index